Leadership Dharma

Leadership Dharma

ARJUNA THE TIMELESS METAPHOR

Raghu Ananthanarayanan

with a Foreword by Prasad Kaipa

Productivity & Quality Publishing Private Limited
Madras-600017

Leadership Dharma - ARJUNA THE TIMELESS METAPHOR

Raghu Ananthanarayanan

ISBN: 978-81-85984-65-0
Reprint 2018

Published by:
Productivity & Quality Publishing Private Limited
Registered Office: 38, Thanikachalam Road, T.Nagar, Madras – 600 017, India
Administrative Office: 2A, Arulambal Street, T.Nagar, Madras – 600 017, India
Phone: +91-44-2384 4512
Email: service@kkbooks.com Web: www.kkbooks.com

Edited by: Devika Khazvini
Prepress by: DSM Soft (P) Ltd, Chennai
Design by: Divya Saxena
Illustrations by: Manu Ananth
Printed by: Manipal Technologies Limited, Manipal

Dedicated to my gurus:
J. Krishnamurti, Yogacharya T. Krishnamacharya
and Pulin K. Garg;
and to
Na Muthuswamy and Koothu-p-pattarai

Contents

Part 2: Arjuna over the ages, *parallels and pragmatics*

Foreword

We live by stories. When the stories that we tell no longer interest us, then we wither away. What evokes passion is something that gives us meaning and stories give meaning to what we do. But stories by themselves don't do the trick sometimes, when the culture in which the story is told is very different from the culture in which the story is born. If that is so, the story has to be re-contextualised. It has to make sense to the people who are reading it/hearing it. In other words, our ancient wisdom – recorded through stories in Upanishads, Jataka kathas, Puranas and Itihasas have to be retold in a way that modern young people can use those stories to reflect on themselves and gain self knowledge. That is how smart people become wise.

Raghu is one such story-teller who knows more than enough about Indian wisdom and is sufficiently deeply interested in the modern IT and entrepreneurial India. He lives with the latest while reflecting on the oldest, at the same time. I have seen it first hand.

My first meeting with Raghu was in Indian Institute of Management Bangalore in early 1990s. I went to Bangalore to do a module on reflective mindset for executives from British Aerospace (BA) (now called BAE SYSTEMS). While my part was only two out of seven – day program, Raghu was doing yoga sessions twice a day for the participants. Most of the participants were new to yoga and Raghu was again great in creating context and generating interest in yoga through stories. I was amazed that most of the participants attended all his sessions.

I assumed that Raghu was a typical yoga teacher but during one meal together, I learned that Raghu was an engineer with a Bachelors and a Masters degree from IIT Madras (my alma mater) and a very accomplished behavioral scientist in addition to being a yoga instructor. He had written books on yoga as well a book on Organizational Alignment where he has integrated seminal ideas from Yoga with the practice of management. He is a pioneer in integrating yoga (and theatre) into process work. I could see why he could connect to 25 foreigners and keep them occupied in an activity that most of them had never experienced before (this is early 90s). He was creating meaning and connection to what they were doing through his stories.

Despite Raghu's interesting yoga sessions, participants were not engaged in the main executive program that they came to attend. They were not used to sitting in the class rooms for long hours and were emotionally overwhelmed by what they experienced in India in contrast to their own lives back home. By the time I was to facilitate their sessions, the unrest in participants turned to revolt and many were preparing to go back without completing their one week in India. I had a choice to make – stay with the design that I came prepared to deliver or use the 'unrest' as a catalyst to dig deeper into their mindsets – either way, I wanted them to reflect on themselves, become more self aware and learn to make better decisions as leaders in the increasingly globalized world. I went with the second choice – decided to throw away my design and started engaging in a live dialogue with them on the changing nature of business and what it meant to them as senior executives. I told them stories of other executives I coached in US, Europe and India and challenged them with deep questions to reflect on. We discussed their busy schedules, lack of work-life balance, constant pressure to perform and increasing competition. We watched movie segments and read a book together called 'Hope for the Flowers' (by Trina Paulus) and discussed how we could 'mind the gap' between our stimulus and responses.

My session was very different from what they had ever experienced and they responded well by going deeper into their psyche. By the end of my two days, the participants were more reflective and ready to engage deeply with the rest of the program. Story does not end here.

Raghu, in partnership with the HR Head of BA, was scheduled to do a session on high-performance organizations. Instead of doing his standard session, he decided to throw away the script as well. He used my session as the story and got them to reflect on what happened to them in that session. He helped to pay attention to their own subtle shifts in emotions and belief system and through his questions, interpretation of my session and its connection to yoga sutras, he did an improvisation session for them. In other words, they learned about storming, norming, and performing through their own case study and that session was a phenomenal success. Raghu helped participants to connect the dots between who they were, what they did in the office and how Indian experience could make a difference to them. As a result, participants went away excited and obviously performed well enough that BA continued sending new batches of participants to IIM for the next 15 years.

Arjuna's Penance is about awakening Arjuna in all of us and helping us to integrate lessons from Mahaabhaarata into our lives and work. But awakening takes place in the reader not in the writer. First, the reader has to connect, then engage, then become aware of different personalities to choose from and then make the choice. Once the reader chooses to be influenced by a character – in this book by one of the Paandavas – then, the story begins to take place inside the reader's consciousness and the author has to keep that connection alive till it transforms the reader. Raghu does an excellent job in creating a story, weaving in lessons from Mahaabhaarata, and making recommendations to readers to connect, engage, become aware and gives tools for them to transform themselves.

A book like this is difficult to write – you have three responsibilities – tell the story of contemporary leaders that readers can connect with.

Then tell the story of the Paandavas in the context of contemporary leaders. Finally, you have to connect the readers to both leaders of today and leaders from yesteryears. I believe Raghu has done a great job and now it is up to you, the reader, to spend time reading, reflecting and reading again in an iterative manner to perform your tapas – to awaken the Arjuna in you!

PRASAD KAIPA

July 7, 2013

Campbell, CA

ACKNOWLEDGEMENTS

This book has been many years in the making. Its beginnings lie in trying to convince Pulin Garg to work on it, and that was many decades ago. Filling in the lacuna left behind by Pulin was a very important impetus to writing the book. Srinivasamurthy has been a constant source of encouragement and push to write. Sashi's willingness to look at each version, comment on it and discuss ideas has made it possible to keep persisting, version after version. Ahalya has also been a great help in shaping the dance analogies and all the way to the final editing. Arundhati's review of the first sharable version brought the voice of Draupadhi into the picture.

The two people who made a substantial contribution to shaping the book are Gopalakrisnnan and Prasad Kaipa. Gopal engaged me in a constant dialogue as he helped rework the book, made me question many things, sharpened the focus of the work and made me re-write many passages. The flow of the book owes much to Gopal. Prasad critiqued the almost-final version and helped to make changes that make this very interesting, but complex subject more accessible.

Divya and Manu Ananth have put in a lot of thinking and effort to illustrate and design the book. The enthusiasm and commitment with which they went about their work helped me see how timeless the Mahaabhaarata is and how important it is to the young minds of today for it to be reinterpreted in contemporary terms.

Prologue

Tradition meets modernity through the hearts and minds of individuals. Many of those who were born around the early years of Independence have had to find their peace with this inner confrontation. I was brought up in a fairly liberal home; however, stories of the heroes of our struggle for Independence were always in the air, as were the retold mythologies. I remember my very formidable Grandfather becoming vulnerable and self reflective as he read out the stories from the Raamaayana to his grandchildren. At the same time, studying well and getting into elite institutions was a constant pressure. When I did get into IIT Madras, I am not sure who was more thrilled, me or the family. Many of my uncles were the first to go abroad to study, and the fact that many of them excelled at their study while retaining the tradition was a matter of great pride.

Perhaps because of this or perhaps because this is a shared struggle of many Indians, I have come across this inner threshold as a critical inflexion point in the lives of many leaders. My work has spanned many sectors from development organisations, working with the downtrodden, to craft groups, to small and medium sized family businesses, to large Global Indian Corporations. Sooner or later the leader has to bridge the gap between his inner core that is deeply impacted by his familial context, and his knowing mind that is filled with concepts and ideas he has learnt in a modern schooling system.

The knowing - doing gap is therefore a chasm between two different world views, two different ways of understanding what it means to be human, what it means to be a hero unto oneself.

It is my humble opinion that while this is an important issue for any Indian growing up today in a world that is becoming more and more global, it is of vital importance to the leader, whatever the context in which he/she is exercising leadership. In my mind I am conversing with a person who is a leader (or is part of a leadership team) on the threshold of shaping his/her organisation to meet global challenges. It is only when you have explored your Indian roots and found a harmony between your inner meaning-making core and your capabilities and talents that you can unleash your greatest creativity and highest potential. I am therefore sharing a narrative of such an exploration.

How do you readers join me in this conversation?

While the written medium precludes a face-to-face dialogue, may I suggest the following;

>> *Read the book slowly and talk about it to a close friend. Treat the protagonist of my narrative, Ranjan, as your alter ego.*

>> *Build your own narrative as you go along. I am hoping that the sharing of my own struggles and discoveries will evoke you, nudge you, surprise you, anger you and so on.*

>> *Be open to these waves within, but address the surge of emotion with your own reflections.*

>> *Stay with the questions that are triggered when you read and treat my answers as one possible alternative. Learning takes place between the question and the answer! And treating your answers as working hypotheses will enable your learning.*

>> *I have suggested exercises that you can use as a mirror to your own inner processes.*

>> *Please take the time to work with them as you go through the book.*

>> *I think a brief sharing of some of my encounters that have awakened my inner theatre of the tradition-modernity drama will be useful. It will spell out my biases as well as the roots of my thoughts.*

I had not yet sprouted to the height suitable for my age, when I was in my 5th standard, so I was a bit short and puny. Fr. Malon was big, towering above me at 6'4" and fairly wide in girth. He would stand at the foyer that led into the school at every recess to ensure that no one played truant. I was the lone guy walking out after lunch so he stopped me and demanded "Where are you off to young man?" "There is a festival on at home and I have to get back early for it, I have asked for leave Sir" I said. "So you are off to pray to your monkey gods is it?" he said. "You have no right to say that father" I countered trying to stand up to my full height!! I was promptly caned before being allowed to go home. It has taken me many years to understand that I was wrong in what I had said. I should have said, "No father, we don't pray to our monkey gods, we play with them".

Meeting Dharampal (the author of several books that go into Pre-British India, and a Gandhian freedom fighter) was a shock. His question to a few of us who had the good fortune to have been mentored by him was "What will you do after you graduate from IIT? What kind of an India will you build? Will you build a great nation by running behind the tails of the west? A part of you is deeply immersed in your own culture, its meanings and world views, will you lobotomise that part of the brain and mind as you embrace a western idea of development? Will you reject what is new and turn your back on knowledge that is vital for our development?" I don't think I will ever answer this challenge fully, but it has been the theme of my quest. This led to seeking out respected gurus and teachers and I spent a decade learning Yoga with Yogacharya Krishnamacharya. I chose Yoga because the principles and insights enunciated in Patanjali's Yoga Sutras are the basis for all Indian spiritual ways, even when they differ on matters of theology. I also spent many years in intimate contact with J Krishnamurti at this time in my life journey.

Pulin K Garg was another important mentor. Pulin was one of the pioneers of T-Group work in India. He went on to develop what he called Identity Based Explorations that brought together the lab modality with Upanishadic dialogue. His rallying call was "I am a child of two cultures, and out of this cauldron I must forge my Identity as a modern Indian". His methods of enquiry and exploration took as much from the tradition of western psychology and sociology as it did from a profound scholarship of Indian scriptures.

This book is an offering and an invitation to share some parts of my journey, and hopefully to trigger your own.

"To play is to learn" Piaget has said and that is true of our psyche as much as it is of the world of concepts. Our gods are archetypes and metaphors to be played with. One has to sit through one of the more traditional koothu (traditional dance-drama) portrayals in the areas surrounding Gingee fort to understand this fully. The yearly re-enactment of Arjuna's Tapas (Arjuna's penance) or the whole of the Mahaabhaarata is an exciting mixture of the serious, the sacred, the comic, the pragmatic and the cathartic. The community involvement is deep, every action of the hero is discussed and compared with what happens in the village. The Sutradhar keeps this thread between the everyday reality and the dream-mythology space alive. So much play and so much learning! In each locale, the tale has interesting twists, new heroes and villains. When one looks further, one discovers that all of these heroes and villains are part of the region's history and the sub plots of the Mahaabhaarata recounted are metaphors of historical traumas. Generations have played with the gods!

The characters of the Raamaayana and the Mahaabhaarata are with us every day and every minute. They stare at us from calendars, they come in disguise through Bollywood and Kollywood, and they are part of everyday conversations. In the eyes of children, Bala Krishna is the mischievous child stealing butter, who then grows into the irresistible Gopi Krishna as an adolescent, and a great hero winning battles as a young man, and becomes a spiritual mentor as he drives Arjuna's chariot. Finally one realises that Krishna is the deep indigo colour of endlessly evolving space where the entire universe is. "That's why lord Naaraayana's avatars are indigo blue" one is told.

The only time when the heroes and gods don't play with us is when we become rational and scientific. Mythology loses its magic and one realises later that with it, one loses touch with the dream state of one's own deeper psyche. So it is with shock that one listens to a talk by Prof. Pulin Garg about the psychological process of choice making, by evoking the Mahaabhaarata heroes, in the halls of IIM Ahmedabad!

"Management is supposed to be rational," you start to argue. "And where do your thoughts, ideas, assumptions and conclusions come from?" you are asked, not exactly in a polite way! The old friends are restored to you, and discussing one's inner turmoil finds a language. "I am karna" you realise one day and a whole process of discovering your dreams and passion gets triggered.

Today one hears of first person, second person and third person learning. First person learning is subjective and is a narrative where 'I' am the protagonist. In discovering my subjective process of encountering reality and making meaning I gain autonomy and mastery over my responses and choices. In discovering the language of mythology, Joseph Campbell says, one discovers the path to one's unconscious. Second person learning is dialogic. One is forced to confront one's conditioning, assumptions and conclusions as one listens deeply to another's subjective view of reality. Third person learning is the statistically validated or theoretically explicated objective view of reality. It is only in moving through all three continuously that one has a glimpse of what right action for oneself might be.

In this process of moving outward and inward, one discovers the art of not only growing and learning more and more about oneself and one's world horizontally; one also encounters the adventure of evolving, of moving vertically into ways of thinking, feeling and acting that are radically different from the reality one is conditioned by and one is taught. In the enquiry into and exploration of both the horizontal and the vertical movements of one's mind and the seamless flow between the two lies the way to discover an integration of oneself, and the shaping of one's identity that is not stuck with one's conditioning, one's socialisation and one's acculturation. Pursuing this adventure, while being engaged with the world is the path of leadership. Arjuna's Penance is a mythological metaphor of this path.

The metaphor of a Tapas is particularly apt since an aspiring leader must discover how to be alone, and not lonely; be relentlessly self-critical without being dislocated; be open to intuition and insight without being blocked by the rational. This intense inner work generates dissatisfaction and pain, a kind of an inner heat, a slow cooking! This 'cooking' over a self-generated fire is Tapas. I have modelled the chapters of the book on the steps of Tapas described in the Yoga Sutras called 'ascending the peak of deep wisdom'.

So, dear reader, to prepare for the conversation, take a large chart paper. Draw two concentric circles. The inner circle is the business you head (whatever your area of control and responsibility, is your business and you are its CEO!). In this area, you deploy your knowledge of the people you serve, the way you convert inputs into outputs, the way you motivate people and the way you create value for people who have invested in you. The larger circle is the space you influence. It has people you serve, people who serve you, people who wish to be part of your team and people who see potential value in investing in you. This is the mirror of your work and your relationships in which you discover the leader in you. Let your childlike creativity come through, draw pictures, doodle (try to avoid words) and have fun in letting your mind wander, meander through this life space of yours.

PART 1

Understanding the Paandavas, *discovering the 'hero within'*

PLATE 1 THE FOUR QUADRANTS

Q1, South East, The Judge/King, *Yudhishtra*; Q2, SouthWest, The Warrior, *Bhima*; Q3, North East, The Healer, *Nakula*; Q4, NorthWest The Seeker/Hermit, *Sahadeva*

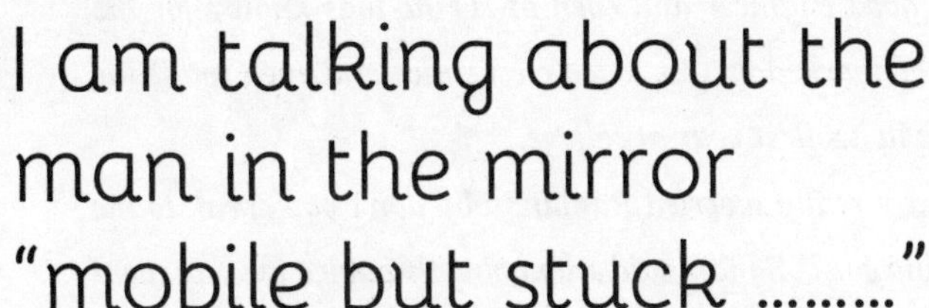

CHAPTER 1

I am talking about the man in the mirror "mobile but stuck ...."

The morning sun was soft and beautiful as it lit up the garden. The birds were chirping excitedly, but none of this seemed to touch Ranjan. It was as if he was sitting within a grey cloud. "What was it that your teacher said about good kings?" Ranjan suddenly asked Sanam and pulled her out of her reverie. Sanam took a while to get the context of the question. "A good king understands that every decision he takes is in the context of a Dharma Sankata*." Ranjan was puzzled. "I have heard you say that before, but I am not sure I get it." "If you are a king, you are in the midst of many conflicting and contradicting pulls and pushes. Many of these are symptoms of underlying dilemmas, Dharma Sankatas, where if you ignored the connected and interdependent realities, you don't even understand the real role of a king."*

"Tell me more."

"Ok let me contrast it with what a bad king is. A bad king is one who attacks the symptoms of a Dharma Sankata with bravado. He treats them as problems to be solved, and in the process creates other seemingly un-connected problems, but creates the ground for deeper problems to emerge. He also said a great hero is one who creates a new ground for action where the Dharma Sankata is resolved."

Ranjan fell silent again, sunk in thought, and the cloud looked darker.

Ranjan was clearly preoccupied as he sat for dinner. His wife Sanam had seen him like this many years ago when he decided to step out of a fairly comfortable job at XY systems, as the head of engineering and development.

Ranjan was a very good engineer and even at IIT he was known for the interesting projects he worked on. He loved electronics and even made his own music turntable in his first year at college.

"I know that you are really worried Ranjan, why don't you speak to me about what is troubling you?" Sanam said after going through a week of silent agony. "But, how will you understand the dilemma I am in?" said Ranjan. "This is not like asking you if you can support me while I take the risks of a start-up." "Try me, and maybe telling me a story will help you engineering types who think in power-point slides." said Sanam. The issues had been worrying Ranjan for a long time and his mind was going over the same ground again and again. "Let's try." he said.

"We are now a two-hundred-and-fifty-crore (50 million $) company. We have three hundred and fifty people and this has been a sudden jump in the last one year. Jagan has been with us from the start. When we started off, the idea of taking up the challenge posed by Sam Pitroda and working in the telecom sector was really heady. India was seen only as a 'body shop', 'sweat shop' and we were really stung by this. XY Systems was a start-up too and became really big but was caught in the services trap. Jagan and I took the plunge; Farookh and Krishnan were very supportive when we said "Can we try something new?". We started a new company 'Mobile Unlimited', set up an operation here and in the US with funding from XY.

"XY Systems gave us a two-year leave of absence from our jobs for the new work. Jagan came with me, and 'Afsal the bean counter' as we called our cost accountant also chose to take the plunge. Getting Jenny on board was so bad for us. She was a very successful 'business developer' person from IBM, but simply could not cope with the start-up. She tried to bring in the IBM processes, that we tried to emulate, but it just made us lose our speed and punctured the excitement. By the time we parted company, the two years were already over! We pursued a VC and got two rounds of funding. But though we had innovative products, the mobile market was still in its infancy. We made good by doing some projects for larger companies while devoting quality time to the R&D. The US operations had to close down and the team consisting

of eight of us came back here. Shanti joined us to head HR. With a two-year experience in XY systems, she seemed the ideal person to bring in the culture that we all admired. Many of us in the management had grown up with very techie, but strong middle class values of thrift, hard work and practicality.

"Within a year of our return, things started to improve. The 50-member team had kept the place afloat through some really heroic efforts and innovative product designing. We lost count of the number of products we had to trash at the last minute, either because the mobiles operation changed their methods or the technology was changed! But, the inspiration we had that we would create a breakthrough in India was a real motivator. And each near success was the stepping stone to the ultimate breakthrough. Mid-way through the year, we got a winner, downloading tunes onto the mobile and instant cricket news!

"That's when the scene really changed. Suddenly, we were across the 'chasm' as Geoffrey Moore describes it. Years of sweating on ideas, living hand to mouth, with all of us and our families involved in making the small business survive. The number of times you and Jagan's wife and Shanti have just been around to cook food late at night and make coffee early in the morning as we worked feverishly to close a project or get a product out!

"Raj Peter came in a couple of years ago and made a big impact. He could actually tell us when to stop tinkering and end a developmental effort and that's what got us the first big breakthrough. All the components were there, but Jagan and I were too nerdy to see how to make a clear offering. Raj got us to work with the service providers and get the billing component right. He was from a service provider and knew the real problem – how to bill and collect for them! The service was a simple thing like the musical ring tone, but the software behind it was not, nor was the billing process!

"In the last two years, things have just grown at a hectic pace. We are now three hundred people! I don't know many of the chaps who walk into my room. They talk of a 'founders' club' and the 'junta' and I have always had an open door! Shanti goes around trying to meet each one and talk to them, but she is inundated with grievances or requests for new recruitment! Afsal was very good at keeping costs under check, but we now have four different areas–the music studio with the 'creative types', the R&D nerds, the service providing

software engineers and the 'hunters' at the sales end. Each needs different treatment from Shanti, each needs a new incentive, each compares themselves with a different company as a benchmark! Very often I find myself playing arbitrator while my team takes stances on various issues. I end up feeling like a 'monkey between the cats'!" Ranjan took a pause. He saw that he was veering away from painting a clear picture for Sanam. He reordered his thoughts and continued, "Let me tell you some of the operational issues. While a software service provider will have about 5 or 6 releases a month, we sometimes have up to 10 a day. Since we have really made great sales on 'greetings messages and tunes', the deadlines are killing. We either have a product with at least a hundred choices and combinations out on the specific date or we just lose chunks of business.

"We realise now that what Raj did was to tie our earnings to the service provider's billing! We now get all kinds of weird requests from sales and they don't always understand the product complexities. In order to be nice to the service provider they say, "Let's innovate an idea". It seems to be just a small tweaking of the product and they have said "yes" to what they think can be made and it's a big sale. The service people say "Oh my God! Not another 'small change'! So their components can't just be used off the shelf. They go and talk to Jagan. And Jagan hits the roof. "Why can't you guys sort out these simple changes?" "The last time we tried, you were very upset with the quality." After an exchange of words Jagan sends an engineer or two off to the 'services'. They work under time pressure since deadlines are very tight. But being R&D people they don't normally work like this, nor can they do a 'chalta hai' (careless) kind of activity. By the time the product is ready, Raj's team is screaming, Jagan is very disturbed and the new service head Hassan has frayed nerves. He has to make 25 releases of similar projects across India! In one of the releases there is a bug and a near-war breaks out between a BD officer and the service project head.

"Shanti can just about cope! Jagan is on the shop floor most of the time and we have not got a new product out for more than 9 months. Small operators are copying us and going to the service providers at lower rates. Meanwhile, the 'creative' studio people not only delay releases, they come and go as they please.

Rashmi was able to keep a great bonhomie and spirit going when she set up the small team. Now the team is much bigger and the work is more of a routine and the bonhomie is missing.

"A year back we had less than 5% turnover, with a small team, but more importantly, really innovative work. Now we hit 25%! Many of the chaps who come in from other software companies come because they have heard of 'new, innovative and cool work'. But what we need is more people at the 'service' end who will assemble 'components' and deliver on time!

"On top of all this the VCs want to go for an IPO. This is their first Indian investment and they want to succeed. "You have a great story," Arun Natarajan, the investors' India Head says, "and anyway that's your deal with us". So they want a new COO and CFO who will "put things in order and administer the place"; they want low attrition or "it spoils the story"; they are bringing in a whole new set of mobile software producing companies from Singapore, Hong Kong and Australia who want to become JV partners. India is growing real fast in the mobile sector and we have pioneered three really innovative products that have a global reach. We gave up on the global scene after the Jenny fiasco. Do we really now want to go global?"

Ranjan now got to the crux of the internal dialogue. "But Sanam, what worries me is, can I make this shift? I see all these people around me, Jagan, Raj, Shanti, Afsal and Rashmi as well as the new employees who were very good till a year or less ago but who seem out of their depth today. Maybe I am the problem because I can't grow to the next level. Suddenly there are Board politics. XY Systems was cool the last few years in sending one of its Board members to replace their VP tech on the Board of Mobile Unlimited. But the VC's are proposing new nominees, and they are asking questions I have never faced before! I see many of the old timers boxed into routine work, may be marking time for the IIPO to be announced! Often, Jagan and I are becoming nostalgic for the early days, that were difficult but they seemed so simple and exciting."

All that was left now was the Big Question.

"So, what do I do, Sanam?"

The morning after

Ranjan and Sanam sat down to have their morning cup of tea in the verandah overlooking their garden. Ranjan had obviously not slept well. "Are you ok Ranjan?" Sanam asked. She added, "Let's go away for a couple of days, for a short retreat and have a quiet conversation". Ranjan was silent for a long while, he sighed and said, "I think that might help". "If you remember, a few years ago I had become entrenched in my dance. My teacher told me that I had practised and performed too often and not turned the dharma wheel enough. 'When you practise and perform, your body, mind and heart fall into a groove. It is like the path cut by the bullock that is tied to the oil mill. Some bhaavas *(states of mind) and their expression start to flow, and you naturally follow this since you feel good. But after a while, this ease is at the cost of a lack of ease and flow in other bhaavas. Your body will not be in harmony with your heart. Some of the* rasas *(emotions) you will embody, others you will fight with. Stop dancing and contemplate, just travel to different kinds of landscapes. Each landscape will evoke different parts of you.' If you remember, this was difficult for me to begin with, but so many new seeds bloomed within, my dance took a new form and our relationship became so much more beautiful", she said as she smiled and winked at Ranjan.*

The *Saadhana* begins

In a couple of weeks, Ranjan and Sanam were driving down to Ramana Ashrama. *They decided that going to a place with a spiritual presence, with basic amenities and no distractions would be just right. Circumambulating the sacred hill was a nice metaphor for turning the Dharma wheel. Ranjan also remembered his father telling him that each of the small shrines on the paths celebrated the tapas of a Yogi confronted with a particular sorrow or affliction.*

Ranjan was silent for most of the drive. He seemed to be lost in a world of his own. Sanam just let him be. After a long while Ranjan broke the silence "I really need to look at things from a very different vantage point. My mind just goes over the same beaten track, the same possible solutions. I am very clear that more of the same will not get me anywhere. If anything, it will take me deeper into the same mess". Sanam waited quietly. She had been in the same predicament before. Advice was the last thing she had wanted. It was only through the deep and empathetic listening of one of her oldest friends that she was able to unhook from the broken record of her inner talk and go inward to truly discover the door to the Dharma wheel.

"I am getting angry and impatient these days. I am finding many of the old friends with whom I started this journey simply hanging on, waiting for me to come up with all the answers. I just want to say, 'Grow up Guys!' but that won't do either." After some more brooding Ranjan turned to Sanam "What do you see Sanam?"

"I don't know anything about business," Sanam began. "I will tell you what I see from a perspective that I can relate to, namely dance, and from the Mahaabhaarata. Maybe this will act as a mirror and help you introspect."

"The way you are right now, reminds me of the warrior's role, say a Bhima. *The warrior is always restless, but when there is danger, when the enemy is sighted, he becomes calm. The rasa of* Veerya *(courage) has found its space and legitimacy for expression. With the warrior evoking his Veerya, the others in his group, who have been knotted up in fear and anxiety find solace. They are relieved, place their faith in the warrior hero and encourage him with songs of valour. The advisors are able to think, the helpers scurry around getting the horses ready and the swords polished. It is almost as if once the role script has been established by a 'leader' all others know immediately what is expected of them". Without realising it, Sanam had sat up on her seat; her face and her eyes grew sharp and resolute. Even in the telling of the role Sanam had evoked the Bhaava in herself. Ranjan watched with fascination.*

"I think you are trying to find the enemy and the source of danger outside you Ranjan. You were past this point a few years ago when Mobile Unlimited was recognised as a leader in your domain. I have watched you play Bhima without conviction and your team played the Sakhas *(friends and mentors) as though by habit. Maybe the space where you are now is not at all the 'dwarfs fighting for survival' kind of battle scene anymore. Maybe you are fledgling giants and the space before you has expanded, except that your eyes are searching for threats and danger when you should be recognising opportunity and open space".*

On hearing this Ranjan fell silent, he became very introspective. He hardly spoke as they reached the Ashram. Ranjan and Sanam settled down, went into the temple and sat for a while in Ramana's room. It was dusk and the sky was turning into a beautiful orange, but Ranjan was lost in thought. Finally, when he was sipping a cup of tea in their room Ranjan spoke. "What you say is right, Sanam. At Mobile Unlimited we have often sat down to strategise for the future, only to get totally animated over some operational issues. We get excited over something a younger colleague can solve, but, though we recognise this, we get drawn to this like a vortex. I remember my professor Pulin K. Garg saying that when organisations and their leaders reach a threshold they 'engage with a problem as though it were a real problem, so that they can collectively avoid engaging with the real problem'. I now understand what he meant. Tactical thinking is easy; the issue seems so real and compelling". Ranjan said with a rueful smile. "I know this well", Sanam commiserated, "When I ran into an inner block, the old dance pieces seemed so inviting, small innovations seemed so important and people liked it. But, the better I danced these pieces, the more I was strangely empty within. My teacher asked me to get back to a few basic questions at this time. Let me explain them to you. He asked me to ask myself three questions. "Who am I?" "Where am I?" "Why am I here?" He said that these are questions that are asked by the key players at each inflexion point in the epic story of Mahaabhaarata.

> Each of you have proved your worth and capability in your own eyes. Can you have a new set of meanings for yourselves? Only then the story will progress. Otherwise, it will wind down to an end.

"Naaraayana asked himself these questions and decided to be born as Krishna, an Avatara Purusha at the turn of the Yuga, when the dharma of the new era had to be redefined. But he also asks himself this question at each step of his life as Krishna, so he plays the role of a common herdsman initially, a saviour when Kamsa (Krishna's mortal enemy and uncle) has to be killed, an exile when he goes to Dwaaraka, and as a charioteer in the war. Maybe you and your team are not a set of 'dreamy-eyed inventors fighting an *unresponsive system' anymore. Each of you has proved your worth and capability in your own eyes. Can you have a new set of meanings for yourselves? Only then the story will progress. Otherwise, it will wind down to an end."*

Ranjan and Sanam sat absorbing the beauty of the magnificent orange sunset. "'God always reveals himself to man through rhythm and order.' my teacher would say", Sanam reflected. "'Touch this in your dance, touch your inner order and rhythm and let it flow. The dance will be beautiful, and your audience will also feel this. This is Saatvikam. *You are now stuck with* Vaachikam *where you have understood the operations of your dancing style and need to find appropriate avenues for expression. It is time to trust your inner creativity and go beyond your present accomplishments, let go of the self you have discovered' he told me before he asked me to stop dancing for a while."*

Ranjan said, "I think you are right Sanam. My team and I are still a bunch of kids excited by the start-up dream. I must search within and see if this is whom I wish to be, who we wish to be as a company or can we find excitement in a new dream. If we can't find this meaning in Mobile Unlimited, we must sell and start on a new and exciting idea again. We have to become incubators, really dig deep to find a great new meaning larger than all of us".

It is time to trust your inner creativity and go beyond your present accomplishments, let go of the self you have discovered

Ranjan said. "Sanam, whenever I think of giving up the inventor/start-up persona, I get a flood of new dreams, but I am also anxious. I have invested in the fighting-warrior-entrepreneur Ranjan for so long, how do I drop my shield, my sword and my armour? What will I pick up or wear instead? I feel vulnerable." Sanam and Ranjan sat in front of a small shrine for a while. Sanam spoke. "All that I can say is that this is the time when I have to summon my faith in myself. I remembered how scared and vulnerable I felt before my arangetram, *the first time I danced on stage. I felt my body would give up on me, I would get my period, I would forget all that I had learnt. 'Go in child, dedicate yourself to* Nataraja, *(the God of Dance) and start the dance' my teacher told me. 'Till now you had dedicated your practice for the performance, now learn to dedicate your practice to the Shiva inside your audience. Only till this point can we be with you, now you take your first steps into a space that you will create on your own. Thank all of us who brought you here and step over the threshold, the* Ambalam *(the divine space) is waiting'. These words ring in my ears every time I get ready in the green room. Can you be vulnerable again my great warrior? Can you find your Nataraja to dedicate yourself to?" Time seemed to stand still; both Ranjan and Sanam were quiet for a long while before they started to walk again. A chanting group was way ahead. A family with a group of excited young kids was approaching when they started to walk again. This group also went way ahead of Ranjan and Sanam before they sat down to rest. "I think the dream of creating a Dharmic and competitive business will excite me and my team. I must dialogue this with the group. All of us have been rebels of a kind, we neither like the way most organisations control their employees nor the way they deal with resources." "Explain Dharmic" Sanam challenged Ranjan.*

"I can articulate two principles now Sanam. One will go something like 'ecological ethic': whatever we do as a business we must be carbon positive. Our idealism and our innovative juices will flow with this larger purpose. The other idea that is germinating in my mind is 'autonomy and creativity'. We started Mobile Unlimited trusting our creativity and wanting to be autonomous. We guys can't be clones of other organisations. The Angel Investor keeps throwing benchmarks at us. We resent this, but, we are getting defensive, we are losing our faith in ourselves and running away into seemingly compelling problems to solve. Our real issue is to define 'why do we exist?' in ways that exceed 'creating innovative products'. We have done this, and done it well".

"This sounds wonderful", Sanam said reflectively. "But, when I came back from my sabbatical with the idea of making every dance piece I chose into the one that would reflect the angst of women today, not only were there many critics, my musical instrumentalists were confused. If you remember, my violinist could not make the shift, and I had to search hard for a new one. The percussionist could adapt, the taala *(beat) had not changed much, the meaning and bhaava underwent real change" she said, her voice lost in the depths*

of her own introspection. "Yes, we could still be innovating new products in the domain, but now we are building an organisation that is innovative, not just a conventional organisation with innovative products that will milk the markets to make the investors happy!" said Ranjan with a new joyousness in his voice. "Small adaptations and improvisations were not enough anymore". "The larger meaning of dance had to undergo a change for me to find my heart" Sanam joined in, "the smaller innovations flowed easily".

As they walked along Ranjan broke into conversation every now and again. "We had dedicated ourselves to proving our worth, now we must dedicate ourselves to creating products that will really make a difference to the lives of our customers", he said thinking aloud. "Maybe we stop all our CSR activities and just find young people to work on products that will help rural India and rural Asia". Then after a while, "We have to deal with the 'shareholder first' idea of our California based Angel Investor. This is the Arun Natarajan I have been speaking about, who says he has come back to help India. Maybe he also needs to spark his dream. I must start a whole new dialogue with him". Then a little later, "You know Sanam, I was feeling very dissatisfied with the way we were running hard just to stay at the same place these last two years. Now I can set a direction and a rainbow to run towards. I am still anxious, but an excitement is welling up. Lots of dialogues and discussions and debates lie ahead".

Sanam fell silent and after a while she said, "Ranjan, when I found my new path, I was not just a dancer anymore. I was seeking communication with my audience at a very different level. People saying, 'I like your dance' was not as inspiring as young people saying 'you have touched something within'. I hear you talking like a Bhima with replenished energy. You can't play the new role from an old persona".

A long silent walk followed this exchange. They sat in silent introspection at the halfway shrine and the next one. "Tell me about roles, you keep coming back to this," Ranjan said as they sat down at the next shrine.

"Do you remember our trip to Greece?" Sanam began slowly. "Epidaurus where the great amphitheater is situated was also the

centre for healing. Changes inside and outside must go together, and one must act from this more complete self within the society. This is also what all our Samskaaras (the rites of passage) are all about. There is one important difference though. Western theatre treats the stage and the actors as belonging to a different time and space from the audience. They are modeling a hero, inspiring the audience. In Indian theatre, the stage is part of the 'here and now'. When we start our dressing up we are also starting a meditative process. We lose our everyday selves step by step and become vessels for the divine energies that are latent within us to fill us up. This is very explicit in Kathakali *(the dance-drama form of Kerala). The stage has a backdrop of a cloth with seven colors representing time. The main characters dance from behind this 'time screen' and go through birth pangs before they become fully visible. Each of these archetypal heroes has come down to this time and space, in doing this they are seeking to awaken in each one of us the seeds of these heroic energies. The drama that then gets enacted with music and dialogue is a reflection of the inner drama that each one of us is experiencing, our dharma sankata, our tears, our affections and our hopes. The rasas (Veerya/courage, Sringaara/love, Karuna/compassion, Bhayanaka/fear, Bibhatsa/revulsion, Haasya/humour, Raudra/anger, Adbhuta/wonderment[1]) are evoked in the problematic space, and resolved so that they can find expression in a new way. So a role is not a 'mask' the way a Greek drama would see it, but an inner archetype that expresses itself and relates with its counterparts through the person". After some thought Ranjan said, "If I hear you right, I must find within me new ways of expressing and relating that are not like Bhima and Raavana (the villainous King of Sri Lanka from the Raamaayana). I must explore the Nakula and maybe Arjuna and maybe even Krishna if I must create a new way for my team and myself. What it means is also helping them find new complementary roles so that all of us can find a new rhythm and order as well as a new meaning".*

"It is clear to me now" Ranjan said with conviction, " I am now heading an organisation that is a leader in its domain, I have to be a steward of many peoples' lives and dreams, not just a warrior battling for myself. I have been wearing this robe and mask for a couple of years now but inside me I don't

[1]The conventional understanding of the *rasas* is that there are nine *rasas* or the *navarasas*. But the *naatya shastra* states only that there are the eight *rasas* as stated above. The ninth *rasa* or *shanta*, has been added on in the later years.

fill this space. Arun, the Angel Investor, is speaking to this mask, and I am replying from my Bhima self. I hear challenge and the war drum when that's not the music that is playing. How deeply distorted our minds and hearts become when we don't grow inwardly! We really have come around full circle in Mobile Unlimited, but we are still stuck in our old personas, no wonder we feel like we are on a tread mill. We never felt that way before, every day was new and exciting, every day had something to teach and we were eager to learn."

Notes to myself

1. Talking to Sanam was so good! I wonder how much of the tension she has been carrying silently. No wonder the home was tense and we were both irritable. Even lovemaking was becoming like a chore.

"We are just a habit like saccharine;
I am habitually feeling kind of blue;
but each time I try on the thought of leaving you I stop;
STOP and think it over"

I sang the Simon & Garfunkel lines without knowing what they meant. How much I need her with me! And to have her listen with love and patience, prodding, questioning the way only a woman can!

2. If Sanam is finding me boring and irritable, my team must feel the burden of the way I am. How will we find the energy and the space to make fundamental changes?! Examining the reflections of myself in my actions and my relationships reveals to me all my imperfections, lacunae and my acts of commission and omission. This is disturbing and painful. I realise that only in staying with this dissatisfaction with myself do I light the intense flame of Tapas in me.

3. This reminds me of the Gita "Seedanthi mama gathrani..."
My body burns etc., etc., (Bhagavad Gita Ch 1.29)

Ah! That was a statement of a personal anguish because of the long list of Dharma Sankatas! Arjuna stated all the intertwined dilemmas, and how he is at the centre of them. No wonder the

Bhagavad Gita is considered the great teaching. Arjuna is the hero who has to learn how to act and resolve these Dharma Sankatas. Maybe that's why the Bhagavad Gita starts with "Dharma Ksherte Kurkshketre sama veta yuyutsavaha...." (On the battlefield that was also the ground of Dharma the two armies faced each other on...)

It was an inner battlefield as much as on outer one. Maybe the Kauravas never saw the inner dimensions and that's why Krishna is with the Paandavas, while his army is with the Kauravas.

I now have a starting point. Let me place myself at this point:

That is me! Jagan and I have been a bit like Jobs and Wozniak! That's a great idea. But though we have started a biz, we are still behaving like team leads!! We have hit upon a great product, we don't know how to build a great organisation. I brought him into this with me, as I have done the others. I better wake up and really learn to lead them. But I need to discover who I am and why I am here today! How much energy I feel to know Sanam is with me fully.

This is where my team is. Close to me and around me, that's great, but are we really aligned and convergent? Do we like working with each other? What are the tensions here like the ones I was creating with Sanam!

Now it is time for you to look at your mirror:

Try and write the story of your business. Let me help you get started. Keep a set of post-it notes with you and as you answer these questions for yourself, write down the answers that strike you. Write only one statement per post-it and make them short sentences.

How do I feel at the end of my day?

☺ 😐 ☹ **Excited** because I have talked to my existing and prospective customers and learnt something? Talked to people at the cutting edge of technology and got into discussing our practices? Met a few associates of my organisation and learnt about them, what makes them tick, their aspirations and the way they look at our organisation? I have a clear idea of what value our company offers to each of our stakeholders today and in the future.

☺ 😐 ☹ **I feel satisfied**. I have solved a few problems and I am sure they will not bug me again; dealt with some of the conflicts between departments and people. However, I am left a little worried because it has been some time since I had a satisfying discussion with my team regarding the future. The top line and bottom line will be healthy, but I am confronting cash flow issues. We are offering value to our customers, but I am not really sure if I have a compelling proposition for them. I know that we ok with our through put, but I don't know where the levers of value are, and where the wastes are being generated.

☺ 😐 ☹ **I am tired**. I am encountering the same type of problem every day. We seem to be lurching from one survival threat to another. I can predict what my team members will come to me with, and their stances vis-à-vis each other. Customer requirements surprise me. I sometimes even feel angry that they don't seem to understand what we offer and how it can be used. I have no time to look at operational improvements. There are new associates I meet and don't know who they are. I don't even seem to have time to say a few words to them. I dread a meeting with my finance people.

Now take a walk down memory lane. Go back to the time when you dreamt of your career. What excited you about it? What were the nightmares? As you look at the years that have gone by, what were the incidents that have left an impact on you, on your team and on your company? Who were the players? What do you recall of them? Do any conversations stand out? Who or what were the enablers and who or what were the disablers? Where did you get your resilience from and what did you celebrate? What makes you feel heroic about your journey?

You must have written at least 50 post-its with one or two lines on each. Now we play with all of them, take a chart paper, and a few crayons, draw, write and build the narrative of your journey. Spend a little extra time and expend a little more attention on the inflexion points. Be sure to re-experience your feelings as you run the movie in your mind.

Put this picture away for a few days, come back to it and look at it again as if it is a new story. Now ask yourself the questions "*Who am I?*" "*Where am I?*" *and* "*Why am I here?*" You will be surprised at the clarity that will emerge! Have fun!

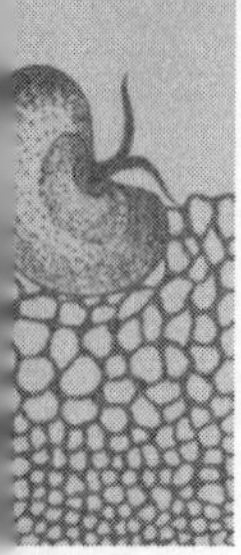

CHAPTER 2

Uncovering the Ground

For a few weeks after the retreat to Tiruvannamalai *neither Ranjan nor Sanam sat down for any serious conversations. Ranjan was introspective. "I have been sharing my thoughts with the team," he said one morning over tea. "I am taking Arun Natarajan to dinner. I am going to have a serious conversation with him. I want to see if he is a mercenary who has come here to do what he thinks is necessary to make a business grow, or is he really searching to find a new paradigm? I will be late returning home tonight, don't wait up for me."*

Silence hung heavy for a week, and then a determined looking Ranjan told Sanam, "I am very intrigued by the Mahaabhaarata heroes. Arun is also keen on seeing what changes can be brought about by using some of our ideas. I have asked my old friend and classmate who is now a professor of management to help me. We used to be fascinated with our teacher Prof. Pulin Krishna Garg (PKG) and his concepts of role archetypes based on Indian Mythology. Ananth Saptaparni (AS) has now taken his place as the head of Organisation Behaviour. AS has promised to spend a whole afternoon with me. Arun has said he will come too.

"When I look back at our first forays into Pulin's theories I remember that we did not always listen. The western ideas of time and death are very different from ours and he always insisted that we must find a way of re-anchoring ourselves in our own mythology. He often said we are children of two cultures, European and Indian. We can either make this a great resource or tear ourselves apart. 'Many of you are 'Macaulay's children', he ranted often; you have internalised disrespect for our learning and our genius. You forget that the British and the

Mughals before them came to India for its wealth, its science and its technology. More that 30% of world trade was out of India and the famous Damascus sword and the Samurai swords were made from steel made in Salem'. We mostly fought with him in class, but many of us were impacted. We often argued his ideas furiously, back in the hostel".

Ranjan was excited when he came back from the meeting with AS. He had already told Sanam that on Sunday he would discuss the theories put forward by Pulin. On Saturday he went into his study and worked through his notes. He would emerge once in a while to ask Sanam about some obscure story from the Mahaabhaarata. Sanam was intrigued and was really looking forward to the 'presentation'.

After breakfast on Sunday, Ranjan set out a flip chart in his study and invited Sanam to come in for 'the session' as he called it. "I am going to test out my presentation to my team, so it will be a little formal. We found in our earlier discussions that a lack of rigour in our understanding of the Hero's journey was allowing us to escape from the harsh light of examination. I will first go through my reconstruction of the discussions with AS, and then I want you to tell me how you see it from your perspective."

Ranjan set up a white board and started his presentation with a framework to explain this new universe that he had first learnt from Pulin.[1]

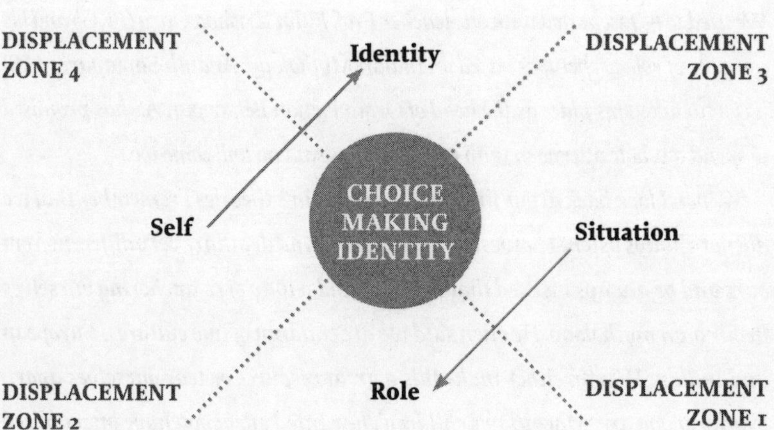

Figure 1: The polarities and the tensions:

[1]***CULTURAL IDENTITIES AND ACTION PROPENSITIES: The Paandavas in perspective.*** *Prof. Pulin K. Garg in his "Primer on Role and Identity" [A primer on Process Work: The ISISD Perspective; Gopal Khandelwal. ed. 1990] speaks of cultural identities and their implications on patterns of action. Ranjan's presentation is a revised version of that paper.*

"Before I begin to describe the framework, there are also some key terms that need to be defined here", Ranjan began. With this, Sanam noted that his demeanour and tenor took on a different colour from his earlier tentative explorations.

BEHAVIOUR is a function of the self in interaction with the situation. These behavioural interfaces become coded in patterns depending on the culture of the organisation at any given point in time. This we shall explore in each of the quadrants and zones of displacement as seen in Figure 1.

SELF: The Self relates to the internal reality of the individual. It triggers evocation and the impulse to act and learn from within the individual, leading to the discovery of skills, capacities, value stances, etc.

SITUATION: This relates to the external reality in which the self must interact with the external world of systems, structures and norms. This includes the worldview, and expectations of others in the outside world/organisation.

THE AXES: The horizontal axis represents the polarity between the inner and outer realities. When the self or individual interacts with the system or situation [external reality], a tension is created. It mutually affects the learning and impressions both about the self and the world at large.

IDENTITY: Identity is anchored in the self. It is a cognitive map that gives meaning to the self in the world and in one's own feelings. It develops over time from the learnings and impressions about the self, with the contours of the map changing with each subsequent engagement. *This idea of self essentially answers the question "Who am I?" As it becomes more entrenched, all incoming experiences from the environment are filtered through it to provide meaning.* It includes individual values, frameworks, choices, wishes, experiences, learning, etc.

Sanam was doubling up with laughter. "I never knew you could become so professorial," she said, "all you need is a pair of spectacles, and a beard!" Ranjan stopped, looked at her and said in all seriousness, " 'Good theory is the best practice' a great philosopher has said. AS says that I am not only at the end of my old behavioural modes, I am also devoid of a new way of thinking about my world and myself. I am determined to work on my thinking with the help of AS and my passion and feeling with your help."

'Professor' Ranjan continued:

> **ROLE:** Role is anchored in the situation. The learning and impressions that one gains about the situation one finds oneself in, develop into a perception of one's place and position in the world, i.e., one's role. *The concept of role essentially answers the question "What does the world expect of me? How do I respond to these expectations?"* Roles are defined in terms of the tasks, ethics and norms of the organisational culture. These are often developed in response to demands made by significant people in the system. From these expectations, an implicit 'model' of how one plays social roles gets imprinted in the mind. The vertical axis thus is the axis between the polarity of Role and Identity.
>
> When a person enters a new situation, he cannot anticipate its challenges. Thus, the encounter is inherently filled with a choice-making tension that requires the integration of the identity and role.
>
> "Will I act from the location of my identity from an introspective stance or will I act from my role expectations and relate to others?"
>
> "Do I act from the demands of the situation or from the aspirations of the self?"
>
> This tension is deployed through action. Some actions are self-oriented while others may be system or situation oriented. For example, a person who tends to be a 'bargainer' in most situations is being self-oriented, whereas a 'controller' is system-oriented.

These patterns of response that are woven into the process of choice making become the Role-script or the Role-identity of the person.

"So how does this affect the way the individual responds to the situation?" Sanam asked. This question gave Ranjan pause. He then went on to explain the concept further.

Choosing an appropriate response to a given situation requires that the individual deal with this tension. He has two choices before him, depending on how well he is able to harmonise the self and the world. Typically, he can avoid this tension by resorting to pre-determined habitual stances, dictated either by role or identity propensities. The tension then gets displaced into one of the four zones: Self-identity, identity-situation, situation-role or self-role. The pattern of displacement would depend on individual propensities as well as the organisational culture. The patterns are neither good nor bad in and of themselves; and are essential to keep the current organisation functioning. It is a rare individual who can choose to locate himself in the centre of the map, facing the tension between the polarities of the self and the world. He seeks to harmonise and balance between the polarities by enquiring anew into the nature of the self and the system to arrive upon the emergent truth.

THE MAHAABHAARATA AND THE ROLE METAPHORS

The role archetypes have been beautifully etched in the characters of the great Indian epic the *Mahaabhaarata*. The five main protagonists [Paandava brothers] illustrate the concepts of integration and displacement of the role identity choices that individuals make, and their peculiar action propensities – the way they deploy their energy.

The story essentially explores the tensions that unfold between two branches of a royal family: the *Paandavas* and the *Kauravas*.

The Paandavas are the five sons of Pandu who represent five stereotypes of personality. The Divine Personage of Shri Krishna guides their path. The Kauravas are the 100 sons of Pandu's brother Dhritarashtra. The trials and tribulations of the Paandavas, while wielding righteous power in the face of grave provocations by their cousins, forms the body of the story.

Sanam was now in familiar territory. She found herself able to add to the perspective by saying, "The Paandavas are symbolic of the five sources of energy – earth, water, fire, air and ether. The 100 Kauravas are a symbol of the fragmented world enveloped in desires and conflicts.

"That is why the climax of the story juxtaposes the Dharmic (Life enhancing) forces led by the Paandavas and the Adharmic *(Life depleting) forces led by the Kauravas in the battlefield. The famous Bhagavad Gita (Song Celestial) is set in the moment when the war begins. Arjuna (one of the Paandavas) seeks to know from Shri Krishna how one discriminates right from wrong and what the commitment to truth implies. "What is Dharma? What is right action?" he asks, "On the one hand stand my teachers and my cousins, and on the other is the cause we fight for. I am confused."*

This interjection was a perfect moment for Ranjan to take a short break in his presentation. "Sanam, why don't you continue to input your understanding of the characters and role scripts as I make my presentation? Your perspective on the five elements will definitely shed new light on this concept. In fact, for this next step AS also wanted to be a part of the presentation as he felt that he could add new dimensions that he has been developing over the years. I have invited him to join us and he will definitely be thrilled to hear your inputs too. He should be here soon."

Soon AS arrived and after the introductions were made, the three sat down to continue their ideation. Ranjan began, "Let us now look at the role archetypes and how they unfold. The personalities of the five Paandava brothers exemplify the five archetypes of the Role-Scripts or Role-Identities described in this framework. We begin with the first-born, Yudhishtra."

Role and Situation: Yudhishtra

When the role identity is displaced on to Zone 1, namely between the Situation and the Role, the symbolic identity that emerges is that of a **King**, who anchors and epitomises **system-centred appropriate behaviour.**

Yudhishtra, the first archetype, represents this role-identity. The counter-point is set by Duryodhana the Kaurava cousin. In the role of Yudhishtra, the individual becomes fragmented between knowledge and action. He has deep knowledge, is wise and has a comprehensive perspective. He can determine what is right and wrong. This ability to make choices is bound by the location he takes between the external situation and the role expectations.

However wise he may be, in his action, he is role bound. He acts in keeping with precedence, so as to maintain the continuation of the past for good role performance. He will not do anything that has not been done before or that which is not in keeping with the 'book'. He maintains the policies and practices of the organisation, so that his actions are routine and even hackneyed.

In making a choice in the current 'moment of truth', he does not make an active choice, but falls back on a programmed set of choices, confined by Role tasks conceived in an idealised context. He aims to be a model of perfection and is coached and trained to behave in appropriate, prescribed ways. In his aim to remain correct and beyond reproach in his actions he does not break prescriptive boundaries even in the face of adversities. He prefers to be respected rather than be seen as manipulative for selfish reasons.

Ranjan then turned to Sanam. "This is where you come in with your understanding of the elements. How do you understand the role of Yudhishtra?" Sanam took a moment to reflect on this and then began, "Yudhishtra is related *to the earth element. He is bound and limited by the situation. He is imprisoned by the 'shoulds' and 'musts' prescribed to him. In a sense he finds it difficult to move freely or offer flexibility in any situation".*

"The self does not grow except in ways that the system allows within bounded roles. ***The self is bounded by and situated in the system".*** *This was AS. "Sanam, your insight is fresh and extremely clear. And since the two of you have created the basic frame of the role archetype, I think I can bring in a new perspective too. I call it fragmentation."*

Ranjan continued:

Yudhishtra does not bring his own knowledge into the system, and only acts within prescribed and given boundaries. His knowledge remains vested in the self and he withholds his sagacity from the system. He is also fragmented from his personal feelings and intuition, continuing to act in the same manner to ensure continuity even if it might cause disaster to him personally and the system that is dependent on him for leadership. In his focus on precedence and procedure, he loses concern for individual well-being, and sensitivity to human emotion. All his actions become restricted to those required by the role and he absolves himself from the responsibility of being responsive to the situation.

In the Mahaabhaarata, the critical turning point in the story is the game of dice between the Paandavas and Kauravas [represented by *Shakuni*, the Kaurava's uncle]. Yudhishtra is warned by Krishna of possible foul play, but still goes ahead. His reasoning is that the rules of the game require that an invitation to play must not be refused. In the process, he does not pay attention to and disowns intuition and feeling, represented by Krishna. Yudhishtra also remains fragmented from his own unconscious attraction to the emotional excitement of gambling. He is indeed defeated, resulting in humiliation. He loses his position and kingdom, affecting not just him but his four brothers and his wife.

The important thing to understand is that when Yudhistra locates himself in this choice-making mode, he fragments himself. He gives up the 'tension and potential'-filled centre and prefers the comfort of looking at a polarised mode, a partial mode. Maybe he realises it is partial and then he will be open to finding complementary modes. Or, he is blind to the polarising choice he makes and believes it is the whole.

Sanam felt compelled to come in at this point. "This makes sense. In art, we usually find the nuances of a character emerge clearly when juxtaposed with a counter character that shows different, maybe even darker, shades of the main character. In a sense Asuras *are counterpoints of* Devas. *So the counterpoint of this identity is* Duryodhana."

Ranjan continued to explain this concept.

Duryodhana derives his power only from the system that is inherited. He is the legitimate contender for inheritance, but is continuously under threat of losing it. He constantly compares himself with his peers, and fears being inadequate or insufficient. As a result, he always wants to be in command, and is continuously aggressive. He directs not just his own energies but also those of the system to consolidate his position. The 'control-compliance' mode of behaviour is a strong undertone of this role script. Duryodhana is the shadow of this identity archetype.

"The Yudhishtras are therefore either the well controlled and impeccable upholders of the system, or become the insecure controllers who are protecting themselves through the self-centred manipulation of the policies and procedures of the system," Sanam helped Ranjan conclude.

AS listened keenly and said, "That was a very lucid insight. But let me now anchor all of this in a contemporary context. Let me paint the management style of a Yudhishtra-type manager."

The primacy of control is the overriding theme here. The managers who echo this model come from families where grandfathers have had the most dominant role. Their fathers are self-absorbed or exiled to escape from their own dominant father. They are also often the oldest sons. Yudhishtra represents the standard operating procedure in the organisation. Without him, there is no structure and the whole system will collapse. In organisations, these people are honest, sincere, hardworking and loyal. They represent the changeless face of the organisation; and are the pillars of strength in routine and stable functioning. They are quietly indispensable and meticulous in the completion of their work. They often form the administrative function of the top management, who maintain the structure and processes needed for daily functioning. However, a Yudhishtra's tendency is an inability to respond adequately to crises or the unexpected.

They represent the changeless face of the organisation; and are the pillars of strength in routine and stable functioning

As leaders, they tend to over-supervise their subordinates. Yudhishtras have a dedicated team, who they patronise. Yudhishtras tolerate their failure and inadequacy as long as the prescribed methods are adhered to. However, they are unlikely to invest in the growth of the subordinates as a result of which they remain mediocre. However, this team performs well when the situation is stable because of the Yudhishtra's own strength of convictions.

Conversely, managers who echo the Duryodhana side of this role-identity are continuously insecure and anxious about being displaced. Though they have perspective, and can anticipate the future, plan and execute their agendas, they become caught with internal conflicts and protective of their self-interests. This causes them to create procedural barriers when none exist and make people rebellious, while protecting themselves through status and rules. One redeeming quality is their generosity to people who support them.

No one is a pure representative of any one type, but we have a propensity to be one or the other. Under stress, or duress, we tend to fall back on these propensities. Therefore, developing a facility with behaviours that are not spontaneous is not easy. Finding places where one can practise them is helpful. This is like a sportsperson

seeking a practice space in which to become proficient in their areas of weakness. Most of us have the behavioural skill in us. However, the context of our growth and the habits we have internalised lead us to favour some skills and let others atrophy. For example, I am very disciplined and deliberate in my interpersonal interactions but find formal situations dry and deadening. I avoid them or react to them. Among friends I can be the joker of the pack!

So, ask "Mirror, mirror on the wall, do I flow this way or not at all?" And if the mirror does not reinforce your fond and wishful ideas about yourself, do not break the mirror! Have a small conversation with it, write down how you see yourself both in agreement and in disagreement of the statement. Ask your friends. But do not, I repeat do not treat this as a level 1 to 5 rater! Behaviour does not lend itself to measurement the way weights and lengths do! It lends itself to observation, description and dialogue.

We will set up the mirror for you after each Paandava hero is discussed. Go over the statements once more after you have completed the lot, and choose the five you flow with and five that block you. Value yourself for what you are! Look for practice spaces in which to nurture other parts of your self if it is important to you. Otherwise, flow with your natural propensities, complement your blocks.

I am now summarising the discussions of the Yudhishtra archetype.

YUDHISTRA

☺ 😑 ☹ *I value structure and stability. I value the framework of roles. I avoid the exercise of authority for my own advantage. I stay within the legitimate boundaries of the system while making demands of my subordinates.*

☺ 😑 ☹ *I take my duties and job responsibilities seriously. I am especially careful and controlled in formal situations. I do not take liberties with my superiors.*

☺ 😑 ☹ *I value the standards set for role behavior and expect everyone to play by these standards. I dislike the uncertainty and messiness of unstructured situations*

☺ 😑 ☹ *I am conscientious and display a strong sense of loyalty to the organisation.*

☺ 😐 ☹ *I value procedures and rules. I stay within the framework of processes and policies laid down. I expect others to respect processes, policies and procedures.*

☺ 😐 ☹ *I believe that power and authority are given by the system and must be exercised in a responsible, dignified and dispassionate manner. I avoid politics. I am impersonal and correct.*

☺ 😐 ☹ *I respect tradition and see a value in following the norms and practices of the system.*

☺ 😐 ☹ *I respect the formal divisions of functions and authority in the system. I am a good administrator.*

☺ 😐 ☹ *I respect the status that one acquires by virtue of one's position in the structure. I consolidate my position and build my career through carefully planned and incremental steps.*

☺ 😐 ☹ *I set aside my emotions and intuitions, or control them if necessary so that my actions are within the frameworks provided by the system. I seek the advice of wise people when in doubt.*

"Ranjan", AS continued in a different vein, "this is a great discussion we have here. It is helping me delve deeper into my own understanding of some of these concepts. Let us follow this style in exploring each of the subsequent archetypes. You make your initial presentation, and then let Sanam bring in her emotive, artistic perspective. I shall continue to apply it to today's context of business."

Self and Role: Bhima

Let us look at the space in the lower left quadrant of the map. When the tension is displaced into Zone 2, i.e., into the area of self and role, the symbolic identity that emerges is that of a **Warrior** who anchors and epitomises a passionate and energetic **action for the system**.

Bhima, the second archetype, best represents this role identity. He is a person of great strength, with many appetites and action potentials. He lives lustily and loves deeply.

He is adventurous and takes up causes. He is very emotional and given to outbursts. He is easily provoked, reactive and impulsive. When evoked [provoked] into action through challenge or in the face of a crisis, he can respond with extraordinary strength, can be relentless and completely focused in achieving his goal.

People operating from this zone tend to be lone heroes. They set themselves against insurmountable odds in action and often act as trouble-shooters. They are self-reliant but need to be rewarded with recognition, appreciation and affection. They suffer from strong feelings of exclusion and tend to fight for inclusion.

Sanam now took the baton from Ranjan. "Bhima is related to the element of fire. He is energetic but his energy and meaning are derived from his commitment to the system and his belonging to the system, much as fire depends upon the fuel that feeds it."

Ranjan then added, "The self grows through the demands and challenges placed upon it by the role requirements of the system. ***The self is shaped from (out of) the system.****"*

"This is where I can now come in with the 'fragmentation' perspective," said AS. "This role-identity is reactive and fragmented from reflection and thought. Bhima disowns reasoning. He does not have the ability to set goals and direct himself purposively, unless triggered by the system. While responding powerfully when provoked, he is bored with routines of ordinary life and tends to become self-indulgent. He is ruled by impulses and when thwarted, reacts with rebellion.

"This role identity is also fragmented between impulses and wishes, socialising norms and the drive to assert oneself. The Bhima personality does not place priority on the method used, but merely on the outcome. Differences are not tolerated, and the discomfort of others remains unimportant as long as his wishes are met.

"In the game of dice mentioned above, Bhima remains silent when the wife of the five brothers, *Draupadi*, is staked and lost. He remains silent through the utterly humiliating episode where *Dussasana*, Duryodhana's brother tries to strip Draupadi in the court, forcing her to seek help from Lord Krishna who prevents the humiliation through divine intervention. He is seething inside but locks in his rage. He reacts with anger only after the event, when Draupadi asks him what he as a husband ought to be doing".

Sanam said, "Ah!! See why the fight between Bhima and Jaraasandha *broke out. Bhima's counterpoint model is Jaraasandha in Mahaabhaarata. When Jaraasandha is born, the right and left parts of his body are already vertically fragmented: with the right representing the socialised self and the left, the impulsive self. Jaraasandha's propensity to act is triggered by subjective impulses, disregarding situational appropriateness. In the counterpoint the individual becomes self centred, extractive and manipulative. Jaraasandha tends to be highly unpredictable. Jaraasandha is the shadow side of this identity archetype.*

In organisations, these are individuals who play the role of trouble shooters, hunters and explorers

"Bhima can, therefore, be highly integrated, sophisticated and self-directed, operating from well regulated power, when he is helped to anchor himself in the right role; or he can go on the rampage and become disruptive and destructive."

"Absolutely," said AS. "Let us examine the management style here. It will shed further light on this Bhima identity.

"In organisations, these are individuals who play the role of trouble shooters, hunters and explorers. The Bhima is the defender/protector of the organisation and its members, and stands against the dangers and threats of the environment. He does great feats, but only when challenged. He tends to set himself against great odds and insurmountable barriers to action.

Bhima is often a lone performer, and rarely encourages good teamwork. However he tends to gather a group of hero-worshiping followers around himself. In superior positions, Bhima is a hard taskmaster and drives his team relentlessly, inspiring terror. Most people tend to avoid confrontation with him. Bhimas tend to value work that is physically evident and based on experience. They have poor appreciation for intellectual processes and sophisticated knowledge.

The manager, who echoes the Jaraasandha aspects, becomes an unpredictable and reactive 'rebel without a cause' in the system. He is very impatient and can create crisis when there is none, or easily become prey to the manipulations of the cunning intentions of others". With this AS concluded the discussion on Bhima.

BHIMA

☺ 😑 ☹ *I am strong, decisive and action-oriented. I am protective of my subordinates and I expect their loyalty to me.*

☺ 😑 ☹ *I am hard working and loyal to the interests of my superiors. I am resourceful and trustworthy; I will get things done.*

☺ 😑 ☹ *I am willing to state my opinions and make demands of my superiors if the situation needs it.*

☺ 😑 ☹ *I am aware of my needs and drives. I like taking risks and operating on my own.*

☺ 😑 ☹ *I act as a trusted agent. My interest lies in being available to those who run the organisation and I am ready to use my talents as they see fit.*

☺ 😑 ☹ *I understand and deploy the personal exercise of rewards and punishments.*

☺ 😑 ☹ *I am alive to power and influence in the organisation. Politics is a reality of organisations and I know how to play the game.*

☺ 😑 ☹ *I am sensitive, emotional and alive. I like vibrancy in my team. I like to celebrate success. I hate failure. I am however not very fond of analysis and see it as a lack of courage.*

☺ 😑 ☹ *I value competitiveness, and believe that real talent and capability must be rewarded.*

☺ 😑 ☹ *I love the excitement of working out tactical moves. the anticipation of an engagement with challenges makes me come alive.*

"Ranjan, how are you going to deal with the characters of Nakula *and* Sahadeva? *They are relatively invisible even in the Mahaabhaarata."*

Ranjan was silent for a moment. "That is why I struggled to gain a complete picture here. It is also probably why my managers who reflect these role archetypes constantly get overlooked and feel undervalued. Let us look at Nakula first and see how it goes. It might be useful to bring to your mind the figure I drew to start with. Nakula is the one who occupies the top right quadrant."

Identity and Situation: Nakula

If you recall, we looked at how the living reality constantly challenges a person to make choices and respond from the right location in the inner space. When the tension is displaced into Zone 3, i.e., between Situation and Identity, the symbolic identity that emerges is that of the **Healer**, who epitomises the attitude of sacrifice and **service to the system**.

Nakula, the third archetype amongst the Paandavas, represents this role-identity. Nakula acts from the premise that the organisation is more important than the self. He does what is required in a necessary situation without being invited to do so, but because of an inner commitment to uphold the system.

The key word for Nakula is facilitation. He permits disagreements and arrives upon consensus through negotiation; as long as the task gets completed. However, these disagreements are kept within closed doors, so as to maintain the invulnerability of the system.

His focus on 'serving the system' causes him to sacrifice himself for the system and he ignores his individual feelings in the process. In this sense, he is selfless. He plays any role that the system requires for its maintenance without requiring benefits. He holds all the negatives within the self and attributes the positives to the system. He becomes the invisible infrastructure-builder for the system; who is not recognised for his contribution. He is the much desired team player always supplementing and complementing others.

Sanam came in here. "Nakula is related to the water element. He flows and invisibly nourishes everything around him. His role is life-giving, and in many ways, he sacrifices himself to the needs of the system."

"His self grows through service of the system. This truth is expressed as **the self is for the system**", Ranjan added. It was now AS's turn to bring in the fragmentation within this role identity.

"Nakula's self is fragmented from feeling and action. In action, he is superb, very efficient and totally in command. His own aspirations are never apparent. He does what is required in the situation. Though he does not apparently seek benefit for the self, he expects the organisation to recognise his contribution, while remaining silent about his disappointments.

"Amongst the Paandava brothers, his role was to look after the horses and swords. But nothing is known of what he felt about his role, his thoughts or indeed about anything else. No credit goes to his contribution. Instead, it is Arjuna who enjoyed fame and the consequences of victory; Arjuna is the hero who gets the women and the honour, but Arjuna would be nothing without the preparatory work of Nakula.

Nakula acts from the premise that the organisation is more important than the self

"I would find it quite difficult to find the counterpoint to Nakula in the Mahaabhaarata," Sanam felt compelled to add here. "My only recourse would be to look through the other great myth, the Raamaayana. Would Lakshmana, *Raama's brother fit this? He gets completely entrenched in the service of Raama."*

"The counterpoint of Nakula is not available in Mahaabhaarata as you rightly pointed out," Ranjan continued from Sanam. "Lakshmana becomes the invisible extension of his hero, his elder brother Raama. He does not anticipate the future, cannot respond to crises in the face of which he becomes inadequate unless directed by Raama.

"He dedicates himself to the dictates of his master and displays fierce loyalty only to this commitment. He withholds all personal feelings. In the process, he becomes a loner who tends to be snobbish, and is capable of ruthless manipulation to achieve the goals of his master.

"When his brother [Raama] goes to the forest, Lakshmana accompanies him without a second thought. Raama however is accompanied by his wife, while Lakshmana leaves his own newly wedded wife behind, devoting his life to the service of his brother."

AS, now excited by the rounded character analysis of Nakula, moved into exploring the management style.

"The manager who echoes this role-identity is the silent, tireless, committed, task-centred worker. His critical role is to convert the waste and toxicity of the system into manure and fertility. He will do what needs to be done, though he tries to remain within the prescribed boundaries of the system; he will be willing to take risks if the task so demands. The system colludes and ignores his deviations because of his accomplishments.

"His collaborations are end-oriented and lack emotionality. He evokes help when he needs it but bargains hard when others need help from him. He is ruthless and yet very sweet. The managers who opt for this model rarely succeed in the No. 1 position. They get disoriented, and their functional efficiency becomes eroded. They lack a strategic perspective of their own and end up as echoes and shadows of the leader they dedicate themselves to.

"Managers who echo the shadow side become the hatchet men of their heroes. They unquestioningly make the hero's goal their own and this often makes them blind to the consequences of their choices to themselves, others and even to the system they serve. Their world is circumscribed by this one purpose of serving their master. They only seek the love and recognition of their chosen hero.

At the end of his analysis of Nakula AS now said, "I did not realise that so much was possible with Nakula. Bringing in Lakshmana as the counterpoint was very interesting. Let us explore Sahadeva in the same vein next".

"But why have we skipped over Arjuna?" Sanam was a bit confused here.

Ranjan replied, "I had the same question when I was first introduced to the archetypes. Arjuna is actually the balancing centre. So let us look at him, at length, later on."

NAKULA

☺ 😐 ☹ *I value equity and team work. I am focused on the group purpose. I am focused on creating the infrastructure needed to get the job done.*

☺ 😐 ☹ *I value the attitude of service. I am open to ideas and suggestions from the team. I am willing to give the lead to others when they show greater expertise or ability for the tasks at hand.*

☺ 😐 ☹ *I am alive to the prerequisites and preparation essential for task effectiveness and efficiency. I invest time and resources to create capability.*

☺ 😐 ☹ *I value technical competency and effective teamwork. I value people with a strong commitment to contribute.*

☺ 😐 ☹ *I often tend to sacrifice my own needs for the common cause. Sometimes this leads me to feel used and unappreciated.*

☺ 😐 ☹ *I communicate well in discussions of task requirements leading to appropriate action. I motivate the team to perform through a personal commitment to goal achievement.*

☺ 😐 ☹ *I am proficient at being a team developer; I invest in creating a sense of safety and belonging in the team.*

Role with Identity: Sahadeva

We now come to the last quadrant, the interior of one's self. When the displacement of the tension is into Zone 4 or Area of Self and Identity, one gets the symbolic identity of the **Hermit,** who limits his interaction with the environment to the minimum on his own initiative, who however is a keen observer and is **the theoretician of the system.**

Sahadeva, Nakula's twin brother, best represents this role-identity. Sahadeva is committed to observation and insight. He is acutely aware of reality and is a data bank of the knowledge resources. However, he does not impact the world using these resources, unless invited. In this sense, he does not come alive in the situation, but remains a spectator.

Sanam came in here with her input. "Sahadeva is related to the air element. He touches the world ever so lightly and is a dry intellectual. He neither shapes nor impacts the world in a visible manner. He takes the location of a 'witness', aloof and alone."

"The self grows inwardly and may be characterised as **the self apart from the system**", added Ranjan.

Sanam then continued with her understanding of some of the other characters in the epic. "The other person of this type of role-identity is Vidura, *the brother of King Dhridharashtra as well as his observer/advisor. He is a person of great wisdom and understanding. However, when the war between the cousins erupts, he refuses to take sides and act, but shuts himself up within his home, completely cut off from the action. Did you know that Sahadeva is actually Vidura's favourite amongst the brothers? Vidura often acted as his mentor on many occasions."*

AS now took over in exploring the fragmentation.

"While Nakula is a silent participant, Sahadeva is virtually invisible in the epic. No one knows much about what this prince actually did. He is fragmented between action and knowledge. One version of the story goes that Sahadeva ate his father Pandu's toe and became clairvoyant. However, he is warned by Krishna not to speak from this intuition, else his head will blow up. He therefore becomes the jyotisha *(the astrologer)* who is able to predict the entire war but cannot act to change its course, or even reveal his knowledge.

"As a result of this fragmentation, Sahadeva loses touch with his action potentials and is alive only to his learning abilities. Since he gives up all action, he does not have any knowledge about his own self. He cannot apply his deep insights to the organisation or is not interested in doing so, though others may use his understanding effectively. Hence he loses all sense of relevance and responsiveness".

"The counterpoint of this identity also is not clearly available in Mahaabhaarata. However, the psychological role model of Hanuman, *a servant par excellence, from Raamaayana is probably a good counterpoint".*

Sahadeva loses touch with his action potentials and is alive only to his learning abilities

Sanam now continued with the character of Hanuman.

"The story of Hanuman goes as follows: when he was a child, he thought that the sun was a ball for him to play with, and flew towards it. Indra, *the King of the Gods, fearing the destruction of the natural order, hurled his thunderbolt at the baby, who fell down and became unconscious. At that time, the child was cursed to forget his enormous power till a time of need arose. Only when he grew up and had to cross the ocean to reach Lanka, where* Sita, *the heroine of Raamaayana was imprisoned, was he reminded of his power. Hanuman however was a greatly learned person.*

"Thus, the counterpoint of this role identity has tremendous reserves of power and potential. But he does not value them enough. These resources are only harnessed under direction or persuasion, through an invitation and a beckoning. At all other times he is invisible, a part of the background. The difference between the role-identity of Sahadeva and that of the counterpoint of Hanuman is one of location. While Sahadeva is located in the system, where everybody bosses him around, Hanuman is located in the individual relating to the system. The inner urge to express and discover one's true potential is very strong in both; however with Hanuman it becomes an individual quest."

AS took over from Sanam now.

"Sahadeva's primary role is to convert experience into knowledge. Typically in an organisational context, these individuals shine in areas that primarily require research and reflection.

"The manager who operates from this role-identity becomes everybody's errand boy. He is seen as a good performer under [often heavy] supervision since his tendency to become self-reflective leaves him tentative in action. Once in a while, he surprises his superiors by his astute and erudite perspective, and appropriate choice of action. While these observations and actions might be noticed, he as an individual does not get much credibility, unless he is in a role that is primarily one of knowledge creation.

"He awaits bestowal of recognition, and rewards, from authority: he does not actively seek it. Amongst peers, he acts as a cathartic valve for others' burdens or heartaches, or performs tasks that are boring for them to do. He does not create tensions, conflicts or threats. In fact, he remains invisible unless he is needed.

As a leader, he is afraid of ownership. His lack of responsiveness in action might come across as insensitivity to the concerns of his subordinates.

SAHADEVA

☺ 😐 ☹ *I value learning and knowledge. I am self- reliant and expect the same of others.*

☺ 😐 ☹ *I am vitally interested in the development of my own potentialities and open to learning. I respect the needs and values of others and I am willing to give help and contribute to their learning.*

☺ 😐 ☹ *I am excited by the challenge of experimentation and discovery. I believe that the pursuit of knowledge for its own sake is important.*

☺ 😐 ☹ *I tend to be an observer in most situations. I give a lot of space to others and do not interfere unless invited to join in.*

☺ 😐 ☹ *I tend to be a loner, and enjoy a deep conversation with people who show a genuine interest in things I am interested in.*

☺ 😐 ☹ *I value high quality work done with care that goes into creating products and services of high intrinsic worth. I dislike acting in a hasty and haphazard manner.*

☺ 😐 ☹ *I have concerns and doubts about how I am received by others. I tend to withhold my doubts and concerns and get withdrawn when I am troubled.*

☺ 😐 ☹ *I am a proficient knowledge creator; I like to get immersed in study and research leading to acquisition of skills and knowledge.*

Now go back and look at your own propensities, look at what you tend to do under stress, and what you dislike being forced into.

AS, Ranjan and Sanam now took stock of all that they had discussed regarding the four brothers. The task of looking at Arjuna now remained. This was definitely an exciting prospect for the team. Ranjan now began with his understanding of the hero, Arjuna.

THE BALANCING CENTRE: ARJUNA

The four princes [and their role identities] represent the four pillars on which the organisation resides in the present. Yudhishtra represents the control and compliance of 'true soldiers' of the system. Bhima is the adventurous explorer and hunter. Nakula is the unrecognised maintainer. Sahadeva is the observer and thinker.

They represent internal adjustments that the organisation makes constantly to ensure that it functions daily, given the present knowledge. They continuously monitor the organisational functioning and act in a way that the organisational continuity can be maintained. While these are essential for daily functioning, these four role-identities can only uphold the present.

The tension of balancing these four essential roles and anticipating the future is held at the intersection of the 'Role-Identity' polarity and the 'Self-Situation' polarity. This is the location of choice making in the here and now and the location of constant questioning of the nature of response and the emerging reality. This location in the Role-Identity map is personified in Arjuna, the fifth archetype. He is the questioner and integrator. He is the one who faces Dharma Sankata, the need to make a choice between two equally valid or right choices (and paradoxically two equally unpleasant choices). This is more difficult than the choices that Yudhishtra makes between what is clearly right and wrong, Bhima's immediate response to challenges, Nakula's focus on service and Sahadeva's choice of observation.

> He has a great deal of potential and resources but must choose between self-oriented action and system-oriented action. Through this choice he provides initiative to the rest of the organisation.

Arjuna is the quintessential hero of the Mahaabhaarata, beloved of the people of the kingdom and the favourite of Lord Shri Krishna. He is a skilful warrior and an ardent student. He faces the ambivalence of the central position; continuously looking at what is emerging. He does not shy away from asking the fundamental question, "What is the way forward? Is the present paradigm sufficient?" however uncomfortable or difficult this might be. He is willing to explore the unknown and moves the organisation through dialogue and negotiation rather than operating on the 'musts'. Thus he is the one who stands between the two armies arrayed to fight, stopping the war to debate on the emergent reality with Krishna.

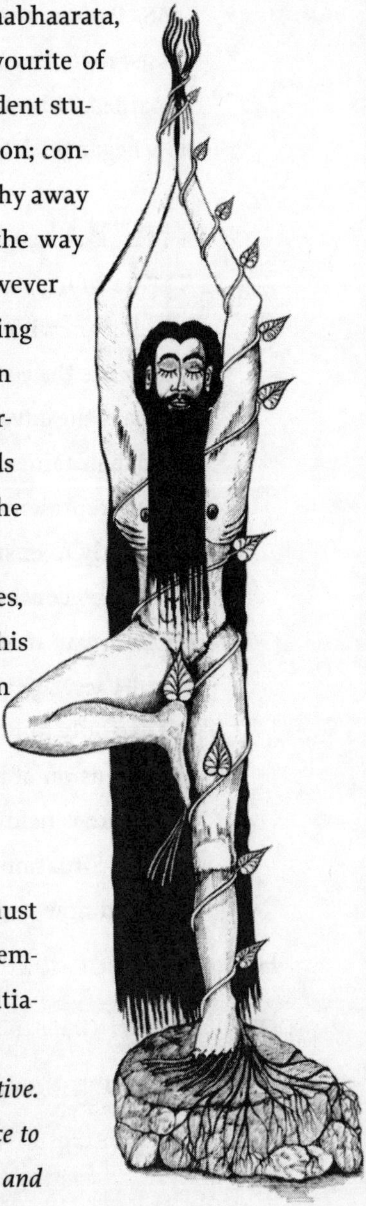

He seeks to integrate and balance all opposites, including his feminine and masculine sides. This aspect is particularly clear as Arjuna takes on the role of a woman when the brothers are exiled after the loss of their kingdom in the famous game of dice. He is thus a good warrior/archer and a good dancer too! He has a great deal of potential and resources but must choose between self-oriented action and system-oriented action. Through this choice he provides initiative to the rest of the organisation.

Sanam listened keenly. She now brought in her perspective. "Arjuna is related to the element of space. He gives space to express and attempts to integrate all the diverse pushes and pulls of living. The key word that describes his living dilemma, of self and the system is 'simultaneity'. He searches for the elusive 'and' in every moment."

"His underlying rule for existence is, '**the self and the system must find a simultaneous growth**,'" said Ranjan.

AS once again brought in his point of view.

"Arjuna is continuously caught between the choice between self or the system; and with lack of assurance of knowing which system he belongs to: the affiliative or the rational, the given or the emerging? He is fragmented between action [goal] and understanding, between passion and will. For each choice, he pays a price and suffers the agony of discovering the right way. The need for deep enquiry and making a balanced choice sometimes restrains the people who play these role-identities from getting into action. Arjuna can get enmeshed in doubt and questioning leading to hesitation or procrastination. At times, Arjuna needs to be pushed into action from an external source or event. The wise Arjuna seeks the help of the right mentors, the Krishnas of his life.

Sanam now said, "Is this character then not akin to Karna? *I should think then that the counterpoint to the role of Arjuna is his eldest brother, Karna. Karna is disowned by* Kunti, *the mother of the Paandavas, at birth and is cast away. He is found and reared by a lowly subject in the kingdom. Duryodhana recognises his immense gifts and befriends him, offering a sense of belonging, recognition and affirmation.*

"Karna is the mightiest amongst the sons of Kunti, and displays courage and integrity. However, like the proverbial 'ugly duckling', he is caught in self-doubt. He is forever in search of his own legitimacy, a search for belonging to his true family and struggles to express his true self. He resolves his ambivalence by a complete surrender to the one who offers compensation to this painful inner search. In the process, he gives up his ability to use his vast resources for himself. He becomes a pawn in the hands of the person who 'claims him as their own' and affirms him. Karna's actions and choices then become inappropriate and destructive both of the self and of the system. His enormous generosity and devotion get misplaced."

It was now AS's turn.

"The managers in this role-identity carry a great burden of institutional tasks. They are actors, rather than policy makers. They are quick to articulate the negatives of policy. While they tend to procrastinate in general during crises, they can also quickly mobilise during crises when they get the right insight or the right advice. They perform best in fulfilling tasks of integration, orchestration and change, since any action of theirs needs to hold the entire organisation in mind. They tend to take up very difficult assignments if their conviction is clear.

"They are committed to the organisations and derive their satisfaction from this commitment. Since they tend to be proud, they do not curry favour, and instead stand aloof. Given their ability to hold divergent viewpoints, they also carry a lot of tension and have to work very hard to find the right balance. However, they suffer injustice in silence.

"Some of the Arjuna types become stuck at middle levels of management in organisations. They often witness the rise of their juniors above themselves. When these two internal blocks to timely action [hesitation to act and self-doubt] are resolved by the individual, the Arjuna leadership qualities start to grow. He can absorb the tensions of the centre, facing the risk of expressing himself anew, and being disowned by the system. He seeks new ways of interpreting reality, and challenges himself to find new responses. He is able to re-fashion his identity and role appropriately, and strikes out into new paths."

Ranjan looked pleased with this presentation, "I have actually got it fairly clear in my mind, and Sanam listened to this right through" he thought to himself.

Sanam now felt that there was a link she could add to the whole presentation. "I like this very much. This fits well with how we look at heroes in dance. I am not sure all the details of the work style make sense to me, let me just tell you where it makes sense to me. Each of the five heroes has a dominant Rasa *that runs through all their actions.*

"Bhima for example has to confront the rasa Bhayanaka (dangerous and fearful) and gets easily aroused into Raudra (anger or rage). If these rasas are inappropriately evoked, the group will get into anxiety and panic and the individual will be fighting windmills. The person may also be experienced as scary and anxiety-provoking. I can see how a Yudhishtra has to deal with Bibhatsa (revulsion) most of the time. He has to sift through the pile of refuse and keep removing the decaying, the impure and the undesirable. Nakula is acting out of Karuna (compassion) and he can easily take on the pain and suffering of the

other in a misplaced sense of caring and concern. This rasa is often seen as a combination of the essences of Daya (benevolence) and Dukha (sorrow).

"Ranjan do you remember the short film we saw of how the caterpillar, about to emerge from the pupa stage, struggles to tear open the cocoon?" Sanam tried to bring a clear picture to mind. It is often much easier to reach understanding, when the mind can see a picture. "They also showed how an artificial cutting of the cocoon, thinking it relieves the suffering, actually results in a distorted and incomplete butterfly, with incomplete wings and an inability to fly! That image gets evoked here somehow.

"Sahadeva is the one who experiences Adbhuta (wonderment and curiosity). If each of them becomes restricted to these rasas, they will not only fragment the life space, they will have no emotional and psychological bond! They will become captives and victims of their chosen spaces, while simultaneously becoming adept at them. Krishna is often seen in dance as the complete hero, since his life shows the exquisite and most appropriate unfolding of all the nine rasas and therefore is the epitome of Shanta (serenity), as is the Buddha. Arjuna often gets caught with Shringaara (love) and loses Virya (courage) at the battlefront. I know how easy it is to get caught with these fragments. Looking for the seeds of all nine in us and nurturing their expression is so difficult. I found Shringaara very difficult, since in our family all sensuousness was denied. We tended to be strict and austere. Sexuality was a complete taboo. If I had to really evoke the sensuous and the sexual feelings that are part of Shringaara, a voice in my head would make me feel a little ugly and guilty. I found Veerya, Roudra and Bibhatsa much easier!

"I hope this talk of rasas helped. How are you going to use all this knowledge?" Sanam asked as she came out of her reflections.

AS was now intrigued by all this talk of rasas. "I feel that this can be worked with quite beautifully in a workshop setting, especially if I were to use theatre as a medium. Why don't we try this with your team?" he asked turning to Ranjan.

Ranjan was thrilled. This was a new impetus for him. He and AS immediately set about fixing a time slot.

"Our team has become quite dull and task bound. It is now time for some Play".

Notes to myself

1. Having Sanam and Saptaparni to dialogue with is great. I am not so lonely any more!!

2. The unflinching gaze into myself has melted the dross that clouds my perceptions. It has revealed to me the nature and form of the stances I take, as I stand on the ground I have created for myself.

3. "Karmanehyapi bodhavyam." Thou hast to know of action, of other than action the context of action in order to understand the true nature of action (Bhagavad Gita Ch 4.18)

4. Let me see what my map looks like now:

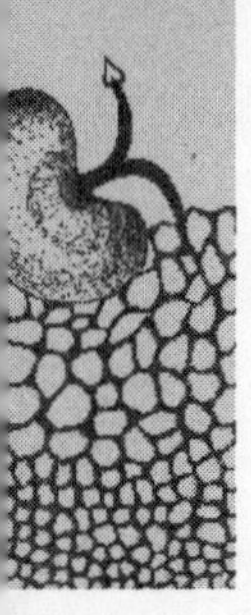

CHAPTER 3

Examining the Seeds that were Sown

In a week's time, Ranjan set up his study again, brought out his notes and took Sanam through the dialogue. "I will take you through the ideas that AS added. AS is very much into theatre you know and he brought in a more grounded perspective to the heroes and called them 'the masks managers wear'. He gave some examples of people he had coached who typified these heroes, but he stayed with the five we already discussed". Ranjan put on his most professorial manner and started, "Let me take you through the workshop step-by-step":

The workshop started with AS asking people to make a choice out of 5 statements. "Which of the 5 will you be able to do with conviction if you are allowed only one:

1) Anchor the rules and procedures, ensure predictability
2) Anchor passion and be willing to fight
3) Anchor team work and ensure equity and reciprocity
4) Anchor learning and experimentation
5) Anchor questioning and doubt"

The discussions suddenly took on a very different dimension since it was obvious that we were looking at our own selves through the stories

We then took up stories of the five Paandavas and enacted them. We chose one or two of our favourite stories of each hero. We found that bringing in the ways in which the heroes had gone incognito towards the end of the exile period added a great deal to delineating the character. The discussions suddenly took on a very different dimension since it was obvious that we were looking at our own selves through the stories. The playing out of the dramatic episodes was great fun and we became animated like little kids again.

After the role-play AS said, "We will come back to the choice. Let me first explain what the choices mean. I am going to talk about the 5 Paandava heroes:

THE MASKS OF MANAGERS

What do these heroes look like today? The field in which they operate is not the *Kurukshetra* (the battle ground) of yesteryears. It is a far more complex space called a business organisation. We will look at each of the heroes separately and emphasise the propensities of each of them. Obviously, each of us is a combination of several behavioural tendencies though we may show a greater affinity for one or the other.

YUDHISHTRA: Primacy of Control

We first look at Yudhishtra for many reasons. He is the first-born and has the dubious privilege of being born into a context of adults. The world he enters is a well-ordered and functional world and most problems have answers. Persons with a Yudhishtra identity value control and order. They are therefore not only self-controlled, they seek order outside themselves. Often the first-born finds that she/he has to play parent to younger siblings. Modelling the behaviour of the elders and passing on tradition becomes almost a compulsion.

The Yudhishtra-Manager is therefore one who relies on procedures and policies. Job descriptions, laid-down processes and documented rules are a key to his feeling of security, and confidence that he can face problems and find solutions. The solutions are to be found in 'the book of rules'. The Yudhishtra-Manager is therefore an excellent administrator. She/he tries very hard to understand and interpret the rules and policies in as objective and rational a manner as possible. She/he would be extra careful to ensure that personal biases, likes and dislikes do not enter their decision-making process.

This propensity comes at a cost. Self-control becomes a prized practice. She/he expects, likewise, that other managers 'leave their egos and emotions at the door' when they come into their rooms. They guard emotions to such an extent that they become cold and display a 'poker face'. This often leads to loss of touch with their emotional selves and they find it difficult to find self-replenishment.

The Yudhishtra-Managers are at their best when the context does not change at a fast pace. Since the Yudhishtra-Managers depend on precedence to help them make decisions, change is disconcerting to them. However, their predisposition to look for stability and security pushes them to set rules and to follow a discipline. This can be functional if their supervisor is a decisive person and can guide them in a step-by-step fashion. If the supervisor is impatient or unclear, the Yudhishtra-Manager will prefer the known path and hold on to the written word. She/he does not see that following the 'tried and tested method' is also a risk! One is betting on the probability that the future will be very similar to the past. But, in the world of the Yudhishtra-Manager, order and stability are the norm. The aura of dependability that they project, because they have a solid set of policies and precedence to follow, can lead to a false sense of security and complacency.

The Yudhishtra-Manager is obviously very successful in stable contexts and where procedural rigour is essential, for example, in the finance function, or the Quality Assurance function. Their key word is efficiency, and they will be efficient, this could however be at the cost of responsiveness to the emergent reality. They also tend to be status conscious. Since they value self-control, conflict is anathema to them and competition is shied away from. “Deserve, don’t demand” is a key principle. “No one is indispensable” they will say very often, but they might be unconscious of the fact that they create indispensability and power by being custodians of the rule book. Status could well become a defence for the Yudhishtra-Manager.

The word ‘Role’ would therefore mean task, job description, status, conferred authority, conformity to expected sets of behaviours and norms. The Yudhishtra-Managers are therefore very successful as judges, administrative heads, finance professionals and managers in stable contexts. Growth would mean more of the same; increases in trust, stability and status. Credentials, alumni references, and pedigree will mean a lot to the Yudhishtra-Managers, and will influence their interactions and recruitment decisions. Confronted with business challenges they would look at structural changes and redefining procedures and they would rarely question the fundamentals. The dependence on control and the need for predictability will predispose the Yudhishtra-Manager to try and drive change through the use of authority, changes in policy, and reporting relationships. Motivation through recognition, increase in status and entitlements, will appeal to the Yudhishtra-Manager. They would look for new formulae that address the new situation! Discovery and the thrill of risking failure in the pursuit of the unknown are not for them.

The focus on right and wrong, the reliance on procedure and the like, make the Yudhishtra-Manager blind to underlying tensions and invisible realities

The focus on right and wrong, the reliance on procedure and the like, make the Yudhishtra-Manager blind to underlying tensions and invisible realities. They would therefore seem a bit naïve in situations that require political sensitivity and manoeuvring.

The Yudhishtra-Manager will be a very reliable friend, and a respectable citizen. However, the feelings and emotions that lie repressed could get expressed in righteous indignation, judgements and accusations, or feelings of being let down. While they have answers for every problem others confront, their fount of wisdom often goes dry when they have to answer their own dilemmas. At these times the Yudhishtra-Managers could become very dependent on teachers and parental figures, or lose their sense of stability and become very anxious.

BHIMA: Primacy of Dynamism

Bhima is the second born. Where Yudhishtra is caught in dependency, Bhima tends to become reactive and counter dependent. Our Bhima-Managers value action. They get restless with too much analysis and positively resent rules and boundaries. One must see Bhima-Managers in turnaround situations to appreciate their true genius. They revel in the danger of the situation; celebrate the heroics needed to turn the situation around. They take to people emotionally and offer as well as expect intense loyalties. Their dislikes are also based on gut feel, and are often very strong. Entrepreneurial situations are their forte. The spirit of adventure and exploration brings out the best in them. They are great tactical thinkers who think on their feet.

The Bhima-Manager who is not led by a dynamic and charismatic leader can become very demotivated and sometimes self-destructive. She/he gets bored easily and procedures are seen as roadblocks, documentation and rigour as a complete waste of time. "Give me the next challenge and let me go" he seems to be saying all the time, leaping at opportunities and engaging with challenges. Back-of-the-envelope calculations that indicate broad directions and an attitude of "act now figure out as we go" characterises their compulsion for action.

The speed of decision-making, love of challenge and emotive relatedness, makes them blind to the difference between roles and the self. They are very authentic and passionate. In leadership positions therefore,

Bhima-Managers can be very charismatic, magnetic and attractive, but also very demanding and insensitive to anything but the heroic goal that they are striving for. To them it is taken for granted that "you are with me, you are my person and therefore you and I think, feel and act the same way!" The lack of differentiation between role and self will be problematic to others when the Bhima-Manager is in a position of authority. When she/he acts from conviction and seeks robust discussion and dialogue, the others caught in issues of boundaries and appropriateness will feel uncomfortable and intimidated. The Bhima-Manager learns through debate, and builds up competence through engaging in mock battles. The way the Bhima-Manager learns is through trial and error, and modelling action based on their heroes. The Bhima-Manager loves a good battle and will be willing to accept the other's point of view if they have the tenacity and the ability to wrestle him down! The fact that he trusts and respects only those who can fight for their convictions and be passionate makes him either a hero or an oppressor in people's minds. "Act like I do" he seems to demand, he is blind to the oppression this can cause. The fact that having an army of echoes and shadows of himself is a weakness is not something he easily perceives.

There are no roles in the Bhima-Manager's dictionary, only situations to be encountered and areas to be explored. The Bhima-Manager is in an arena most of the time. Growth to him is an opportunity to fight and win, cover new ground and move on. He is prone to trust affiliations, 'old boy' networks and relationships, while dealing with people and recruiting managers. He is likely to see them as belonging to his group and could be blind to their real strengths and weaknesses. This often works well in start-up situations when the cohesiveness and bonding of small groups work towards breaking new ground. This is a time when the tensions of managing paranoia and decisiveness, speed of judgement and immediacy of group action, trust and robust confrontation become the keys to success. However, this intense focus on action and bonding tends to create issues of inclusion and exclusion. Newcomers to the group will find it hard to break into the founders' club. The Bhima-Managers believe that pride and challenge are great motivators that can inspire others into following them into adventures, and taking risks, and making great sacrifices in the pursuit of heroic goals. Binding them within roles and norms is a very difficult task; it is possible to reach them only through the heart.

Bhima-Managers are great friends, they love to entertain and love to be loved. They are often larger than life, and spread a childlike innocence and enthusiasm around them. They often talk of heroes and warriors, dream of great victories. They are very successful sales people, entertainers, entrepreneurs and explorers. Most books about successful start-ups are built around the Bhima-type initiator. However, without the dedicated infrastructure builders, one would not have heard of these heroes. The other part of the story is boring in comparison and often gets glossed over.

NAKULA: Primacy of Method

Nakula is like the third born. In many cultures, the third born is trained as a priest or a doctor. The parents have spent time on the first and second born, and the third born often becomes the odd one. Aware of one's own lacunae and the pain of others, Nakulas tend to be self-effacing people serving the needs of others.

The Nakula-Manager is likely to be a team worker, driven by the purpose of the group, and willing to do whatever he can to make the team succeed. The Nakula-Manager is naturally open to co-operation and is skilled at complementing and supplementing skills and competencies that are required to complete tasks. The Nakula-Managers are often great problem-solvers and infrastructure-builders. They rarely seek the limelight. Having the key resources and being competent gives them a sense of power and security. Logic and rationality are valued; creativity in solving problems is celebrated.

Nakula-Managers are very sensitive to the context and believe in situational leadership. They are therefore indispensable to the entrepreneur as he enters the stage of consolidating early gains. However, the larger-than-life, powerful Bhima-Managers can put off the self-effacing Nakula-Managers, and the patient work of building the foundations and creating the wherewithal for the grand plans of the entrepreneur may never materialise. Almost all great teams in the fashion world, the world of sunrise businesses, breakthrough technologies and the like have come out of the teamwork between an inspired Bhima-Manager and a dedicated Nakula-Manager.

Though they are team oriented, for the Nakula-Managers the team exists for a purpose and once this is accomplished, they will have no problems in moving on to the next purpose that deserves their attention. Past achievements mean little except as testimony to competence. Private agendas are definitely out, since sacrifice to the larger cause, and the group, is paramount. 'Service before self' is their rallying call. The focus on building infrastructures predisposes the Nakula-Manager towards a rigour of processes. Their focus on problem solving and creativity predisposes them to constant improvement. They are the ideal leaders of a TQM or a lean initiative! Nakula-Managers perform well where the goals are clearly stated and they are given autonomy to define the how's, mould the team and coach the team members to perform to their best.

Nakula-Managers tend to be committee focused and value consensus building and questioning. This could be seen as slowing down the response to opportunity, but they make up the apparent time lost in not jumping into action under-prepared. Through the rigour they establish and the team spirit they nurture, they ensure a steady and reliable action that avoids waste of effort, time and resources. Their tolerance for learning and approaching the new challenge methodically is critical to steady growth. Nakula-Managers are the tortoise that beat the hare to the finishing point! Steady, methodical and goal-focused, they build as they grow.

Roles are flexible and defined by the purpose. No task is too small, no relationship is permanent, and status does not enter the picture, since Nakula-Managers value equity. They learn by applying theory and principles and therefore go into basics while confronted with challenging problems. Larger and more impactful problems motivate them. Being invited to be part of path-breaking and significant task forces is seen as recognition of their competence and contribution. Defining and redefining larger, more challenging goals and discovering robust processes, is their idea of growth.

Nakula-Managers are great coordinators and very reliable. They are the ones who keep families ticking and ensure that parties and picnics are fun. Their self-effacing nature predisposes them to stay in the background and when they are taken for granted, they tend to feel used. They become instruments of the purpose, and tend to be discarded once the task is done. Respect and mutuality are very important to the Nakula-Manager.

SAHADEVA: Primacy of Knowledge

Sahadeva is the last-born. Usually, the family has no real roles or expectations from the last-born; they are expected to grow up on their own. The presence of elder siblings makes things easy at one level but very difficult at another. Learning becomes easy, as there is always someone to turn to, or some model to imitate. But, this ease also takes away the pain and endeavour necessary for a discovery of one's real worth and identity. Sahadevas are loners in search of their true selves.

Sahadeva-Managers are the proverbial researchers. They value knowledge for its own sake, and go to great lengths to establish valid knowledge. The immediate use or application of the knowledge is not of interest to them. The intellectual challenge and the sense of self-actualisation in grappling with a field of thought, is all that they care about.

The Sahadeva-Manager understands the need to interact, to share learning and insight. However they like to do so in settings that are intimate, secluded, and have the seriousness of enquiry. After such an interaction they need time to introspect and reflect so that they can digest the knowledge and make it their own. In fact it is this propensity to be alone and preoccupied with intensely personal searches, that makes them seem unsociable and gets them nick-names like 'the absent-minded professor'.

Sahadeva-Managers cannot be led easily. They are seekers, and very self-driven. They search out areas of enquiry that are meaningful to them, and pursue the enquiry single-mindedly. They are not interested in leading others. They are seeking knowledge and truth, and can be dogged and competitive in this pursuit. Freedom to pursue their path is key to the Sahadeva-Manager. They offer their resources for research and administrative efficiency, but remain uninvolved. Many scientific establishments make the mistake of giving the Sahadeva-Manager positions of authority and leadership. Very few can make the adjustment and often become a liability to the management, and a loss to the field. When a group of Sahadeva-Managers come together, it is like the gathering of prima donnas. Each is an expert in his chosen field, and often lacks the ability to dialogue and debate. Making a presentation of the theses or hypotheses to be critiqued by others is their way of peer interaction and learning. Sahadeva-Managers are very successful researchers, designers, analysts, and specialists. Without them the modern organisation is lost, since all advances in business are ultimately advances in technology. They would love to create wealth for themselves, but their real motivation lies in breakthrough knowledge and thought. Growth lies in creating lasting, aesthetic, and profound knowledge.

Sahadeva-Managers have few friends, but to those who know them well, they can be delightful companions. Their keen sense of observation makes them astute and they can be very humorous, with a brand of humour that would be subtle and incisive. They are very reluctant to offer their insights or discoveries lest they be found erroneous and lacking sufficient rigour. This sometimes makes them over cautious.

AS stopped here. "Let's understand these four heroes before we come to Arjuna. He is a different dimension altogether, we will come to Arjuna when we have examined these four managerial actions and the kind of organisation you have created".

THE DANCE OF THE MASKS

These four orientations seem to be universal. In his book 'The Gods of Management' Charles Handy uses the Greek archetypes to describe the four types and the descriptions are almost identical. Carol Pearson talks of the King, the Warrior, the Healer, and the Hermit. Again these have a great similarity with the four Paandava heroes. Though we have described the behaviours of these types in isolation, they are neither found in their pure forms nor do they function in a vacuum.

Most organisations seem to be created by Bhimas. Or at any rate the way the myths are built, the founder tends to be painted in heroic terms, with the metaphor of challenges and victories. Initiation and breakthrough into new ground is certainly Bhima-Manager behaviour. The Bhima-Manager tendency to move on from one challenge to another does not create the ground for building long lasting institutions. When the wise Bhima-Managers team up with resilient Nakula-Managers we have the beginnings of Organisation Building. The entrepreneurial zeal of the Bhima opens up opportunity and makes progress, and the Nakula-Managers quickly come in and build methods and processes to nurture and foster the conquered spaces. We find this pattern repeated in history. Genghis Khan has often been portrayed as a marauding Barbarian. He was a fierce warrior but recent portrayals of his methods reveal an astute inclusiveness, a healing of the wounds suffered by the conquered people and the creation of stable governance. The Mongols stayed on in Afghanistan and the Middle East for hundreds of years and were the Mughals who invaded and conquered India. Babur made the early conquests, but it was Akbar his grandson, who was able to bring together the Warrior and the Healer, who established the empire.

The ability of the Bhimas and the Nakulas to work together is a prerequisite for the Yudhishtras to enter the scene. One rarely comes across a Bhima-Manager/Yudhishtra-Manager team that is stable. The need for seeking adventure and the need for security and stability do not mix easily. The paradox is, however, followers as well as the average citizen need safety and security. Long term survival and growth cannot rest on a nomadic pattern of existence. This may be why Alexander could not hold on to the lands he conquered, whereas the Roman and the Ottoman empires lasted for a thousand years. When the Dynamism of the Bhimas died down, these Empires became stagnant and then they died. This is clearly visible in Mughal history. Akbar's reign was followed by many years of stability, good governance and peace. When Aurangzeb came in with his brand of reactive leadership, and a need to establish a Muslim state, there was large-scale insecurity, rebellion, fragmentation and collapse of the state.

When the initial consolidation happens between the Bhima-Managers and the Nakula-Managers, not only the Yudhishtra-Managers but also the Sahadeva-Managers find space. No group can evolve and grow without the theoretical insights of the Sahadeva-Manager. The early problem solvers obtain solutions through trial and error, as well as from passionate engagement. They can rarely explain why something works. The rest of the team observes, learns, and sets down a method. The theoretical underpinnings are still not clear, only the practices and the injunctions are clear. It takes a scientific mind to uncover the math and physics of the 'why'. The moment the 'why' is discovered and explained, a technology gets defined and the methods proliferate. Also, the ground is now created for pushing the frontiers of the existing capabilities. Knowledge has grown this way and history was made by the Bhima-Managers who used the new technology.

In the future, the importance of the Sahadeva-Manager and Nakula-Manager is bound to grow. We have seen that some of the most successful entrepreneurs in the last decade were tandem teams. It was Steve Jobs and Steve Wozniak who created Apple. Both shared traits of the Sahadeva-Manager, they were innovators with a passion for learning and experimenting. Steve Jobs was also a demanding Bhima-Manager and that brought the fighting qualities to the fore. The wider the knowledge base needed to create a product or service, the greater the need for teamwork among experts. The team as a whole will have to exhibit the fighting qualities of a Bhima. The world is clearly moving towards an exponential growth of knowledge. Innovation is the key driver of business. It is therefore inevitable that the Sahadeva-Manager and Nakula-Manager combination will form the core of successful businesses in the future.

This pattern is not only evident in history, it is repeated in organisations as well. Ichak Adizes ("Managing Corporate Life Cycles", Dr Ichak Adizes, Adizes Institute; 08-2004) has done extraordinary work in studying this phenomenon.

Go back to the story you wrote about your organisation's journey. Try and identify the key players who have shaped your organisation with you. Write down the feelings that have been generated in the interface with them. Often those behaviours of others that are most frustrating are reflections of our own behaviours. It may be some reaction we have triggered in them, some aspect they are pointing to in us that we are reluctant to see. We sense the need for supplementing and complementing our selves, but the changes we need to make in order to accommodate, to value these different ways of making meaning and making choices needs to be worked at. This then generates a sense of 'damned if

I do accept your invitation and bring in my best, and damned if I don't, and withhold my best!!' Great leaders find the energy, the wisdom and the commitment to recognise these double binds and evolve beyond them. They create genuine spaces of dialogue and collaboration with people who are different from themselves.

EXCELLENCE AND THE SHADOW

Our four heroes are the archetypes of human behaviour. What will make a person excel in one of these archetypes? We will look at a few case studies to unravel this.

We look at the career of this person we will refer to as Bhaskar who is a Bhima-Manager type. Bhaskar was a young and very successful Human Resources and Industrial Relations manager who had been drawn to the challenge of turning around an ailing organisation in the Agro Industry. The organisation had a long history, and was a very well known institution. It had stagnated for a long while and had recently been taken over by a Business Family. The initial attempts to revive the organisation, through bringing in financial discipline and sales discipline, were successful. It soon became apparent that the organisation needed 'right sizing'. The Family promptly dispatched its Bhima to clean the 'Aegean Stables', who in turn assembled a small team of Bhimas and Nakulas. Bhaskar was offered this very difficult task and took it up as a challenge. His dedication to his leader was total.

The initial processes were difficult, and needed more input than mere rigour: a close study of past performance, a discussion of attitudes, and potential to identify who the real contributors were. Then came the painful part, which was to ask people to leave. Many of the ones who were found redundant had stagnated for years, and were probably unemployable. Also they were middle aged and had families to support. Bhaskar went into the task, steeled himself for the ordeal, and started wielding the sword on behalf of the organisation. The other managers and the leadership team held him in awe and in some ambivalence. Soon Bhaskar was being secretly referred to as 'the Butcher of Bilbao'. Towards the end of this terrible chapter of the turnaround story, Bhaskar came to know about this nickname. He was deeply hurt, but he hid his pain and carried on with the task. Within about a year of this event, Bhaskar's performance started deteriorating, he was moody, irritable and the joyous person who was the 'life of the party' had disappeared.

Bhaskar then sought help. He went through a practice of yoga, and at the invitation of his yoga teacher cum coach, he went through Process Work Labs. He continued to be coached by his yoga teacher/process worker. As he started uncovering his feelings, Bhaskar got in touch with the core issue that was draining him emotionally. "Those b.... just fled the battlefield!" he burst out one day to his coach. "They pretended to be with me, but just left me alone to be the bad cop while they were the good cops. They could not stand the bloodshed they had authorised. Bloody b..." It soon became clear that behind this anger was guilt. "I can still hear the weeping of grown men asking 'How will I get my son through college? How will I get my daughter married to a good person?'" He could see that the treatment meted out to him by others was a reflection of their own fear and envy of his strength. "But, I did it all for our good, why did they desert me?" this question was the most difficult for him to come to terms with. A set of people Bhaskar saw as 'my people' had taken protection under the idea of appropriate roles to be played in the organisation, and had not been willing to stand by him in his most difficult hour. Like a great Bhima or Hercules before him he had to fight the bloodiest battles alone.

When Bhaskar came to see that the oppressor/executioner was the inevitable other side of the coin when one is a warrior, he could release himself from guilt and resentment towards the 'cowards'. He slowly found his conviction to act, recovered his zest for life and went on to become the President of the organisation. He pioneered many innovations in operations and governance, befriended the farmers' community. He also created a very stable partnership between the organisations, the farmers in the area contracted to supply agricultural produce to the factory, agricultural research agencies and the government agencies. He is now a well-respected adviser to the Industry lobby and the government. But for him his great achievement is "I created a community where in the beginning, there were only warring parties. The farmers love me for this and I will do whatever I can for them".

The Mahaabhaarata has a fascinating section where the Paandava heroes have to live incognito for a year. Metaphorically, they are invited to examine their shadow sides before they can emerge as complete people. Yudhishtra lives as the Kings' gambling companion, Bhima as the cook, Nakula becomes the stable boy, and Sahadeva the cowherd living all alone in the forests of the land!

Beauty parlours often have mirrors that magnify one's face and therefore put a spotlight on its faults. Shadow areas of the self are very difficult to see for oneself, but others can see them easily! Also many of them are unintended, and an inevitable part of the positive behaviour. The warrior is a brutal killer too. Imagine a warrior who worries about getting hurt. Let's take a trip through the key statements in this story.

BHIMA

☺ 😐 ☹ *I hide my cowardice. I expect my subordinates to play along with the facades I show.*

☺ 😐 ☹ *I become a sycophant of my hero figure, and an unquestioning instrument in his/her hands.*

☺ 😐 ☹ *I pretend to be courageous to impress my bosses.*

☺ 😐 ☹ *I become compulsive and greedy.*

☺ 😐 ☹ *I become ruthless and enjoy the sense of fear I create in others.*

☺ 😐 ☹ *I use my charisma and my ability to reward others in ways that reinforce me.*

☺ 😐 ☹ *I get entrenched in the 'what's in it for me?'*

☺ 😐 ☹ *I like to hype up situations and pump up enthusiasm even when it is hollow*

☺ 😐 ☹ *I am contemptuous of losers. I sometimes cheat so that I don't lose.*

☺ 😐 ☹ *I cover up my lack of foresight with an urgency for action.*

Let us now look at the unfolding of a Nakula-Manager. We will call our protagonist Neil. Neil was taking over the reins of a very successful technological company. The founder CEO had taken a small boutique consulting division, and made it into a powerhouse. But, he also brought with him his own sharp likes and dislikes, preferences and prejudices. He either loved people or disliked them, and this was returned heartily by the recipients of his attitudes. Neil was able to understand the man and become the bridge between him and the organisation. He absorbed the tensions and the toxicity; converted potential blow-ups into creative dialogues and built the platform for growth.

When the transition did happen and Neil became the second CEO, he faced the same danger of many who take over from charismatic founders. People compared him with his predecessor and found him very down-to-earth and pragmatic. Many of the accomplishments that were built on the hard work of Neil were attributed to the brilliance of the founder. The company was flourishing, but many of the essential functions like finance and HR were not built up to be robust. The accent on technology and sales had been very high.

Neil had to confront many things within the self. His self-effacing service to the organisation had not only made his contributions invisible, but also, predisposed him to remaining in the background and doing the institution building work. Initially he felt 'used' as an instrument by the founder. He had to come to terms with the reality that the other side of the coin of the service focused Healer/ Institution builder is the Martyr. The one who sacrifices his life for the larger good but is forgotten and taken for granted. Once Neil came to terms with this reality, he was able to see the immense gift he had for creating stable teams and practising situational leadership.

Initially he felt 'used' as an instrument by the founder. He had to come to terms with the reality that the other side of the coin of the service focused Healer/ Institution builder is the Martyr

After a period of introspection, Neil chose a small team to work with him as part of the CEO's Office. He astutely selected a Bhima to front-end business expansion, a Nakula-Sahadeva to work on internal strategies of building people and infrastructures, and a Yudhishtra to anchor the finance function and make it efficient. The team decided to launch a series of initiatives and in a couple of years converted the early gains of the Founder into a powerful platform for growth. The organisation has grown exponentially in the last few years and is a leader in its domain.

NAKULA

☺ 😐 ☹ *I devalue myself and allow myself to be exploited in the name of being an organisation person.*

☺ 😐 ☹ *I use the idea of service to cover up my own ambitions.*

☺ 😐 ☹ *I am very uncomfortable with centrality and give up what is rightfully mine in the guise of being humble.*

☺ 😐 ☹ *I feel resentful of being used, but hardly ever let others sense my anguish.*

☺ 😐 ☹ *I often tend to complain and whine in very private settings.*

☺ 😐 ☹ *I carry the pain of the systemic hurts that people experience.*

☺ 😐 ☹ *I sympathise with them and nurse them. I find it very difficult to seek help for myself.*

☺ 😐 ☹ *I blackmail myself with my commitment to the team/organisation and avoid all confrontation even when I know that the confrontation and demand is important. But when I do express my disappointments, I become reactive and start blaming.*

The Yudhishtra-Managers are great consolidators. They are necessary when change for its own sake is undesirable, and creating a strong foundation is called for. These are the leaders who oversee steady growth. Let us look at the career of Yeshwanth who is a Yudhishtra-Manager.

Yeshwanth was a very respected and seasoned finance professional who had grown to head the operations. He was known to be meticulous and methodical. He interacted only with his direct reportees and went on a daily inspection of the works. His 'daily rounds' were feared by the rest of the organisation; "how does his gaze fall on exactly those areas that are non-compliant?" they wondered.

Yeshwanth found his elevation in the organisation stalled once he reached the position of Operations Head. His enthusiasm to maintain the daily discipline was waning, and he discovered that some of his team members had learnt how to 'beat the system'. Surprises would hit the organisation where the records showed no deviations.

He came into the coaching process very confused with what was going on. "The world is not what it was anymore," he started, "and people don't respect the wisdom of experience. They come up with new fangled ideas and flavours of the month and don't understand how it disturbs the operations". It was not easy for him to see that the changes being proposed by the head of Sales and Marketing were in response to the demands of the customers. The customers were facing an uncertain context and were not able to make clear commitments or projections. The costs associated with the changes and the wastes in inventory, when orders were suddenly changed, stood out in his mind. The difficulty in predicting markets, and the need for technology to anticipate latent needs, and create solutions did not strike him as critical marketing tools.

Yeshwanth was getting very unpredictable and angry and this upset him even more. He saw his anger as righteous and being triggered by the capriciousness of others. It took a lot of effort to introduce Yeshwanth to self-reflective thinking. He was used to thinking and feeling the way he ought! To come to terms with the spontaneity of the feeling world was to play with fire. He came to realise how he had become a captive of the injunctions and rules that he lived by and how change and uncertainty made him anxious. Doing something 'wrong' was a constant preoccupation. Doing what was given, the 'should' or the 'must' as he heard it from authority was safe. When he could see that these were the inevitable realities of the King archetype, and that being in constant touch with the bad and the undesirable was the constant companion of the Judge in him, Yeshwanth started to appreciate and value the stability and the goodness he brought to the system by being hypersensitive to that which must be kept out.

Coming to terms with the shadow side of the Yudhishtra-Manager archetype and owning up to his own inner world of feelings and confusion released Yeshwanth to value what he brought into the context without being defensive or protective. He was able to be more open to the demands of the market place, less judgemental and far more approachable. He forged powerful working relationships with the Board, and when the situation changed, and the board saw the need to have a steady hand at the helm, Yeshwanth was made the CEO.

YUDHISTRA

☺ 😐 ☹ *Without structure I feel lost, so I compulsively impose structure.*

☺ 😐 ☹ *When situations go out of my control, I become very judgmental of others.*

☺ 😐 ☹ *I find myself imposing standards in punitive ways.*

☺ 😐 ☹ *I become a proxy of the organisation and compel conformity.*

☺ 😐 ☹ *I become confused and angry when the written policy is not followed faithfully.*

☺ 😐 ☹ *When I find the situation or people acting in surprising ways, I wish to purge the system of the uncertainty, and impose order.*

☺ 😐 ☹ *I wish to eliminate all 'strange and odd' people from the system.*

☺ 😐 ☹ *I resent power and authority that is not formal and become entrenched in finding rules and procedure to stymie this.*

☺ 😐 ☹ *I sometimes find myself throwing all caution to the winds and becoming a gambler! I let my feelings overwhelm me.*

Sahadeva-Managers rarely create large organisations, except when their technological insights become the starting point of new organisations. Even here the Sahadeva-Managers tend to stay with their research and not get pulled into the rough-and-tumble arena of action.

Let us look at the journey Sarah took in her life journey. Sarah was an artist, a very talented filmmaker. She started her career making insightful documentaries on very difficult and controversial subjects. This combination of talent and social responsibility attracted the attention of the US Consul General and Sarah was recommended for a scholarship to study and work with some of the very best film makers and teachers in the US of A. On her return, she was surprised to find that a prominent film producer was eager to start a television production house and offered Sarah the lead role in setting this up.

Sarah was thrilled. Here was the opportunity of a lifetime. "I can really influence the medium as it grows," she thought and plunged into work. She selected independent professionals like herself and started creating scripts and pilots. Soon she was in business, two of her ideas were taken up and the serials were aired.

Very soon, all kinds of small irritants started to surface. Sarah found that the production value of the work turned out was not to her expectations. She started to supervise the work more directly. Her need to go into the depths of the characters and demand authentic performances meant that there were budget overruns. The level of investments did not allow for the kind of infrastructure that Sarah wanted. At first the financiers were willing to go along, but it soon became evident that the artistic temperament of the team and the demands of high efficiency did not go together. Sarah would fly off into fits of anger when the members of the support staff were not responsive. When cost overruns were pointed out she kept insisting that these were temporary phenomena and that the viewers would learn to pay for value. It is true that Sarah produced some of the best work in the TV scene in India. Many of the serials were purchased for reruns abroad. But the path of artistic self-expression and business pragmatics did not converge. Sarah felt that she did not understand enough, went into study and intense discussions with peers and critics. Slowly her conviction deserted her and she took a sabbatical to "introspect and rediscover the spring within", as she put down in her letter to the financiers.

Sarah went into a period of travelling alone. "Just me and my camera" she said. Her first work was to document the plight of the victims of the Bhopal Gas tragedy. She came back from this '*pada yatra*' troubled and rejuvenated. "I am essentially a loner, why did I get pulled into the role of leading and managing?" She found great meaning in the researching of the area she would document, ensuring its veracity and making an impactful film. She realised that the shadow side of her intense need to discover the truth and to state it, was a fear of being accused, and the fear of being found wanting.

The more she tried to avoid these possibilities, the more she found herself treading a vicious cycle. She was avoiding the accusation that her reading of public taste was inaccurate. So she put more effort into production quality and authenticity. The more perfect the final product in her eyes, the more it won critical acclaim, the less accessible it became to the general public. When this reality struck her that the pursuit of self actualisation and the love of truth go hand in hand with being misunderstood and being seen as elitist, she was able to re-evaluate her priorities. Being exactly right but totally misunderstood or understood only by a very few was not her idea of filmmaking. Working for perfection was her preoccupation. What she saw as errors and lacunae were not even noticed by the lay viewer.

Sarah then moved into a time of "studying people and how they respond to form and sound". This study took her away from self-absorption and opened a new world of possibilities. Sarah decided to become a communications consultant and an independent filmmaker choosing her films on her terms. She has built a small boutique consultancy and is winning acclaim for her sensitive portrayals of Indian reality and the vernacular culture.

SAHADEVA

☺ 😑 ☹ *I procrastinate and withdraw from action.*

☺ 😑 ☹ *I get caught in analysis-paralysis.*

☺ 😑 ☹ *I am never sure when experimentation is enough. Learning needs application.*

☺ 😑 ☹ *I tend to become a spectator and get lost in my own world.*

☺ 😑 ☹ *I love my loneliness and use it as a cloak to avoid the rough-and-tumble of life.*

☺ 😑 ☹ *I get hypercritical and nitpicky.*

☺ 😑 ☹ *I have a tendency to become a skeptic and a cynic, and this further blocks my action.*

☺ 😑 ☹ *I love abstraction and enjoy the idea of being an academic.*

"The team was fascinated by this portrayal" Ranjan said as he finished his brief recap and sat down to sip a bit of tea.

"But there is no mention of Arjuna" Sanam said, sounding a bit disappointed.

"AS has asked all of us to ponder over this question and he has promised that our struggle to understand the Arjuna within us was key to our taking the next steps." Ranjan said. "I am waiting to have a chat with you on your favourite hero".

"I must say you have been a good student" Sanam said "I can understand why your friends called you 'Kodak' in college, I am sure you repeated AS word for word to me!"

"No, this is from my collation and reworking of the discussions, but I am pretty satisfied with my gist. I thought I was losing my ability to listen and understand. What was great for us, Sanam, is that we were able to self-reflect as we discussed the Archetypes with Ananth Saptaparni. I am a Bhima like you said, but it is not that simple. Jagan has a lot of Sahadeva in him. He chose the alternative that said 'anchor experimentation'. But, it became clear to us as we were examining our actions and their consequences, that Jagan and I have become a tandem team. That has made us very good together, but when we are alone we exhibit a bit of the extreme of the archetype, almost as though we have got used to the other person covering up, like a doubles team that clicks! I am shocked by some of the feedback I got. I realise that I trust Jagan's thinking so much that I don't give the thought of others enough weight till I hear Jagan. What was happening to me was that I was not thinking through, but leaning on Jagan, and he in his turn was giving up his action orientation!

"AS asked us to look at some key events and then said, 'Now go into it again while asking in doing what I was doing what was I really doing?'" This is a really powerful question. It was like an opening of a door and we understood what 'role' meant. "What you do at the surface is often the task, the relationships and dynamics created by the way you carry out the task is the role".

"AS then explained to us that we were so caught up with the task of problem solving, we did not look beyond this. Apparently this way of understanding a

situation by examining the action, its context, and its subtle dynamics is recommended in the Gita.

"Shanti came through as a Yudhishtra and that was quite difficult for her to take! She thought she was more of the caring type, and it took some courage for her to admit that she was acting from an ideal, more from the 'should' than the spontaneous feeling. Afsal turned out to be a Nakula, trying very hard to adjust with the chaos and keep the cash lubricating the system. We all thought he was such a great team player. The cost to him and the system has been enormous and we guys have simply not been cost conscious! He has tried to bring in some discipline, but got pushed by our crisis mode and allowed all kinds of unintended problems to take root.

"This brings me to the big one. AS said that if you are a leader, 'everything that happens in the organisational space, whatever its cause, is your responsibility and you must ask yourself the famous question, 'How am I part of the problem?' If you don't, you convert the live issue, the on-going drama into a 'problem out there.' ' It took us a while to figure this one out and longer to admit to it. Clearly, the marketing vs. production vs. product development was a consequence of our not realising that we had grown into a size where we had to decide whether we were a product company or a service company!

"This is when we stopped and AS said now I want you to ask yourselves the question, 'Who is Arjuna?' and left us with some homework. He wanted us to reflect on critical moments in our growth as managers so far and try to examine the shades of the archetypes in our role propensities. The fact is that there are no clear black-and-white demarcations. We can be more than just one archetype in the way we interact with the world.

"I have been really excited and troubled by this task. I have also taken it a step further and begun to ask myself, 'What kind of an organisation have I created?' First, it is clear to me that we have exhausted the dream we started with as individuals, and as a team we were so excited with innovating and taking products to the market that we have never asked ourselves the next question: 'What space do we want to occupy in the world? What will we stand for?' Secondly, Jagan and I have spent hours critiquing the earlier organisation we were in. But, we have assumed that we are now creating a

great system. Maybe we have avoided asking and finding out what we have really done. It is so difficult to become vulnerable and ask, 'how have I messed up?' But, I must have the courage to do that today." The decision to take the dialogue further was set for the following weekend.

Ranjan came back late on Sunday evening looking very happy but sombre. He took the morning off on Monday. "Let me share with you what came up," he told Sanam. "It was really difficult," Ranjan began, "We easily identified with the positives. My Bhima-like ability to take on challenges was discussed. Jagan's Sahadeva-like curiosity and thirst for knowledge was also easily acknowledged. What hit us in our face was how all of us disliked the Yudhishtra mode. We would all say we need order and need procedures, but all of us hated to be bound down. Also, as we started looking back, it came through that one of the reasons we were together was the shared feeling of being boxed in by the organisations we were in earlier. You must remember how restricted I would feel in my earlier employment, and how resentful and unhappy I was. My progress in that place was at a huge personal cost. All of us had felt that way, and the risks of a start-up were a pleasure compared to the feelings of being boxed in. Each of us in our own ways undermined any predictability and procedural discipline. We loved the crisis. What hit us was how easily we found the urgency or a crisis to focus on and used it to become warriors. Sanam, I just didn't know how to build an organisation; I don't have the patience to see a foundation laid and a building come up brick by brick. You remember Jenny who came in from IBM when we were in the US? We made Jenny unable to function. She was also unable to help us create systems; she just demanded systemic functioning and was simply unable to handle the ambiguity of the start-up. We invited her in too soon and probably also sabotaged her efforts! Raj Peter has been unable to do much after his fixing of the billing issues. We saw it as a problem to crack and a crisis to overcome. Rashmi was intellectually excited, I was fired up, and we really helped the systems and processes to come up. This made us

What hit us was how easily we found the urgency or a crisis to focus on and used it to become warriors *grow and enabled us to serve customers. But neither Jagan nor I have had the patience or the foresight to really take the process further and invest in the 'back-end'. Not very heroic work Sanam, and we have constantly been excited by challenges. We realised how the Yudhistra Shanti and Nakula Afsal have suffered silently. AS helped us to see how we have created the subtle rules of our culture. Firstly, get the customer (does not matter how). Secondly, be a hero in spite of the system (if you can't, don't be a block). Next, scramble, work hard and deliver (be really busy).*

"So we recognised only the heroic salesmen and the great problem solvers as our assets. No wonder we kept getting these great orders that were a nightmare to deliver. The sales heroes loved the front-end battle to beat the competition, the problem solving heroes loved the scramble and Jagan and I loved the whole hustle and bustle of this!

"We just did not see how early strengths had become the reason why we could not go beyond the initial surge. It was very painful to realise how we had got stuck in our style and never saw its dysfunctional sides. We were just doing 'more of the same,' as AS said, when we came to a place where we needed to really transcend the culture and the practices that brought us to the threshold. More of the same meant running behind the next big order, the next interesting innovation and not building an unquestionable depth of expertise and excellence in any one area. We were great tacticians, we won every battle, but we did not develop a perspective, we did not build deep capacity. 'You really have to understand Arjuna,' AS said at the end of the day. So I must sit with you Sanam to talk about Arjuna."

That evening AS dropped in to discuss some of the ideas about Arjuna with Sanam. "Why do we need a whole and separate time for Arjuna?" Sanam asked as AS stood up to leave. "I think it is important for me to share some of my thoughts about Arjuna so that your explorations can be meaningful." AS began after some thought. "Sanam, your understanding of the heroes can be very helpful. I guess we are clear that the Paandava heroes are archetypal figures. The Arjuna archetype is the one at the centre of the Chakra Vyuha, *he is the one who knows how to go into the vortex of life, and come out!*

However, this journey is fraught with great danger. Therefore Arjuna is the great hero who often seeks the counsel of Krishna, the archetype of one's deepest wisdom and purest intent.

Therefore Arjuna is the great hero who often seeks the counsel of Krishna, the archetype of one's deepest wisdom and purest intent."

"I must digress a bit and return to the four heroes we have discussed so far before we can go ahead," AS continued after a brief pause. "Yudhistra, Bhima, Nakula and Sahadeva are the pillars of the society as it has ordered itself. Yudhistra is the one who is the pillar of Justice. He is an exemplar of discipline and self-control to the point of self-sacrifice. Bhishma, the patriarch of the family, is another face of this archetype, the one who upholds the ways enunciated in the age of Raama, the Dharma of the old Yuga that is being challenged by Krishna the new avatar! Bhishma forsakes enjoyment, femininity and vulnerability when as Devavrata he promises not to marry or have progeny. This is his idea of his duty to his father as a good son! He is a rigid upholder of the rules of conduct and the law, he refuses to question them, and his own inner struggle to uphold them as well as the pathos of his choice are glorified. The Yudhistra mind has no Dharma Sankatas, no doubts, no dilemmas, only the letter of the law to follow.

"Bhima has no doubts either, he is the exemplar of the ones who will fight and lay down their lives for the land, the community they love. Nakula likewise will go out of his way to heal people. These are people who have felt the oppression of the current authority figures, or who have been wounded in battles. He does not question the social order that causes these hurts. Sahadeva is content with where his curiosity takes him, seeks knowledge, but does not ask who uses it or how. It is the great science given to us by the Sahadevas that ends up as weapons of war! Since none of these four heroes question society and its present order, but excel in fostering it they are its pillars, the pillar of Justice, of Might, of Healing and of Learning!"

"I see why the solidarity and obsession with which we as a group followed our cherished goals first helped us to surge forward, and then started to take us down a path of slow decline and decay," Ranjan reflected. "We put in heroic effort, sacrificed much and kept at it come what may!" he said and laughed.

"I am happy you can see the pathos of this in a lighter vein," Sanam sounded relieved. "I hope all of you see how your sacrifice actually affects your spouse," she added only partly in jest.

"That brings me to the three aspects of the Arjuna Archetype, and why he experiences Dharma Sankatas, the dilemmas of living and the paradoxes inherent in any societal order we come up with," AS continued where he had left off. "Karna is born of the Sun God. He is as great a hero as all his brothers, but he is a social outcaste. That simply translates to seeing Karna as a potential disrupter and anarchist as viewed through the lens of rigid norms and dogmas of the social order. He is the holder of its 'untouchabilities'; he is dispossessed of his legitimacy to act from his true potential. The true Arjuna can see this, and that is why he articulates his deepest doubts about the reasons to go into battle at Kurukshetra. Draupadi is a symbol of all that is considered vulnerable and precious on the one hand, but also all that is weak and desirable. She is the feminine aspect of the patriarchal order of society that at once protects and oppresses the weak. The heartrending scene of Draupadi's disrobing reveals this aspect of the social order in its most depraved form. This is also reflected in Arjuna's anguish as he asks, 'Why this war? Should I fight at all? Do the consequences justify it?' All his questions are reflections of the Dharma Sankata. If one wishes to uphold society, one fights for the right as defined by the society in its present levels of wisdom. If one does fight, one perpetuates the oppression and adharma inherent in its present order!"

"That's very insightful, AS. The Mahaabhaarata is then a story of the glory and beauty of a society if its ways are followed, as well as the unintended suffering and pathos when it is followed! It also starkly describes the violence caused by a greedy and self-centred interpretation of the order and the practices of a society. Arjuna, Karna and Draupadi represent this simultaneity of the best and the worst. It is only through Tapas that the Krishna mind gets revealed, a mind that can go beyond the double binds and forge the new emergence by engaging with the depth of suffering and sorrow engendered by the present order," said Sanam, now in a deeply contemplative mode.

Notes to myself

1. Whew! That was something! I thought Leadership was all about tasks and skills. Without Saptaparni, we guys would have been judging and beating each other up for things that are our nature. I have to now set the tone and really understand people's propensities in behaviour and not just skills, before I define role.

2. I realise that I am the unfolding of the seeds and weeds I planted in myself. There is great hope in this realisation, I can therefore reorganise myself.

3. "*Dhyaytho vishayaanpumshah sangraseshu upajayate....*"
When a person dwells upon an object, attachment is born, out of attachment comes desire and from desire anger is born. From anger comes delusion and delusion leads to a loss of memory. The mind is then incapacitated and the person goes towards his destruction. (Bhagavad Gita Ch 2.62)

4. OK back to my map:

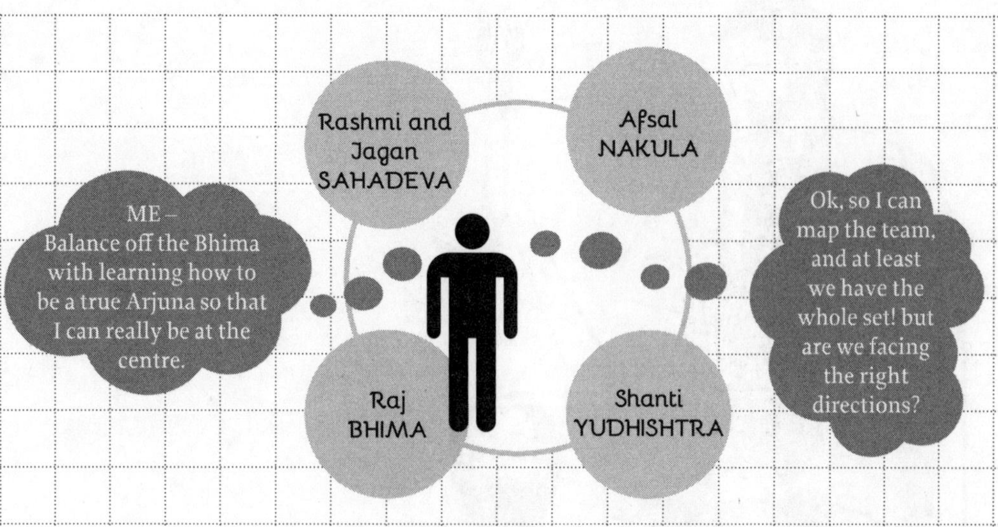

Ok now let me do some "architecting of the organisation" as Saptaparni will call this. What are the challenges, and who is best equipped to respond?

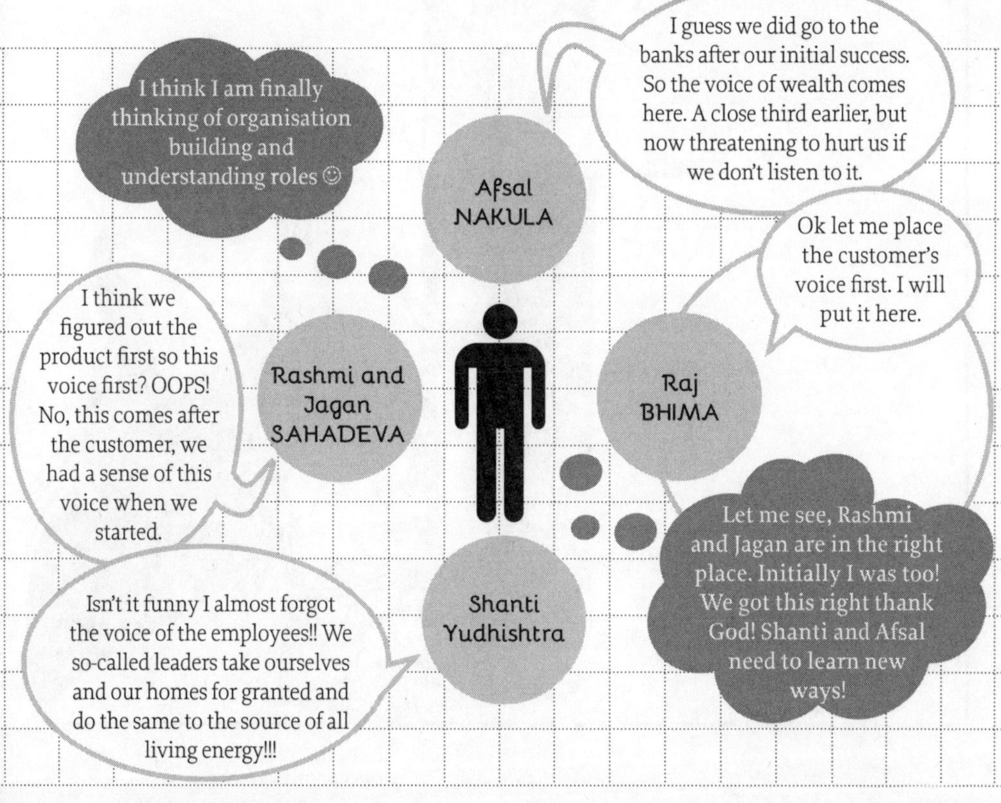

I think I am finally thinking of organisation building and understanding roles ☺

I guess we did go to the banks after our initial success. So the voice of wealth comes here. A close third earlier, but now threatening to hurt us if we don't listen to it.

Afsal NAKULA

Ok let me place the customer's voice first. I will put it here.

I think we figured out the product first so this voice first? OOPS! No, this comes after the customer, we had a sense of this voice when we started.

Rashmi and Jagan SAHADEVA

Raj BHIMA

Let me see, Rashmi and Jagan are in the right place. Initially I was too! We got this right thank God! Shanti and Afsal need to learn new ways!

Isn't it funny I almost forgot the voice of the employees!! We so-called leaders take ourselves and our homes for granted and do the same to the source of all living energy!!!

Shanti Yudhishtra

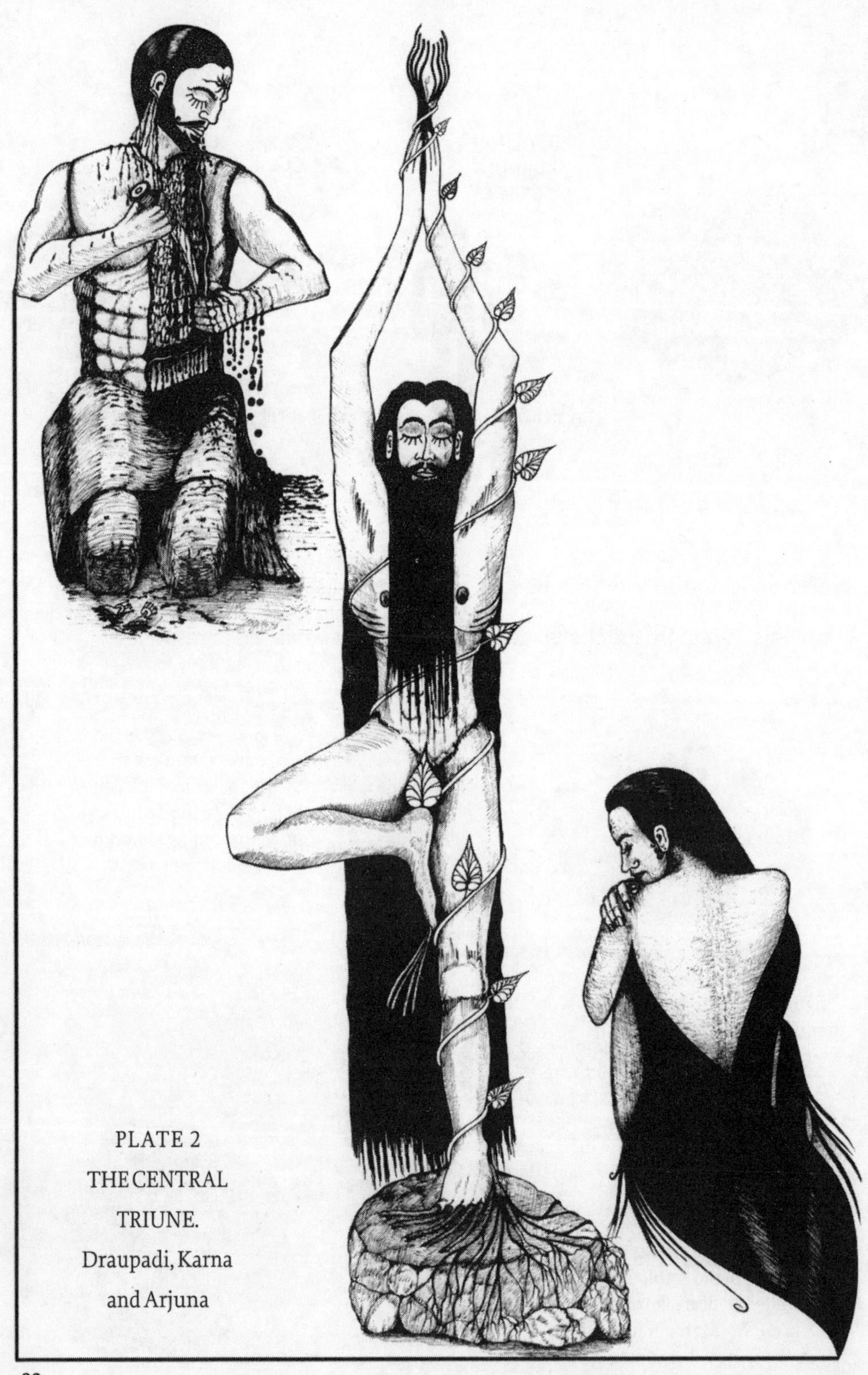

PLATE 2
THE CENTRAL
TRIUNE.
Draupadi, Karna
and Arjuna

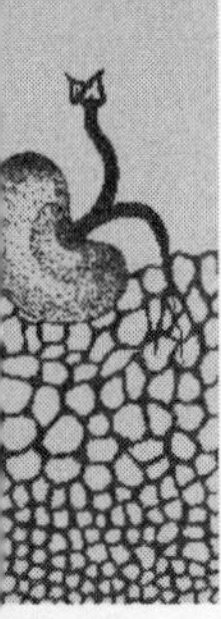

CHAPTER 4
Composting and Tilling Again

Ranjan was getting restless and pushed Sanam to find the time to sit with him. The following Friday saw Sanam and Ranjan drive down to Mahabalipuram. Sanam had insisted that the right setting for her to reflect on Arjuna was in the vicinity of the magnificent mural sculpture of Arjuna's Tapas and the temples to the Paandavas. AS could not make it till the next day, but Ranjan was eager to take time off and converse with Sanam. The time he spent in these reflections was becoming very precious to him. It became very clear to him that without deep inner work, all outer changes in behaviour were unsustainable. He had to discover leadership from inside out!

"I am going to tell you a few stories. The perspectives AS shared with us have helped me relook at the heroes. I have also tried to 'be' the archetypes from the dance recital context. I have to get into their character as I don their masks," Sanam began when they settled down at dusk after a slow walk around their favourite sculptures. They had admired the sculptors at work and every street in the little town had a stonemason's workshop. It was now Sanam's turn to become the storyteller. The musical sounds of the hammer and chisel that sculpted the rocks was slowly subsiding and the waves of the sea were replacing the rhythmic hammering. "I must tell you that I am a little partial to Karna," Sanam continued, "he is after all a Paandava too, caught with the Kauravas like the tiger that grew up in the company of wolves. He suffered all his life with an inner realisation of his true potential, never really

acknowledged or affirmed, in a way that reflected his conviction of who he was. We will come back to him soon, for, as AS told us, no story of Arjuna is complete without the tale of Karna, who is his equal in every way, nay even his superior, but stuck with the stigma of being a 'sutaputra' a low-born while Arjuna was the much-loved favourite". Sanam paused for a few moments. "There are two aspects of Arjuna that stood out when I looked at him from a fresh perspective. There is an aspect of Arjuna that helps to create a balance between the four unique personalities around him. The ability to be both a Yudhishtra and a Bhima, for example, helps Arjuna be a facilitator and a bridge between them. How will four artists, each a master of a different instrument, harmonise and create a coherent whole without an orchestrator of great ability? But this is only one half of Arjuna. While he sees how he is similar to his brothers, he must see how he differs. His task is not merely to maintain the social character of the present he must see beyond, he must help the present evolve towards a greater future."

ARJUNA'S TAPAS

The Paandavas were languishing in the forest after having lost their kingdom in the infamous game of dice. One day a mendicant, who had a message for Arjuna, sought out the brothers. The mendicant's message was very clear: "Prepare for battle. Duryodhana will not give you an inch of land. He will not keep his promise". The mendicant also brought this message from Krishna: "To defeat Karna in the battle field, practise austerities and acquire the *Paasupathaasthra* (the Divine *Weapon*) from Lord Shiva". It was clear that Arjuna was the one who would go on the adventure to acquire the *weapon.*

Arjuna was not sure why he was chosen. He was deep in thought and just as the mendicant was about to leave he said, "I want to ask some questions, to clear my doubts. You carry the words of Krishna and are a wise man. Tell me, why am I the one to go on this arduous journey?"

The mendicant drew a line on the ground. He set himself directly in front of Arjuna on the other side of the line and said, "Where does the question arise from?"

"I am not as disciplined as the wise Yudhishtra," Arjuna began. "Yudhishtra is not only wise and just, he is tireless. He never deserts his duties. He is in perfect control of his senses and his passions".

"But look closely Arjuna, look deeply into Yudhishtra's mind and heart. Don't you see him resolutely follow the path already laid down, even when his heart cries out? He guards himself from encountering life, lest he get carried away, lest he abandon the righteous path, lest he condemn himself by the same yardstick he uses to pass judgment over others. He tires, because he is constantly sifting out the right from the wrong, the good from the bad and, like the scavenger who keeps the city clean of debris, he keeps the dysfunctional thoughts and deeds of society out, and protects the good through the rule of law. And like the scavenger, he cannot stop the debris from being created, he can only clean it out. He must stay with his commitment. The stability and security of the land lies in his hands. He holds the sceptre, the symbol of justice; he holds the book, the symbol of wisdom, not for him the journey into the uncharted and the new. It is only for him to manage with dignity the call of his heart, and the pain of constantly discriminating the good from the bad and throwing the bad outside the boundaries of society".

Arjuna felt compelled to react to this. "I understand him. I often sit with him in his lonely moments; I hear his inner dialogue. I know also that when I question some of the ways and traditions he upholds, he withdraws saying it is not for me to ask questions, it is not for me to pursue doubt, it is only to uphold the systems of law and the practice of righteousness. The people of the land have a sense of certainty and order with Yudhishtra".

Arjuna was now in thought. "Then why should not Bhima go?" Arjuna asked. "He is brave and powerful, he fears no adventure, his love and passion are unbounded".

"That is true," said the mendicant. "He is the most loyal and the most loving person. He is a true warrior, ever prepared to protect the weak, to guard the land against enemies, to explore new lands and find new ways of gaining wealth and dominion. He is fierce in battle, shows no fear of death, and this disregard for his own safety is what terrorises his enemies and emboldens his own men. But, when the crisis blows over, the intensity of the battle has ended, Bhima turns inward and he worries. 'Am I loved with as much passion as I love them? Am I secretly feared and are people wary of my power?' Often, he is pulled by contrary passions and impulses, unable to make choices, unable to comprehend, he waits for the 'respected other' to show him the way, unlock the wasteful conflict within, and focus the energy in action. His deepest worry is that like the butcher who takes away the life of innocent animals, bathes his hands in blood as he cleans the dead animals and places the edible flesh for sale, like the executioner who in an act of finality rids the land of dangerous criminals, is he too, more feared than loved?"

"Yes I know these things that you say are true. I have often sat with Bhima, as he shares his doubts and pains with me. I know that he loves passionately and very few can love with that intensity. He is loyal to the last drop of his blood and very few can be that devoted. It is the very distance between his intensity and the energy others bring in that leaves him with doubt and pain. Emotions trigger him deeply and often cloud his perspective. His readiness to fight, defend and protect also makes him reactive, antagonistic and oppositional. It makes him take stances that are ill considered, makes him pledge loyalty triggered more by feelings than by thought. Lack of action wears him down".

"Such a pillar of strength is he for the people of the land that without him there would be no sense of safety and security" the mendicant added "Without his unquestioned love of his people, the community would be at a loss, too preoccupied with anxiety and danger to love each other and embrace each other, to dance and to feast".

"Nakula is the most reliable, the one who works quietly making up for all our lapses. Never waiting to be asked, he serves everyone, never judging appearances and status. Why not him?" asked Arjuna.

"Nakula is the great healer. With his service and his sacrifice he holds up the ground and strengthens the foundation. Just as the roots, invisible to the eye, hold up the mighty tree, Nakula works unseen so that the land is healed of its hurt and the sorrowful dry their tears. He creates the base, the infrastructure upon which society builds its monuments and its facades. Yet he is seldom seen or heard, often forgotten, since the arena and the stage once created, become the space for the drama that others have to enact. The celebrations and the laurels go to the actors. The days and weeks and months of preparation, the effort and the love that go into creating the context are forgotten, in the heady moments of action on the stage. And yet without the healing hand of Nakula, without the tireless tilling of the ground, the seeding and nurturing of the field, there would be no harvest. Even before the shouting and festivities are over, Nakula has withdrawn into his quiet corner, his sacrifice unnoticed, his offerings taken for granted."

"Yes I have been with him in such moments", said Arjuna. "Wondering whether he has been used and discarded, Nakula's only joy is in knowing that the glory of the visible action comes from the excellence of the invisible ground. He often sees himself as a martyr who has sacrificed himself to the cause."

"And yet without the silent Nakula, the social fabric will tear, the essential everyday routine would go untended. The land would lie fallow, and the sick and ailing left uncared for. The fires are kept burning and the fields ready for harvest, because of Nakula."

"That leaves us with the knowledgeable Sahadeva" said Arjuna. "He observes with care, learns from everyone and every event around him. He can even see how the present will unfold into the future, why not him?"

"True, Sahadeva is a great seeker, though many don't see him that way. Silent, introspective and attentive, there is little that escapes him. He works alone, and fashions implements that few have imagined. He broods and pens down his thoughts, though few

Without his relentless searching what would people do?

care to share them. Often when asked, he answers with such profound knowledge, one wishes he had been consulted early enough. But, he often holds back, unsure if he will be heard. He has visions, but forever the silent hermit, he seems to only care to watch and wait for the future to unfold, in line with his imagination".

"I have often walked with him as he ponders over what he sees," said Arjuna. "But he is unsure of how he will be received and is unable to lead others into action. Perhaps he fears that few will understand him as deeply as he wishes to be understood, fewer still will act rightly, and for having made bold to speak of things into the future and of things unseen by others, he will be held accused and called a dreamer and a heretic".

"Without him, there would be neither science nor technology," added the mendicant. "Watching, learning, searching, seeking and thinking, he completes the picture, keeps the record, and builds up the wealth of knowledge. Both success and failure are the same to him, for they are the basis of knowledge. Without his relentless searching what would people do? Inadequate and incomplete in skills and knowledge, society would languish and stagnate".

Arjuna fell silent. The mendicant waited till Arjuna raised his eyes and said, "So let us look at why me?"

"Arjuna, have you understood who you really are within? Warrior or dancer?"

After a few moments of reflection Arjuna answered, "I am sometimes both and at other times I feel pulled in opposing ways – beauty and action both fascinate me. Poetry and grammar, the circle and the square hold equal meaning".

"Arjuna, have you been clear and certain that you will respond in a known pattern? Have you not questioned and made choices, sometimes from the anchor of rule of law and precedent, sometimes from the flow of passion, sometimes from a sense of service, and yet other times overcome by curiosity because you wanted to learn?"

"Yes," said Arjuna "I have valued doubt and questioning above certainty. Staying uncommitted and examining reality, examining where my responses sprang from has been very difficult, often excruciating. But that's the way I have been. Some called me vacillating and undecided, but not for me the silencing of one voice in preference to the other; not for me the choice of outer over the inner; not for me the choice of the inner over the outer. Often I have had to be the balancing force when I have seen my brothers stay committed to their course of action. And many times I have had to stand in the centre pulling together the four. Sometimes I have felt like the timekeeper for a jugal bandi (a playful collaboration of different musical styles), the conductor of an orchestra between my brothers. Sometimes I have initiated, evoked or provoked them to act when their natures have made them hesitate."

"And Arjuna, what have you felt, and what has been your inner dialogue?" asked the mendicant pushing Arjuna further into self-reflection.

"I have often felt unsure, but acted with provisional certitude, only to have to come back and listen to the voices of the dilemma, each voice seeming to be right in its own context, each sounding *dharmic*, but divergent. The price of choosing one over the other was the greater wrong. In making provisional choices, I have sometimes felt guilty, sometimes ashamed, since I lacked courage, and sometimes acted in a self-centred way, and at others hesitated to assert my truth. And when I returned to a quiet spot and my inner dialogue began, the unresolved dilemmas and *dharma sankatas* came back to haunt me. I discovered a way of standing equidistant from both and holding them both in my view, I learnt to step backward. In doing this I discovered spaces, resources and energies in me that could encompass both, I touched the ground from which both realities grew. I felt elated and whole when this happened, something creative was unfolding. At other times, stepping backward seemed to awaken demons within. Demons that lay in the shadows of my inner landscape, shadows that

And when I returned to a quiet spot and my inner dialogue began, the unresolved dilemmas and dharma sankatas came back to haunt me.

were formed around rocks and walls of certitude, shadows lurking beneath powerful and congealed emotions, shadows lurking beneath the pride of sacrifice and the arrogance of knowledge".

"And Arjuna is it not true that you were able to listen to the sorrows of your brothers, their silent inner struggles only when you confronted your own demons? Is it not true that you sometimes sought to listen to them so that you may hear more clearly the voices of your own dilemmas and the voices of your own shadows? What made you do this? Were you not happy the way you were?"

"The pursuit of beauty and order and truth leaves me forever dissatisfied. As soon as one circle seems complete, I see a reality just outside this circle, a reality that I can see, hear, touch and feel, but I cannot comprehend. These realities do not cohere and converge. Unlike my brothers, who are adept at keeping this circle clean, and hold a constant vigilance of all the factors that distort its perfection, my gaze seems to fall on all of the realities that lie outside of the circle. However much this circle expands, it does not touch these realities".

"And why does this seem important? Living within this circle, its norms, its skills, and its abundance is comfortable. Most people would want nothing more".

"My brothers ensure that all the people within the circle are served well, and they absorb the pain and effort of keeping the circle abundant and comfortable. But, to me this is not enough. A deep sorrow wells up within me. 'There must be a better way', it says to me and once I hear this voice, I cannot rest. This voice is at once mysterious, dangerous and seductive. Perhaps this is why I wander so much; this is why I search out the shadows. My brothers have learnt how to find dignity and meaning playing their roles to perfection while they manage the debris and residues within. This call within me is insistent; it grows each time I turn away. Just as my brothers play their assigned roles and perform their assigned tasks for the sake of all our people, so too do I agonise over the limitations of the circle of the known that we live in, so that all of us may be released from the suffering and limitations we now live with".

"Arjuna now you know why the journey to discover the *Paasupathaasthra* should be undertaken by you. You value doubt and you question; you value balance and integration; you struggle to resolve dilemmas; and above all, the 'quest' is what you live for. Remember, though my warning may be superfluous, that only one whose heart beats for human suffering can undertake this quest. One in search of personal power cannot walk the path of this journey. May your quest be filled with success! And one last word before I leave, it is only when you encounter Karna in the battlefield that this journey will be complete, and you will understand the quest."

Arjuna walked with the mendicant to the bank of the river. He sat himself on a rock even as he wished "fare thee well," to the mendicant. He had much to ponder over. He knew that he had to undertake the journey, to go on a great quest, but he had not asked for any directions, "Where do I start from? Which way do I go?" said Arjuna to the silent dusk as he walked back to his dwelling.

In a few days, the preparations were made. Each of the four brothers prayed for Arjuna's success and offered him gifts to take on the journey. Yudhishtra offered him the ability to be steadfast, Bhima offered courage, Nakula offered compassion and Sahadeva offered him curiosity. Draupadi offered her special prayers too and she offered him forbearance and love.

Arjuna decided to walk along the bank of the river that flowed past their humble abode. He walked slowly with measured steps. He steadied his breath, and in a contemplative state of mind, he started his quest. He noticed that the river took a gentle turn to the north and seemed to point the way ahead. The bird calls seemed to welcome Arjuna, and soon he felt reassured that his heart had chosen the right path.

After a few days' journey, the jungle became thick and the paths seemed to become more and more unclear and deceptive. The bird calls, the animal sounds, and roars, lost their playfulness and innocence. The jungle seemed somehow both enticing and entrapping. Arjuna had the eerie sensation of being followed, that a silent pair of eyes was watching him carefully. Soon he came upon a clearing. He sat down to refresh himself and drink from a pond. He then saw a small pile of fruits neatly laid out, as though someone had prepared the place for him. As he reached out for the fruits, from the corner of his eyes, Arjuna saw a lovely maiden approach him. She seemed attractive and repulsive at the same time. Her gait was sensuous but somehow lacked grace; grotesque was the word that crossed his mind.

The maiden approached Arjuna warily but with the sureness of demeanour that said, "This is my space". When she came close by, she addressed Arjuna directly. "I know you Arjuna. I have been following you for a few days, and I have drawn you to my playground. Rest a little, and eat the fruits I have plucked for you".

Arjuna was tired and the guile of the maiden disarmed him. He rested his bows and arrows to partake of the offerings. The maiden's gaze never left him. Slowly, she began to woo Arjuna. "I am *Perundi*," she said, "I have known about you for a long time. I have spied unseen on you and all your brothers and Draupadi, often from the edge of the forest. My heart pines for you and you alone. You cannot imagine how lonely I feel, and this loneliness has become deep and sorrowful since I have seen you. I have heard many stories about your bravery, and I have envied the women you have loved. I offer myself to you completely and without conditions. Please embrace me and stay with me in this paradise," she entreated.

Even as he listened, Arjuna felt a strange revulsion for her, mixed with compassion. "Lovely maiden, I am on a long journey and a great quest, I cannot tarry. Please find another to love".

As she heard Arjuna's refusal and rejection of her, she became more impassioned. "Arjuna, you cannot fathom how deeply I love you. I cannot let anything part us now that I am close to you". Her entreaties became more insistent and with each insistence Arjuna's discomfort grew and his revulsion became deeper. Yet, he was also fascinated and strangely compelled to continue engaging with her. Soon, the maiden lost all pretence, she openly declared her lust for Arjuna and was prepared to possess him, chase him, wrestle him down and devour him in her need for him. As her lust grew so did she become more grotesque. Fearing that Arjuna might reject her completely, she ran to her brother and manipulated him into helping her possess Arjuna, or to punish him for refusing her.

In a strange way, Arjuna felt attracted by the obsessive quality of the maiden, she was so overcome by her lustful love of Arjuna that he felt affirmed. His own sensuous lust and anticipation of pleasure got awakened and he had to wage a war within. He saw his own lack of steadfastness; he saw how misplaced his compassion was. He saw also, that the part of him that felt attracted to the maiden was the part he would loathe after the passion had ebbed. In the midst of the cacophony, of the outer lustful, plaintive, insistent seduction and the inner awakening of the violent egotistical impulses, Arjuna discovered an anchor within. He saw the power of envy and greed, the power of acquisition and possession, the immense sense of self that oppressive ownership of wealth and women creates, and the energy that comes from competing and snatching away what belongs to another. Arjuna's voice and demeanour took on a new quality. He neither fought the maiden's entreaties, nor indulged in his inner turmoil, but by seeing them clearly and acknowledging the seeds of confusion in himself he said, "Thank you young maiden for showing me your true face, the grotesque face of aversion. Simultaneously you are magnetic and riveting and repulsive to me. You are like quicksand. With every effort I make to get out, I get dragged in, angry with myself, hateful of myself and both my embrace and my condemnation of you are rooted in self-destruction,

In a strange way, Arjuna felt attracted by the obsessive quality of the maiden, she was so overcome by her lustful love of Arjuna that he felt affirmed.

my own greed and envy. I thank you for being a mirror to my soul. Please free yourself of this madness and let me walk my path, wiser and more attentive to myself".

Even as she heard Arjuna speak to her, the maiden felt her madness abate. Her blind resolve to entice and hold Arjuna captive, her fear of being rejected as unworthy, her jealousy of the women Arjuna loved and her fear of loneliness abated. Her fevered need to hold Arjuna and cling to him gave way to freedom in which she could offer her love and let Arjuna choose how he would receive it.

Feeling more sombre and more determined, Arjuna walked his path. Soon the dense jungle with its myriad sounds and colours gave way to a gentle landscape. The trees were not so thick; the undergrowth gave way to grass. Deer and *Chittal* and rabbits calmly grazed on the grass while their young danced around as the birds burst into song. As he walked along, Arjuna heard the soft whispers of a gurgling brook and above, the chirping of the birds, the rustling of leaves and the cadence of the water flow. There arose the cadence of a beautiful voice, singing exquisitely. Sometimes the voice rose clearly and distinctly above the forest sounds in a beautiful melody. At other times it was so greatly in harmony with the birds, the leaves, the water and the animal calls that it seemed like silence split into a myriad colours. Even the way the melody rose above the harmony only to merge back had a rhythm that made the whole song even more enchanting. The voice and the song drew Arjuna down a path that looked more like a garden than a forest. The grass gave way to beautiful flowerbeds, and the eye was bathed in deep yellows and crimsons, blues and violets, pinks and lilac. Arjuna's senses were filled with pleasure. Not only were the flowers a treat to the eyes, their fragrance was delicate and intoxicating.

Arjuna saw the lady of the flowers, *Mohini*, singing softly as she drew him to her. Arjuna thought that he was in a dream. "This is so soft and warm," Arjuna said to himself, "not like the maiden of the jungle, cold and grasping. Such delicate pleasure, that I know not if my senses are alive spontaneously or they are being awakened". Slowly the words of the song became clear to Arjuna. Like a tapestry woven with deep hues of silken thread, the lady of the flowers was painting a picture of a life that she had always dreamt of with Arjuna; A life effortless and subtle, where all of one's senses would be filled, but never satiated. "This must be heaven and I am with an *apsara*," Arjuna said to himself. "I have escaped hell with a lustful temptress and my path has led me to this divine place."

Even as he was starting to feel like a cloud borne into the limitless blue sky, a voice spoke up from Arjuna's heart. "What is your quest and where are you floating away to, intoxicated by sensual beauty and pleasure? The touch of lust was compelling though it made you hard and without humour. The kiss of seduction has made you yielding and poetic. Both are deadly, one awakens aversion and self-hate, the other awakens craving and self-indulgence. Beware Arjuna, listen and look deeply lest you lose your way."

It was a very great challenge for Arjuna to let go of the sensual seduction and find the calm contemplative centre within. The battle with aversion had seemed like an external battle against the vice-like grip of violent emotion, but the challenge of craving was like cleansing oneself of a sweet poison, removing an imperceptible veil that cloaked ones vision. At last Arjuna found his true vision, and with a clear voice he spoke. "Dear Lady, I am grateful indeed for the gift you have given me. The face that I have seen reflected in your song and the flowers in your garden, are like the light young skin that covers a rotting gourd. I can tarry with you no more in this enchanting garden, listen no more to your seductive song. I am on a great quest. I have found new resolve and energy, freeing myself from the hold of your sister and saying no to your kiss of pleasure". Hearing this, the lady moved away. Her song became plaintive but no less beautiful; loss filled the notes where it was once filled with anticipation. Arjuna was able to eat the fruits that the trees and birds offered and drink the water bubbling fresh in the brook without losing the clarity within.

As he walked away from this lovely woman, her voice growing faint in the distance, Arjuna found himself feeling more centred and balanced. The hard and the soft, the passionate and the hateful, the movement towards and the drawing away, vigilance and complacency, masculine and feminine, had all found a resting place. Arjuna felt aware, awake and calm. His gait was fluid, and music sprang forth from his heart. As he walked on, the landscape changed and the forest gave way to vast grasslands. Wild game of many kinds was abundant, as were the lions and other big cats. A small bunch of hunters could be seen in the distance, some stalking their prey and others returning from a hunt. All at once a young and handsome hunter appeared before Arjuna. He seemed to have come out of nature, just magically formed in an instant. He stood before Arjuna and asked him, "Are you Arjuna the great warrior and marksman?"

"Yes," said Arjuna both surprised and flattered that a hunter from unknown lands should know him.

"Are you truly as great as people say you are? Are you worthy of the praise and glory that is showered upon you?"

Arjuna was silent. Even though he had basked in the affection and honour that he had been offered in his life, he was never really sure he deserved all of it. He had noticed how he would become arrogant in response to the praise. He had also learnt how to say to himself, "I am not as good as I can be, even though others think I am", and learnt through practice to better himself. Something about the manner of the hunter and the way he seemed to taunt Arjuna made him bristle within. Just then, a young boar came out of its burrow in the earth. It was startled at seeing the hunter and Arjuna and stood rooted to the spot for a moment.

"Let me challenge you to see who can hunt down this boar," said the hunter, and Arjuna readily agreed. They waited till the boar regained its wits and bolted. The two challengers went off in hot pursuit. The boar was really swift and cunning and Arjuna became completely absorbed in the chase; there was only the boar and the chase, all else was peripheral. With great skill Arjuna went about planning his movements. He carefully avoided the branches and bushes that blocked his path, jumped over rocks and rivulets that came in the way, as the boar did its best to outwit its chasers. Even as he was running behind the boar, Arjuna was able to anticipate its movements, so deep was his concentration. The boar was starting to tire and in a flash, Arjuna intercepted the boar with a well-aimed arrow. The boar faltered and fell. Triumphant, Arjuna leapt up to claim his trophy, only to find the hunter step out and lay his claim too. There were two arrows on either side of the boar's jugular!

"Mine was the first arrow", the hunter said, "I have bettered you".

"No!" said Arjuna, his anger rising. "Mine was the arrow that found the mark."

"How do you know that your arrow caused the boar to die?" asked the hunter.

"Can't you see how deep my arrow has gone? And how true its placement?"

"Your arrow has indeed pierced the skin, flesh and muscles of the boar, but so has mine. How does that tell you that your arrow ended its life?"

Arjuna's anger was growing into a rage. "What futile argument is this? The blood has gushed out from the wound my arrow created, the breath was stopped because of that wound."

"Ah! It does seem that way, but look at my arrow, it has pierced the jugular and the windpipe, but that only proves that the body and breath were wounded. Tell me great warrior where lies the life of the boar that you claim to have killed?" Even as his anger was boiling over, something in the question stopped Arjuna. His challenged pride and his own arrogance in his skill as an archer could not stop the force of the question. "What is life and what is death Arjuna?" the hunter continued. "What gave you the right to kill the boar? Was it your need to prove your might to me? Was it your certitude that no one could compete with you? Was your need to prove me wrong more important than life? Now that you claim to have taken the life away, and claim the boar as a trophy, enliven it."

As he listened to the hunter, Arjuna perceived a silence grow in his heart. "What a profound mystery life is, and how quickly did I decide to take it away? I was so consumed with my own sense of self, my own greatness. I had not a moment of compassion, not a thought for the others. So focused was I on the kill, all my energy, all my life had but one purpose, to end another's life! The beauty of the forest was lost to me, I heard nothing, saw nothing, smelt and felt nothing, my prize and my winning were everything".

"What are you claiming as your trophy Arjuna, the body of the boar, even as it grows cold and stiff or the life that is now gone never to be found again?"

As he listened more intently, Arjuna realised that the hunter was not what he appeared to be. He knelt down and said, "The body of this boar will decay and wither away. What of it will I call mine to own? I know not whence its life comes, and where it has gone, what of its life will I claim as my trophy?"

As Arjuna said these words, the hunter revealed his true form – he was lord *Shiva.* "You have crossed the major thresholds I placed for you and you have passed the tests. You have seen through desire and aversion. You have seen the truth of yourself and your identity. Let me now share with you the secret of the *Asthra (weapon)* and the power you seek. The *Asthra* is not a thing like your *Gaandiva (Divine Bow).* The power is not an energy like your passion. Meditate on the following questions and it will reveal itself to you: "What does human sorrow and suffering mean to you? Do you seek personal salvation or do you seek the true way? Where does your self begin and where does it end? How do you measure time? Where do all the parts of your self cohere?"

Arjuna received the words of Shiva as the flow of Grace with profound humility. Shiva blessed Arjuna and merged back into the void from which he had emerged.

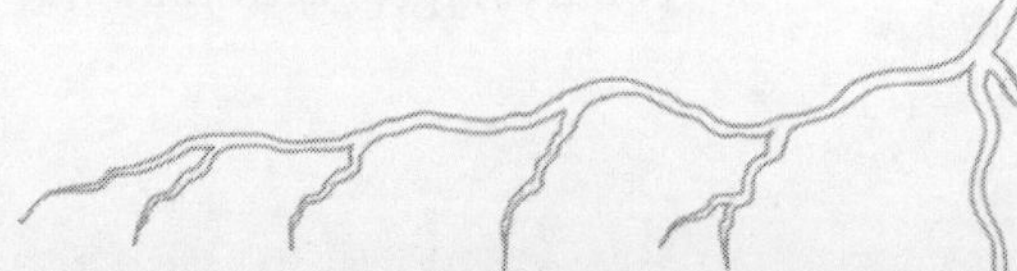

Arjuna is one of the most idolised heroes. What makes one a hero are inner qualities of the being out of which actions emerge. It is not possible to imitate heroic action. So societies value and appreciate Arjuna's brothers more readily than they embrace an Arjuna. Arjuna questions the existing paradigms, seeks to examine Dharma anew before committing to action. He consults his inner guide before making a deision. So, look into the mirror, but slowly, ever so slowly, before you recognise the face! Reflect, introspect and contemplate on each statement and follow your own inner conversation carefully.

ARJUNA

☺ 😐 ☹ *I listen without judgment, and with an intent to understand deeply*
☺ 😐 ☹ *I act from a deep sense of commitment to the whole system*
☺ 😐 ☹ *I ask questions and explore deeply to find answers; I engage in an intense questioning of the invisible practices and process of the organisation*
☺ 😐 ☹ *I enter the unfamiliar without seeking guarantees*
☺ 😐 ☹ *I am willing to be alone in the search for the new*
☺ 😐 ☹ *I value doubt and continuously re-evaluate the present*
☺ 😐 ☹ *I am open and negotiable with the new ways that I discover*
☺ 😐 ☹ *I am a proficient orchestrator and change agent*
☺ 😐 ☹ *I strive to be the change I want to see*

Ranjan was in a strangely excited mood when Sanam completed the story. "I see the way forward for me now," he began. "Instead of jumping into the fray and getting into action, I need to hold back my emotional responses, my desire to create a favourable outcome, as well as my aversion to the unfavourable. I will then be able to see many more possibilities, and create the future that is wishing to emerge. I know what this means. So many times, Jagan and I have found creative solutions when we have stopped battling for it, and let go. We used to love rambling on about anything that triggered us, and suddenly, we would see the obvious staring at us. I understand now why Prof. Pulin Garg would get all worked up when we said 'paradigm shift'. 'You cannot shift paradigms like you shift furniture,' he would say. He deplored any outside-in perspective on behavioural shifts. 'All leadership is inside out,' he would shout, 'To be a real leader and transform the present you must be ready to turn yourself inside-out like Gandhiji did'. He insisted that the following three ideas are critical to leadership: firstly Ashby's[1] *law of requisite variety, secondly Bertalanffy's study of open systems and biological systems*[2], *and thirdly Gödel's Theorem.*[3]

"I might bore you a bit Sanam, but this connection with Arjuna is exciting. Ashby's law is simple. If you don't have the capability to respond to your environment, you will die. A polar bear can't live in a desert. However, human beings have an innate capability that allows a Tuareg to live in the desert, while an Inuit lives within the Arctic Circle. If an organisation must live, it must adapt and evolve as the environment changes. Bertalanffy wrote extensively about open systems. These are systems that are in constant connection with the outside space. This means that the environment is impacted by the system and vice versa. It is a mutually linked connection. For example Jarred Diamond writes that the Easter Islanders flourished initially, but their ways of living depleted the resources of the Island. They did not develop requisite new ways and were decimated".

"I am seeing where you are going with these two, but why talk about a mathematician?" Sanam interrupted.

"Gödel is key to understanding paradigms. Very broadly he said that there will always be problems that can be described by a mathematical system, but not solved within it. To be able to solve the problem, one must look at the fundamentals of the system and redefine it."

"Ok, so how does this relate to Arjuna?" Sanam was puzzled.

"Let me explain. Jagan and I started an organisation based on a technical innovation. We have grown and we have become the pioneers who have changed the business of hand-held devices. But we are still thinking, feeling and acting like we did when we were a start-up! We can see several problems, but we describe them and attack them from an old mind-set. Mobile Unlimited does not have the 'requisite variety' of responses to navigate an environment that it has spawned. Our clones are our major competitors! For an individ-

[1](http://en.wikipedia.org/wiki/William_Ross_Ashby)
[2](http://en.wikipedia.org/wiki/Ludwig_von_Bertalanffy)
[3](http://en.wikipedia.org/wiki/Kurt_Gödel)

ual to grow out of his old frames and really be able to see, feel, think and act from a new 'paradigm' he has to undergo something like Arjuna's penance. He must let go of the present ways of feeling attracted to and repelled by external events. He must let go of his obsession with his own creations. Both Jagan and I don't like the set of problems we are confronted with today. We are in love with our innovations and worse, our innovative techniques. To see this and own up to the fact that I am causing the dysfunction in the organisation that I love is very painful. But if I do love Mobile Unlimited, I must embrace this pain and let it transform me."

Sanam was pensive for a few moments. "I think I understand. I had to really struggle to let go of my identity of a dancer and reinvent myself as a choreographer before I could design my dance dramas. I think you really love your theoretical stuff Ranjan. You must go back and immerse yourself in an academic environment."

"I really wish I could," Ranjan added. "I don't remember who said this, 'There is nothing as practical as good theory,' but it is absolutely true. It is sound science that created transistors, and sound science that helped to create the chip in the first place. Understanding our own inner processes is more difficult but that's no reason why one should not enquire into it deeply."

Sanam and Ranjan decided to take a pause here and savour the nuances of Arjuna's inner journey before attempting to delve any further.

Notes to myself

CHAPTER 5

Weeds and Herbs

The next morning Sanam and Ranjan got off to an early start. They took in the beauty of the sunrise over the sea, its orange glow shining like a halo around the temple on the seashore, in reflective silence. They sat quietly in the balcony of their room sipping their tea for a while after they got back. "My dance teacher never liked manicured gardens. He would say that they were pretty but unhealthy because they had no weeds. 'No weeds, means no herbs!' he was fond of saying. Did you know that most weeds are the base for Ayurvedic *medicines? Apparently they keep out many pests, and make the earth fertile." Sanam said breaking the silence.*

They had decided to wait for AS to join them, so they drifted back into silence, each immersed in their own thoughts until he arrived.

"Saptaparni, you were right," Sanam began diving right into the discussions for the day. "Karna and Draupadi represent all the tortuous experiences of deprivation, discrimination, denial and dispossession that await a person living in the shadow of a society. What are the scenes that most uniquely bring to mind Draupadi and Karna?" Sanam challenged Ranjan.

"Why, the disrobing of Draupadi of course," Ranjan responded. "Let me think about Karna. Could it be when Karna tears off his Kavacha *and* Kundala *(the armour and earring gifted at birth)? Or when Kunti reveals her secret to him? Yes, and the last moments of Karna when his chariot is made to*

sink into the unstable ground by Krishna. And even as he gets down to release the wheel he is shot at, and then Krishna comes disguised as a mendicant seeking all the merits Karna has gathered in his life".

"These scenes are such powerful drama," Sanam resumed, "Draupadi reflects the most undignified way in which a society can treat its women. And Karna is left desperately alone without any support as he clings on to the one possession of his that he has earned through abundant generosity, the merit of giving unstintingly. He is dispossessed of everything, after suffering years of discrimination. It is only when a society can look at its treatment of its women and its own under- class and see that this is the shadow of all that it holds dear, that it can transform and evolve."

"Yes, I can see the importance of this process. As the leader of Mobile Unlimited, I have created a great organisation. But unless I own up to the oppression and the unintended exclusion that I create in order to remain focused on our goals, I will only do more damage than good! Compose a slightly better score, polish the harmony here, add a note there, but never transform it."

"If Draupadi had not been shamed, if Karna had not been constantly discriminated against and dispossessed, neither of them would have nurtured the deep hate within, that fuelled the Mahaabhaarata war," AS joined in. "I am sure a huge amount of resistance and politics in organisations is the result of shame and discrimination held in people's hearts that has no way of being healed."

KARNA'S ANGUISH

Karna was not sure whether having his mother[1] own up to him being her son, was his most joyous moment or his most sorrowful. "I have lived all my life battling within me, knowing that I was not

[1]Karna was actually the first born of Kunti, the mother of the Paandavas. As a young woman she had been granted a boon that whichever deva she called up in penance would grant her the gift of a child. Not realising the portent of the gift, she tried it out one day, calling upon Surya in a prayer. He appeared before her and was trapped into giving her a child. This child was born with a gift of a plate of armour and a pair of earrings that would always be a part of him and protect him in time of need. The young princess in panic over this illegitimate child decided to let him go. She placed the infant in a cradle and let it float upon the river. The child was found and reared by a childless couple.

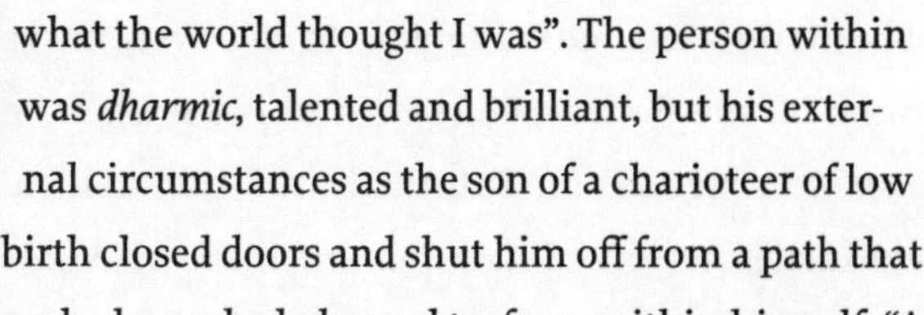

what the world thought I was". The person within was *dharmic*, talented and brilliant, but his external circumstances as the son of a charioteer of low birth closed doors and shut him off from a path that he knew he belonged to, from within himself. "All my knowledge and skill leave me feeling like a thief. It was never offered to me as something that I was meant to learn, and even when I excelled in all the arts, I was never affirmed by the elders."

When Karna showed his prowess in archery, Duryodhana embraced him and honoured him just as he was about to be thrown out as a lowborn.[2] "I was so parched for friendship and belonging that I became totally devoted to him. We both had a common enemy, and that reinforced our friendship. While I am devoted to Duryodhana, I know that my devotion is partly energised by my deep need to be worthy, and partly by the feelings of hurt and vengefulness at being denied my rightful place. My commitment to generosity and compassion has become compulsive because of this."

Karna was born with a gift—a coat of armour and a beautiful pair of earrings. But as he experienced hurt within, the armour seemed to get absorbed into his body and soon became a part of his flesh. "I did

[2]The story goes that Karna won an archery contest that had been set up to display the prowess of the young princes in the land. Their teachers felt insulted that this low-born young man of no real means had beat them all and were ready to turn Karna out of the arena. At this point Duryodhana stepped in and granted Karna a kingdom to rule, making him a prince among all the other princes. This act of generosity won him the undying loyalty of Karna.

not hesitate to become vulnerable, to give away my golden breastplate; I tore it off my flesh and offered it to *Indra* when he came to me disguised as a mendicant. But, the hurt I have felt in being treated as illegitimate, the envy I have felt when seeing Arjuna showered with affection and attention, have congealed into a vengefulness that I cannot forsake."

Karna faced the most agonising moment of his life when his mother came to see him at the start of the war. After narrating the story of his birth and her own plight surrounding it and her continuous battle between claiming him as her son and not disturbing the given structures, *Kunti* begged Karna to spare his brothers. Karna had promised that she would still have five sons at the end of the war. Yudhishtra, Bhima, Nakula and Sahadeva he would defeat but he would not kill. Arjuna he must defeat and kill.

Karna pondered over these feelings of total enmity with Arjuna. "He and I are so much alike and yet so antagonistic to each other. We match each other's skills almost equally, we match each other's knowledge and accomplishments too, but while he is the blue-eyed boy with mentors at every stage, I have had to walk a lonely path. When I did find teachers, I have ended up incurring their wrath, even though I learnt with great humility and diligence. I have ended up being rejected for my birth. Where Arjuna is the beloved, I am discriminated against, where Arjuna is blessed, I am the deprived and the despised, and yet we have always been tied to each other by fate and now I know why."

In a little while, Karna's agitation subsided. As his mind calmed down, Karna wondered if he should follow Krishna's advice and go over to the Paandavas, declare himself to be their brother and end this fratricidal war. He imagined what might happen when he went across. "I will be stopped at the gates and I will be questioned. Yudhishtra will probably lead the questioning. 'You who have always felt resentful of us and have been keenly aware of our shortcomings, why do you come here today?'

'I have resented you and been aware of your shortcomings, because I have been forced to live as 'the other'; as your shadow. I am one of you in more ways than you know, yet you have seen me only through the lens of justice and law, norms and rules. Nay, you have been blinded by them. You saw me not, but only that which had to be kept out, like a good scavenger who cleans out the waste, you have applied the measures written in the books of law and made me an outcast. I come today, the voice of all that has been discriminated against by the laws you uphold, the spontaneous, intuitive self, throbbing with life, beautiful in its own intrinsic order, neither bound nor deformed by the rules and laws that pretend to be impersonal and righteous!'.

"Yudhishtra will then argue, 'I am not the one who can judge the writers of the law, but unless I hear in your voice the unconditional commitment to uphold the structures of the social order, to hold yourself in abeyance and dedicate yourself to preserving the values of society and its tradition, I cannot continue this dialogue with you.' "

"Bhima will probably burst out with his challenge, 'For all these years you have sworn loyalty to Duryodhana, what kind of a man are you that you can forsake the commitment to your friend and benefactor.' "

"Yes I swore loyalty and I do love Duryodhana dearly, but I have been a slave to my need for love and acceptance. So often have I been Duryodhana's sword arm, only to feel within me that I am a mere executioner. Trapped within the roles I have accepted, feeling beholden to the one who embraced me, I have killed my own impulses and my own passion; I have fed my envy and vengefulness on his behalf as much as my own. A battle rages between these two parts of me – one that is passionate and impulsive, sensuous and full of adventure, and the other bound to fealty and to promises once made, to being a willing instrument of the ones that I belong to and love dearly. I stand before you today, having lived

I have resented you and been aware of your shortcomings, because I have been forced to live as 'the other'; as your shadow with this pain secretly, since I lived within the hollow of the man I had become. Shaped by denial of that which is truly me and mine, embraced and owned up by the other. I have suffered deeply with this dichotomy within, not knowing which voice I must listen to. The one that said, 'act for love, act for the ones you belong to,' or the voice that said, 'act for the righteous cause, be a warrior for the righteous cause?' "

Karna's mind then turned to Nakula and Sahadeva. "They speak very little," he thought to himself, "they will surely ask penetrating questions."

"What do you serve?" Nakula will ask. "What do you seek?" Sahadeva will ask.

Karna's mind went over the many occasions when he had taken the side of Duryodhana afraid to ask the question "what do I really serve by doing this?" Blinded by the acceptance he got from Duryodhana, and the rejection he perceived from the Paandavas. "Who do I serve?", became much more compelling. How this service helped him fulfil his secret vengeance was clear to Karna, but in his actions he was the epitome of generosity and self sacrifice.

From his earliest recollection Karna could only remember the searing doubt that he held within. "Am I the person others see and react to? Am I the *sutaputra*, the low born, the one with limited entry into social spaces? Am I the loyal friend of Duryodhana? Or am I who I experience myself to be from within, the warrior with great talents, the compassionate person? Have I become the generous person, often compulsive in my generosity, only so that I may be loved and affirmed for a moment as compensation for the person I am from within, visible only to myself? So often have I strayed far and wide seeking to discover who I am, only to find myself having followed a path that took me away from my being, into an acquisition of skills and capabilities, trophies and accomplishments that were compensations for my own inability to truly embrace myself as I saw myself unfold."

Finally Karna turned to Arjuna in his mind's eye. "What do you truly question?" asks Arjuna.

"Everything and nothing," Karna said to himself. "Looking at all of you and the social norms and practices you uphold, I see the shadow, the oppressive underbelly, the violence that is disowned but glorified by your constructs of culture and society. I see the efforts and ardour undertaken by the underclass, those you can neither see nor acknowledge; the effort they put in to keep your world alive and to eke out the little that keeps them alive. With every effort of theirs, they energise you and impoverish themselves. But, I am caught within, between a vengeful anger and a wish to belong. I am clouded by my resentment and my envy. I see myself distort myself hoping to be seen, loved and embraced on your terms. I hate myself for deforming myself I hate you for the love and adulation you get".

It is not possible to build a system that will have no negative impact. We design systems and enunciate policies hoping to create a context where the members of the system can act with honour and live in peace. Yet, every system has its toxic elements, its ways that prevent some people with heroic potential from discovering legitimacy and recognition due to them.

Ask yourself the following questions:

Are good people, people with high potential exiting the organisation?

Have you had honest 'heart-to-heart' conversations with such people before they left the organisation?

For you to discover what it takes to be an Arjuna, you must discover the underside of the present system. Who are its untouchables? What makes them untouchable? Is it their fault, or is it the ways of the organisation that makes it impossible for these people with heroic potential to feel that the doors of the organisation are open to them?

As the night was turning into day and the *sharanya* of predawn painted the sky with soft pinks and reds, Karna shook himself away from his dilemma. "The four of you I can encounter, I can engage with, forgive and maybe even embrace, but Arjuna, you, I must conquer. The hurt, resentment and envy I feel for you is a self-consuming fire. Vengeance will be sweeter than your embrace," Karna said to himself. Shalya was waiting outside. He was the greatest charioteer after Krishna, bristling under the demand from Duryodhana that he be Karna's charioteer, charioteer of a *sutaputra*, a lowborn. He hated the demand but had to accept it. Karna could see the anger and resentment in Shalya's eyes and demeanour. He saw and heard the omens of his doom. Like a true warrior that he was, he cleared his mind of all these disturbing inner and outer energies, focused his attention on the task ahead, evoked his deepest commitment to his chosen path of action and strode forward.

When Sanam finished the tale, her eyes were moist with tears. The sound of the sea was mesmerising.

Later that evening, AS, Ranjan and Sanam ate dinner still immersed in their own thoughts. After a while, Ranjan made a move to get up, but Sanam stopped him. "Just like all men, you think a hero archetype is only the masculine aspect of the self. Remember that all manifestation is Prakruti, and the feminine principle is the ground from which the forms emanate.

"I am sure you remember that in the period when the Paandavas were incognito, Arjuna became a woman and taught dance. It was in a way a necessary exploration of the feminine side of the central integrating point of the five Paandavas, just as much as Karna is its counterpoint" Sanam continued.

"Ah! You are right. Like a typical man, I too got so caught up with the 'hero' idea; I only saw the masculine – the action side. It was in an intense moment of self-exploration with Prof. Pulin Garg that I saw how deeply I had internalised the idea of a powerful hero. Our family has a proud Kshatriya history. Valour was always talked about as courage in battle," AS quipped.

"We have blinded ourselves with a one-sided view of the more visible and the more active aspects of man. The balance between the yin and yang gets lost when you do this," Ranjan added. And they waited for Sanam to continue.

"I see Draupadi not as the 'woman behind every man' as the cliché goes, but as the 'being' out of which the 'doing' or 'acting' emanates. Draupadi is like the Earth Mother. It is in her that each form of the hero archetype discovers replenishment and through her that they harmonise with the others". Sanam warmed up to her portrayal of Draupadi. Saptaparni and Ranjan settled quietly into their chairs, listening attentively.

"Unlike Kunti who bore the 'heroes' and gave birth to them, Draupadi enters their life in their prime, when the heroes have lost their inheritance. It is her ability to evoke patience and forbearance that lies at the heart of resilience. When active deployment of oneself and the stage for its expression is taken away, one must discover a depth within the self, into which one can withdraw. Without this space that is at once nourishing and regenerative, one will become frustrated and resentful. The masculine, heroic energy will become armoured, brittle, and rigid. This is probably what happened to Karna, when he was repeatedly frustrated and shamed. When he acted heroically, he was shamed for being a Sutaputra, and because he was a Sutaputra, he was denied a stage for action. So Draupadi is also the creator of space, non-threatening and nurturing. However, the patience and the quiet space are not smothering, dull, and self-indulgent. While Draupadi offers a safe space, she does not give up the central dharmic principle. The hero needs her receptivity for replenishment, but this replenishment is also a space for preparation. Is it not Draupadi, with her hair unknotted, who is a living reminder of the betrayal of dharma? Draupadi is a powerful hero, who prepares her men for dharmic battle. In her patience, the purpose and intent one lives for is not forgotten".

Sanam paused for a few moments, AS and Ranjan remained quiet. The pathos of the feminine, heroic being enveloped them.

"It is the ability to be anchored, to receive and to regenerate the hero who has been denied, deprived, and discriminated against, that underlies Draupadi's power". Sanam continued. "As Yudhishtra's wife, she was the

knife-edge on which Yudhishtra placed the weight of his dilemmas, the paradoxes of life, and its irreconciliable polarities. While Yudhishtra appeared in court, sombre and thoughtful, searching for the right decision and the right judgement, what lay invisible to the common eye was the ability of Draupadi to listen to his anguish. Often Yudhishtra would seek out Draupadi when he was torn between the two sides of a Dharma Sankata. Draupadi was the still point 'listening from the heart' as Yudhishtra's mind sought a resolution. After having looked at the various sides to the problem at hand, 'what is fair? What will reclaim balance? What will energise life?' Yudhishtra would ask. And in that silence, Draupadi would share her intuitions. The fear of making a false judgement, the fear of causing chaos, the fear of deadening the world through the use of authority, were absorbed by Draupadi, and converted into wisdom".

It is the ability to be anchored, to receive and to regenerate the hero who has been denied, deprived, and discriminated against, that underlies Draupadi's power

"That is so true!" exclaimed Ranjan. "Is that not what I have done every time I struggled with making a choice? I have asked you to share my feelings of vulnerability, when I hid behind a cloak of impervious objectivity".

"Wisdom and fairness have always been seen as goddesses," AS added. "And did you know that the oracle at Delphi was also the Goddess of Justice, till Apollo displaced her?"

"Some tea before we continue" Sanam said, getting up and pouring herself a cup. "Let's see how Draupadi, the wife of Bhima related to the warrior hero. In my dance choreography, I have found it exciting and invigorating to imagine this part. I imagine that Draupadi felt most loved and cherished by Bhima. She could be impulsive and playful, passionate and emotional. The places where the two could meet, and love each other's presence, were gardens and forests. These were beautiful, unpredictable and exciting spaces. Bhima would become like a child and an adolescent with her, and Draupadi had to find the balance between her playfulness and her sense of boundaries. Bhima could get carried away, and forget his own strength! In receiving

Bhima, Draupadi had to find a great ability to stay anchored, and be the banks through which Bhima could express his impulsiveness and passion. But, she also had to be ready to manage his unpredictability, and direct and channel his enormous energy. A warrior he may be, but Bhima had his fears too. He would often confide in Draupadi his feelings of inadequacy. Draupadi had to listen seriously to the mighty warrior sounding weak and small. 'When do I encourage him to test himself? To prove to himself that he is strong? And how do I listen to the truth of his self-doubt without becoming afraid myself?' Draupadi would ask herself. From her being, Draupadi brought forth compassion and joyous celebration. When Bhima entered an arena looking supremely confident, what the eye did not see was the love and compassion of Draupadi that filled his heart. Draupadi had to contend with Bhima's possessiveness too. Without her he felt empty. But, in discovering his own freedom and love of the world, Bhima released himself from narcissistic self-absorption and found the joy of exploring the world around, entering the new and unexplored with child-like curiosity".

Ranjan became more and more taciturn as Sanam went on with her exploration of Draupadi – the wife of Bhima. When Sanam finished, he took a long time to speak. AS and Sanam waited for him to come out of his introspection. "Much of what you say reminds me of our relationship. Maybe I reflect a lot of Bhima in my ways. I can see what a roller coaster ride it has been for you. The risks I took because I always look for challenges. The number of times I have needed your listening, your resilience and perspective to see me through. This is one more time when I need you to help me walk the tightrope".

It was close to dinner and the three of them decided to meet early the next evening.

"We will look at the feminine counterpoint of Nakula," Sanam began as they settled down after tea the next day. "We will look at Sahadeva also before exploring the Arjuna archetype. Draupadi as Nakula's wife brought forth from herself her most sensitive and delicate aspects. Nakula would often exhaust himself in the service of others, and would find it very difficult to ask anything for himself. It would sadden Draupadi to see Nakula sacrifice himself to be there for others. She therefore made sure that she was able to sense his feelings, and find ways to help him feel valued. Draupadi always knew when she had touched a deep chord within Nakula, since his eyes would moisten with love and gratitude, when she offered a touch of love and affirmation. At such moments, Draupadi would become aware of the deep pathos that Nakula felt for the suffering of people. She would share some of this with Nakula in silent communion. It was not always easy. Draupadi had to also awaken Nakula's emotions to not only absorb the pain of others, but also to challenge and awaken them when they became dependent and self-pitying. This was not the easiest of things to do, because Draupadi would find herself wanting to protect Nakula and take up cudgels on his behalf. Holding back her protective mothering instincts, and yet to heal the healer, called for a lot of wisdom and patience. Awakening the ability in Nakula to use anger appropriately and pro-actively was Draupadi's greatest challenge. She often felt that Nakula suffered more than the person who was at the receiving end of a sorrowful event, and ended up receiving the real punch. 'When is pride an essential ground for empowering a person, and when does it become dysfunctional vanity? When is compassion a gift, and when is it an invitation for dependence?' She would often ask herself. Draupadi, Nakula's wife would often find herself becoming tired and fatigued, not from external exertion, but from reaching out emotionally, and being there for Nakula to reenergise. But her relationship with Nakula was always like a beautiful melody".

When is compassion a gift, and when is it an invitation for dependence?

"We often speak about empowerment, but this is a very interesting perspective" AS reflected. "This reminds me of some of your advice on coaching," Ranjan added. "The feminine side of the person is so important. I am beginning to see why many managers end up getting stressed and struggle to replenish themselves".

The three of them sat quietly for a little while. The sun was setting and the world around seemed to become silent. Sanam began to speak once more as the pink and orange clouds started to turn grey. "Sahadeva's facade of a dry and objective intellectual is very deceptive. As Sahadeva's wife, Draupadi discovered a delightfully witty person. She had to discover the part of herself that held mischief. The curiosity and insatiable appetite for learning and knowledge that Sahadeva deployed went hand in hand with an ability to see the apparently logical and rational, from a very different perspective. To have a meaningful conversation with Sahadeva, Draupadi had to quicken her wit. The range of associations and patterns that Sahadeva could make were wide, and he made them with great quickness, but this aspect came alive only when Draupadi could awaken the prankster in herself. The ability to play freely with ideas and patterns, purely for their delight, brought Sahadeva alive. But, to bring this alive, Draupadi had to discover within her the ability to anchor deeply, and not lose her bearings. She had to offer Sahadeva the reference point as he freely travelled all over, experimenting with the things of the world. His very ability to enquire deeply, and let his curiosity lead him, also made him ask himself 'who am I really?' Often, Sahadeva would withdraw deep within himself. Draupadi's ability to be alone, anchored and not get lonely was central to letting Sahadeva enter his inner spaces. To be a beacon called for a great inner clarity for when Sahadeva was intensely engaged in experimentation and play, as well as when he disappeared into an inner landscape he had to be focused.

"I know what you mean" AS said. "I do this to my wife every now and again. I get so lost in my research and in tossing ideas in my head that I am lost to the world for days on end. At these times I lean heavily on the knowledge that my wife is not dislocated by the loneliness. I play a kind of a 'lost and found' game with myself. And I want her to be in both places with me!"

"Let us look at Draupadi as Arjuna's wife now," Sanam said. "In a strange way, I can't do this without also looking at what it might have meant for Draupadi to have become Karna's wife. It almost came to pass, had he not been barred from the court based on his birth. In some versions of the Mahaabhaarata, Draupadi is depicted as experiencing a secret love for Karna. It is perhaps the recognition of the two aspects of the disowned parts of a social system, which drew Karna and Draupadi to each other. Karna was after all a Paandava, cast away at birth and having to experience deprivation, denial, and discrimination, from the guardians of a social order. Draupadi too suffered humiliation on account of being a woman. While Karna as a male warrior struggled with having to prove his worthiness repeatedly, Draupadi struggled with having remained a 'context creator' for her warrior husbands. They were two sides of the invisible reality of the social order. One cast away, and the other held within, but both denied the legitimacy of action. The heroism of Draupadi then lies in her ability to experience the hidden and 'shadow' sides of the context, the hidden inner realities of her warrior counterparts, and discover the wisdom and forbearance to transform them into nourishing energies. Perhaps it was this ability of Draupadi that held the Paandava heroes together. She was the palm that integrated the fingers of the hand, gave it convergence and carved out coherence so that they experienced the wholeness of which each of them was a part. I have often wondered whether the Paandavas would have become fragments without Draupadi. Would they have acted in concert, as a team? As Arjuna's wife, this was probably the most important aspect of Draupadi, the role of an integrator. In this feeling of being grounded, Arjuna could own up to his doubts, he could ask the difficult questions, and find a quality of listening in which his doubts did not paralyse him; a listening in which his doubts acted like a rudder, setting the direction. Maybe this is why Draupadi was Krishna's lifelong friend too. Draupadi disrobed, would have exposed the shamefulness of her society so deeply, that it might never have recovered.

The Heroism of Draupadi then lies in her ability to experience the hidden and 'shadow' sides of the context, the hidden inner realities of her warrior counterparts

It would have been as frightening to behold as Krishna's Vishwarupa *(the awe-inspiring all-encompassing form)! The darkest hour they say is before dawn. Perhaps Draupadi held this darkness on behalf of the Paandavas, in dignity and honour, so that they might act for Dharma. All the questions Arjuna had about himself were borne by Draupadi. His discovery of his femininity was enabled by her feeling of being grounded, his ability to act mindfully was enabled by her own mystical self, aware, silent, and deep".*

Sanam's voice became heavy with tears welling up. "The dharma of a Yuga (a millennium) will change only when the voice of the outcasts and the women are heard. And when they speak, the upholders of the old dharma will listen in silence and in shame."

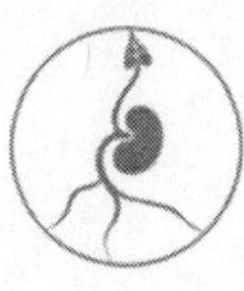

Arjuna was unique among warriors. He was the only one who encountered and explored his feminity. The Mahaabhaarata has each of the Paandava heroes live incognito for a year. Arjuna disguised himself as a woman and a teacher of dance!

☺ 😐 ☹ *Ask yourself how nurturing is your leadership style?*

☺ 😐 ☹ *Does your system have a sense of aesthetics? Does it appreciate beauty and rhythm?*

☺ 😐 ☹ *Are there burnouts that render yesterday's heroes, today's maimed?*

☺ 😐 ☹ *Do you and your team find yourself justifying the unintended fallout of your decisions and actions as 'collateral damage'?*

Notes to myself

1. I never looked at these stories as an inner drama happening within me! How profound its impact has been. In just listening to Sanam embody the heroes whose worlds she was narrating, I think I have had a glimpse of the Arjuna within me. Some seeds have been sown for sure. I never thought preparing to be a leader was such deep emotional transformation.

2. The careful reordering of myself has allowed deeper intelligence and insight to emerge. I realise that 'what I am meant to be' is far beyond my imagination. I have released myself from the prison of my limited thought. I can't change the qualities I am gifted with, but in having an insight into the several aspects of myself, I understand the light and the shadows I create in me. By just reordering these elements intelligently, I can become what I was meant to be.

3. "Draw the bow deep within to shoot the arrow true and fast", I remember hearing someone say. The hub on which the team turns its wheels is 'I'. The more grounded and deeply anchored I am, the more the power and enlivening of the team. Can I make it?

4. "Na dveshtyakushalam...." He hates not evil action, nor is he attached to good ones, he who lets go, and is pervaded by deep insight is in meditative awareness and has no doubts (Bhagavad Gita Ch 18.10)

GROUP
LANGUAGE

INDIVIDUAL
SECURITY

GROUP
SECURITY

INDIVIDUAL
LANGUAGE

PLATE 3 THE JOURNEY

PART 2

Arjuna over the ages, *parallels and pragmatics*

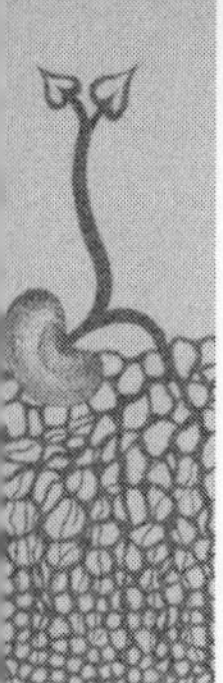

CHAPTER 6
The Doorway to the New Garden

Ranjan was up early next morning and sitting in the balcony of their hotel room, having tea. As soon as Sanam came to join him, he started talking excitedly. "I have asked AS to join us again. He had talked to us briefly about the evolution of organisations, and what he called true heroism of a leader, when we were closing our reflections last Saturday. I called him up this morning, and I have asked him to join us for the day. He has promised to share with us his ideas on evolution. 'It is really the story of Buddha,' he told me as we finished the call and I can hardly wait to hear him out. Sanam, I simply must enter my Tapasya, *I have no other choice. If I don't, I will be chickening out of the most difficult part of the adventure I have undertaken. I must become the leader who offers to the next generation in Mobile Unlimited, the possibility of an institution that can live a hundred years. It should be capable of evolving as it grows. I can't be the hero who broke new ground, but did not create a foundation".*

AS came in time for breakfast, and over a cup of tea he began saying, "There are many stories to tell and lessons to learn. Arjuna is a timeless hero. He has taken many forms and has been born a thousand times. You must let me move between stories to explain some theories, to really understand how you can be an Arjuna. We are not just recounting stories here. "Have you read the works of Joseph Campbell? He has done a wonderful job of looking at myths and stories across the world. One of his best works is the one called The Hero with a Thousand Faces. *It deconstructs the underlying structure of all the heroes through the ages and across cultures. In fact the frame-work I am going to talk to you people about is inspired by the 'Hero's Journey' that Campbell describes in his book. I have been going over the idea of Arjuna as a symbolic hero for all ages. Looking through the evolution of human collectives, I wanted to examine the 'Arjuna role-identity' at each stage, as a change agent. I am going to try something I have never tried before, Ranjan. I am going to have a dialogue with you to see if you really are capable of being an Arjuna. Sanam I need your help. I was inspired to think of this after listening to you. I am going to create a new step in Arjuna's path, a threshold he must have crossed before he met the Hunter Shiva and got the Paasupataasthra. If either Ranjan or I get stuck, please come in and help us."*

AS asked Ranjan to sit in front of him, "We start here, after you the aspiring Hero, the Arjuna wannabe, has taken a great step. You have come to terms with your Perundi, the persona full of aversions and uncontrolled passion. You have also encountered and put to rest your Mohini persona, seductive and full of desires. In front of you there is a large door with a short wall on either side of it. And I am sitting in front of the gate, a wizened old man."

Ranjan sat down, and looked into AS's eyes with intensity and eagerness. "Let's have a conversation, and I am going to see if you deserve to cross this threshold, this little gate." AS said and became quiet.

After a few minutes, Sanam asked, "Are there any signs that tell us where we are?" she asked. AS thought a bit and said, "Yes. There is a small sign on the door that says 'Your first steps to realising your dream lie on the other side of this door... '"

"And who are you?" Ranjan asked feeling emboldened. "I am the gate keeper to the world on the other side," AS replied. "What lies yonder?" Ranjan asked. "Let's first find out if you deserve to go there." AS stood his ground. "What makes you think you can cross the door?"

"I come here weighed down with great sadness," Ranjan was warming to the task "I have many burning questions, but I don't seem to have any answers," he began. "I feel impelled to seek answers while holding an enduring dukha *about the present state. I am unwilling to compromise, collude, and accommodate with it anymore."*

"That's a good beginning", AS said encouragingly. "There are no short cuts or escapes from the alienation as well as a sense of isolation on the journey to become a Hero. Are you committed to being brutally honest with yourself?" "Yes, I understand that I will be leaving behind the security of the group and I will have to seek the answers, drawing deeply from my own resources," Ranjan said. His voice was sombre but determined. There was a period of awkward silence. Sanam broke the silence with a question. "Is there any guarantee that he will find the answers?" "No none at all," AS answered.

Ranjan continued after a deep reflection "I became an entrepreneur because of a compelling dream. I have created an organisation, a world that holds promise, but it is of great concern to me that many of us feel the 'dukha' of this world. It is not only a personal seeking, though I might be awakening to the negatives of the present steady state of the group more acutely than the others. I hear an inner call to walk this path to the end."

AS was moved by Ranjan's sincerity and resolve. "I am going to test you now with a few questions: Do you believe that 'I have the answers and it is the group that has to change'?" Ranjan thought for a while. "I don't think you feel that way," Sanam interjected, "I see you seeking answers because you know the problem, but you don't know the answers." That helped Ranjan articulate himself, "I am part of the problem. Every one of us is keeping the present state alive. If I am demanding, my colleagues are willing to accommodate. When I am down they commiserate. I do the same for them, but these adjustments are mutually reinforcing the present impasse. Maybe the others have found ways of coping, I can't rest till I try to find a way out."

AS sounded very pleased. "Ranjan, you have taken a big step here. The willingness to take the responsibility for your experience of the present, and the responsibility to find a way out is the bedrock of 'the Karma theory' that the Bhagavad Gita speaks about. There is no them, there are no escapes, no postponements."

"Yes," Ranjan started, feeling affirmed by AS. "The cribbing that we do, the small parties we organise to let off steam, the occasional 'Kaizen' improvements we do are ways that help, but they don't change the ground," he added.

"Adult learning is a difficult thing," AS came in. "To find really new ground, one must be willing to 'unlearn'. This admission of ignorance can be terrifying for an adult. When a child discovers something new, he is excited. An adult however is afraid and pays a high price, since his viability is now challenged. The status and power that he commanded from his knowledge is lost when this edifice comes down. He can no longer pretend that he is powerful, and has to admit to his inadequacy."

The three of them sat quietly sipping their cups of tea. AS broke the silence "Let me ask you the next question," he started, "But who are you in this whole drama? Why are you sitting in front of this door?" Sanam interrupted, "Ah! I was wondering when Ranjan would ask this question. I suppose he is too engrossed in his thoughts to ask. In any case let me answer you, I am just the gate keeper to this exciting but dangerous space behind the door. Some call it a jungle, some call it a desert, I don't know. I only know that real seekers have to cross this door, many go in and no one can come out this way, it is a one-way door. I am here to help the aspiring Arjuna find out if he has it in him to really confront what's in there."

"OK, so what's the question?" Ranjan was getting impatient.

"How do you think your group will take this movement of yours into the lands beyond the door?" AS asked. Silence once more, a bit more sombre than the last one.

"I don't think they will be happy," Ranjan began. "I am admitting that I am not the Atlas with all the answers, with the broad shoulders on which their world can rest." "They will feel abandoned," Sanam added, "that's the way I felt when I had to step out of the boundaries of the tradition and try out new choreography. My teacher just said 'This is as much as I know, it is now your search' and here I was thinking he knew everything!"

"But, I think it is important for all of us to get away from this myth that simply because I am their boss I have all the answers!" Ranjan sounded indignant. "Yes, I can see that they will feel anxious, my stepping into this land will clearly say none of us has the answers. They might even feel angry, distance themselves from me, and leave the organisation. Who knows?" "But staying with the façade is a disaster too, Ranjan," Sanam added. "It only reinforces

dependencies. The real dissatisfactions and let-downs will be shoved under the carpet." "Only to explode in our faces" added Ranjan wryly. "Now for the question. 'Do you believe that moving to a land of seeking will allow me to escape from the group and the agony I am experiencing? Or that it will lead to my becoming more powerful?'" AS was unrelenting.

Ranjan was intrigued, he was going to answer quickly, but stopped himself "Mmmm..." Ranjan began, "I think it will ask of me to agonise for the community! Transition to this Space will not mean an increase in power, status or resources. Instead, the heroism in the transition is my willingness to risk my status in the quest for learning." AS seemed delighted with the response. "An individual who is deeply involved with the Community and loves it; who is committed to it strongly, and wishes its well-being; who will take responsibility for its current reality and confront it; only such an individual can move into the land," AS elaborated. "The agony that he feels is from the concern to the 'we', it cannot be a personal search. A person who is unconcerned about the 'we' will leave the community when it becomes personally impossible to continue. Only an individual who is deeply concerned and committed will enter this Space. He takes responsibility for the issues that he and the Community face; and chooses to confront reality directly."

"Are we through?" Sanam asked excited and impatient, "Can we open the door?"

"Yes, I think so, but let me warn you, there are no guarantees of success, no guarantees that the group will respect and love you for going through with the Tapas. How they will receive you once you come back with answers, if you find them, is also uncertain." Ranjan and Sanam looked at each other, there was no hesitation in their "Let's go, why wait?" stance.

"Oops! That was exhausting." AS said, "Let's give ourselves some quiet time and I will take you through an understanding of the whole journey. I think it will be important for you to grasp the larger perspective."

"Is that when we look at the story of the Buddha?" "Yes Sanam, it is" AS answered.

It was past lunch and almost time for the evening cup of tea when the three of them sat together to continue the exploration.

"I will get back into teaching mode," AS now sounded like a teacher in a class room as he began to outline a framework.

THE HERO

When one talks about a hero in a community, organisation or group, one imagines a strong leader who guides the steps of others: The hero is powerful, of high status within the community, with the capacity to make significant decisions. He commands the resources of the community and can allocate them as per his vision. He is invulnerable; and has qualities and skills that are either internal or can be obtained through training. In this sense, he is an end product.

What these accounts do not show is the internal struggle and pathos that goes into the journey of becoming a hero. **This journey is the Tapas.** The hero is willing to be vulnerable. He is not necessarily powerful within the community. Instead what makes him an achiever is his ability to undertake a journey of heroism, a path he traverses, to arrive upon a vision for the group and later work with the group in making this vision a reality. Thus the hero in each context varies. The heroes in this journey require some basic qualities like dedication, concern for the well-being of the group and the willingness to undergo the process of change.

The journey, in brief, is in four parts. In the first part, the hero is a member of a larger group; and is differentiated from the other members since each one has uniqueness but there is a sense of equalisation. He follows the rules of his community, and draws his security from his belonging to the group. His daily actions are in tune with the community's requirements and he follows the norms and hierarchies of the larger group.

"This is more or less the happy story of our early phase" Sanam quipped.

In the second part, as his individual awareness increases about his internal and external reality, he begins to experience greater constriction and dissonance with the norms of the group. However, he is wary of articulating and acting on this dissonance in the larger group.

Such action has the potential to threaten the group, and he faces the risk of being punished for not acting according to group expectation. So the individual begins to express this dissonance through catharsis, within cliques, and in intellectual debates. Any changes that he proposes, however, remain restricted to problem solving and Kaizen, rather than transformative ones. At this stage he might discover that the dissonance between his own experience and the group expectations is not really being answered by the marginal changes he helps to bring in. The futility of such expression, without change in the fundamental reality that is throwing up the systemic lacuna, begins to weigh heavy; and the reality in which he finds himself becomes urgent.

"Ranjan, do you recognise where you were when you called me for help?" AS asked. "It is important that you recognised this point and persisted. Many people with great abilities simply give up, or don't have the heart to seek the answers. They find their coping strategies and remain functional without becoming the best that they can be. Let us get back to the Hero's journey from this point now."

At this point he makes a significant shift into the third part of the journey, where he takes the risk of being alone, leaving behind the security that he obtained from his belonging to the group and he moves into a state of questioning. This shift is dangerous, since he has to unlearn his earlier ways of perceiving and acting in the group, he has no assurance of success, and is likely to face the disapproval of the group. This shift marks the beginnings of becoming a hero; with no guarantee of being one. Having answered the call to look for a new way, to go through the intense search and experimentation that is necessary to discover the new, he might come upon the insight and the vision he seeks. It must be emphasised that he might have a vision that triggers a systemic transformation; that has the potential of moving the group forward, but, equally he may not, and the great idea he grasps in his hand is only an empty fantasy. However he still faces the task of translating this idea into reality, and that can happen only in the same group from which he went away to seek the truth.

"This is the threshold we encountered this morning," Ranjan said in the short pause here. "The dialogue we had has really set my mind to rest at one level, but, at another level, I am seized with the enormity of my task."

He then moves to the fourth part of the journey, where he takes the insight-vision that he has discovered and comes back into the group. Since this vision has the potential of radically altering the group norms and boundaries, he has to negotiate the changes he proposes with the rest of the group. The group cannot accept his word without subjecting it to a rigorous examination, and confronting the 'hero in the making' with their legitimate resistance to the adoption. This confrontation and examination separates an empty fantasy from substantive insight, and separates the villain attempting to profit from the discovery and the hero who is offering a valuable gift. A group that adopts the new without this negotiation can fall prey to exploitation or weak followership. Through this process, his vision is incorporated into the group functioning and the new paradigms are applied. This can be a long process and while working through the resistances and evoking the hope and trust of the group, the hero faces the risk of being villainised and crucified. Only after he has weathered this storm has the hero completed his journey.

"Mmmmm....that's not a great situation to look forward to at the end of all the effort," Ranjan said, "But, I guess one cannot expect people to pay the price of a change just on the say-so of the self-proclaimed hero!" "Yes, the dissatisfaction with the present must be clearly felt and the answers must address them clearly," AS added.

The hero is not one who just discovers new levels of capability and goes back to the group as a transformed individual. Leadership lies in changing the existing paradigm of the group, and helping each member of the group discover enhanced competencies that converge into an enhanced capacity of the community to engage with the emerging reality.

At no point during the journey does the individual have any assurance that he will become a leader. Rather than accepting an increase in status within the existing steady-state practices of the group, the aspiring hero has to be willing to give up his position and belonging in the group. Hence this journey is not easily or comfortably taken. Often an individual would become a hero only when the pathos caused by dissonance between his own awareness and the reality of the community becomes unbearable.

AS stopped here, and said to Sanam "To illustrate this journey, let us draw upon the hero who has inspired millions: Gautama Buddha."

Siddhartha, as the Buddha was called at birth, was the heir to the Shakya kingdom. When casting his horoscope at birth, the king, his father, was told that the child had two possible futures: one was to become a great and powerful emperor and the other was to become a great spiritual teacher who would lead the world on a new path. How Siddhartha became Gautama and evolved into the Buddha when confronted by the universality of human pathos ['dukha' literally meaning compressed/constricted/stressful space], rather than a king, is a classic example of the Hero's Journey.

In common parlance, a king would be a hero: with wealth and power over other people. The path of such a king is relatively easy. However, kings belong to the current space, the space of status, power and wealth within the existing paradigm.

In his journey, the hero is not driven by the need to enhance his status and power, to become bigger, to increase the size of his kingdom. Gautama is brought up in the lap of luxury. While he has doubts about the way the kingdom is being run, the politics and intrigue of the palace, the transitory nature of worldly pleasure, it is only when Gautama is confronted with the four signs, namely, a sick man, an aging person, a dead body, and a meditating mendicant, do the doubts become a raging fire. Gautama cannot rest until he has found an answer to the question, "Why does man experience such dukha?" Gautama crosses the threshold from being a prince to being a mendicant: one who has no worldly power, possessions or status, but only a dedication to the quest, when he discovers that none of the answers available to him address his question in any meaningful way. He is concerned for the well-being of others, and is dedicated to find methods and ways of moving the group forward. He confronts reality as is, rather than as he would wish it to be. For this he not only risks material concerns, money and power, but also relationships such as family, companions and his kingdom. In doing so, he comes face to face with his own fear, loneliness and pathos. He risks the disapproval and disowning of the larger society.

At the end of the story AS felt compelled to add, "Ranjan and Sanam, you have helped me put all this together in a framework for further understanding. I want to present this to you now".

THE HERO'S/HEROINE'S JOURNEY, A FRAMEWORK

The overview

The Hero's Journey can be better understood if mapped on a framework. This framework is drawn on the basis of two factors: the language or the expression and the location of security. On the vertical axis we have as the two polarities 'Group Language' and 'Individual Language'. By language we mean the entire gamut of expression. Group Language is the set of words and ways of expressions that falls within the collective consensus of meanings, both denotative and connotative.

On the horizontal axis we map the two polarities 'Security in the group' and 'Security in the self'. Security in the group would mean that the person experiences a sense of harmony, acceptance, and belonging in the group. All the intrinsic and extrinsic needs of the person are met through this belonging, and through playing by the rules of the group. Security in the self would imply a deeply introspective state, where the person withdraws from the group and does not participate in the group activities, because he experiences dissonance between what the group values and what he values. However, he is comfortable with this difference and the knowledge that the group will not be in harmony with his own reality. The person is, therefore, able to be introspective and engage in a search without the distracting compulsions of belonging to a group, complying with its rules, and conforming to its norms of behaviour, while being at variance with them.

The hero in this journey traverses four worlds. Firstly the world inhabited by the groups he belongs to, the ones he inherits i.e., family, community, nation-state and humanity. He then moves to its periphery, when he experiences the lacunae and dys-functionalities of the world he is born into, but does not know how to make a difference. If he hears a call and responds to it, his real journey begins and he goes into the desert and becomes a seeker. If he discovers what he seeks, he enters the fourth world, that of the mature hero offering insights and impacting the world.

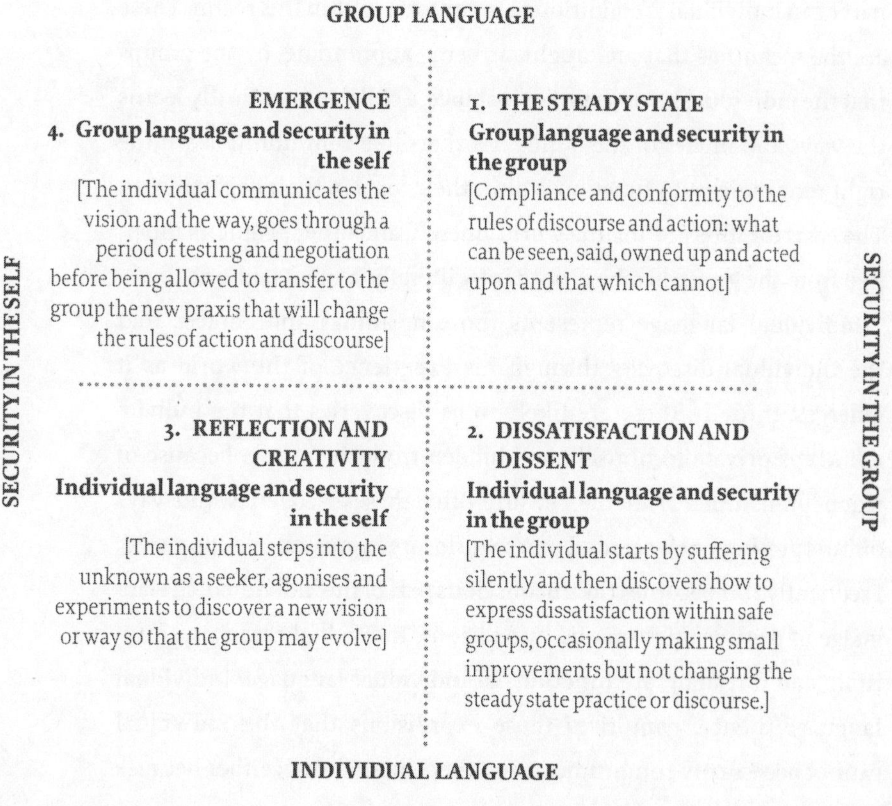

GROUP LANGUAGE

SECURITY IN THE SELF | **SECURITY IN THE GROUP**

EMERGENCE **4. Group language and security in the self** [The individual communicates the vision and the way, goes through a period of testing and negotiation before being allowed to transfer to the group the new praxis that will change the rules of action and discourse]	**1. THE STEADY STATE** **Group language and security in the group** [Compliance and conformity to the rules of discourse and action: what can be seen, said, owned up and acted upon and that which cannot]
3. REFLECTION AND CREATIVITY **Individual language and security in the self** [The individual steps into the unknown as a seeker, agonises and experiments to discover a new vision or way so that the group may evolve]	**2. DISSATISFACTION AND DISSENT** **Individual language and security in the group** [The individual starts by suffering silently and then discovers how to express dissatisfaction within safe groups, occasionally making small improvements but not changing the steady state practice or discourse.]

INDIVIDUAL LANGUAGE

"Am I making sense?"AS asked, sounding uncharacteristically diffident. I want to elaborate each aspect of the framework, but tell me if it is meaningful." Sanam was unequivocal, "This certainly captures Ranjan's journey as I have seen it from close quarters." AS continued.

Language: Group and Individual

Language refers to the universe of meaning making, choice making, and role taking that an individual employs in his living process. It includes not just the spoken word, but includes the meanings, methods, and practices he learns and uses. Thus at the very least, it refers to the common forms of discourse. It also includes the worldviews that the individual is embedded in and responds to.

Group language includes expression that is collectively accepted and openly shared in the Community or group. These expressions are driven by the need to belong and conform to the group. The conscious part of an individual is conditioned to conform within this realm. These are the meanings that are taught, as being appropriate, by the groups that the individual belongs to. For instance, a child automatically learns the ways and modes of the family. Workers in a community learn the right terminology, to function within their roles in their departments. The basis for interpreting the world, oneself, and other people, is inherited from the group he/she is born into, literally, and metaphorically.

Individual language represents those meanings and choices that the individual discovers through his experience of the world as it emerges. Initially, these are likely to be discoveries that the individual keeps private to himself, and hidden from the group, because of fear of punishment, ridicule, censure; often these discoveries, and ways of interpreting one's self and one's world, are repressed or suppressed. Frequently this becomes the unconscious part of the individual, the language of dreams, nightmares, and visions. Individual creativity, intuition, and foresight, are functions of individual language. Individual language, hence, comprises those expressions that the individual cannot necessarily communicate to others in his group; either because they cannot be easily understood, or their expression cannot be tolerated by the group. Induced fears in the unconscious are one reason for this suppression of the new and different ways of responding to one's world. One consequence of moving from group language to individual language is the risk of losing relevance of expression. Every individual is bound to discover such dissonance between the given and the emerging. Some learn to manage the inner struggle that such discovery brings with it through control, others value their creativity and seek expression for their creativity.

This axis is a polarity, since an individual can experience both the extreme locations as well as any point between them at different moments of time. It is possible that some parts of one's meanings lie in the collective consensus, and some lie in a subtle intuitive form, too early for expression. The two are definitely not opposed to each other.

Security: Located in the Self and the Group

The second factor is that of security: where does the individual belong and draw his inward sense of security from?

When the sense of security of the individual is located in the group, the individual belongs to the group; draws support, resources, and safety from the group. Thus the identity of the individual is merged within the group. He acts on behalf of the group, and with group sanction. In return the individual is protected from the consequences of his actions by the group, and is sustained by the group. Families and Communities perform this role.

When security is located in the self, the person draws upon his own resources, to live in the world. He takes responsibility and faces the consequences of his actions. Group support is not essential; and therefore his belonging is often questioned. However, being located in individual security does not mean that the individual is no longer a member of the group, or is not concerned about its well-being. What it does imply is that his predominant reason for action is not the approval of the group. One reason for moving from group security to security in the self is because of a greater difficulty felt by the person, in influencing group norms as well as the feeling of being disowned or punished for being different. However, such withdrawal is never really without a compulsion to protect the self, and therefore does not allow for a passionate introspective search. The difference between a protective refuge in the self, and an anchorage in the self lies in the freedom that is experienced inwardly to direct ones enquiry in the second type, as against remaining preoccupied even when one is off to the Himalayas in search of peace in the first!

This axis is again a polarity, since the two inner states can be experienced by the same person at different times, or to different levels, without being mutually exclusive. Nor are the two states ever nonexistent in the person. Choices are made from time to time, and each has its place in the life of an individual.

Each individual in a community has to contend with moving through the four kinds of universes, defined by language and location of security, for inner growth. The continuous movement and growth of individuals within the community, who seek higher modes of relating, create the journey of leadership within the community. They perform a cycle of actions that traverses four universes. However, most communities tend to get stuck in the steady state, and therefore become stagnant as well as oppressive. Leadership in such communities tends to be of the Yudhistra type, where administrative efficiency, control, and compliance, are paramount. Bhimas and Arjunas are seen as rebels, and Sahadevas feel suffocated. Nakulas are welcome in this state of affairs.

"Let's examine this through the Buddha story" AS began after pausing to see if there were any questions.

I. THE STEADY STATE: Group language and located in the group

> When his father, King Suddodhana, heard from the
> astrologers that his son Siddhartha was born to be

> a great king, or a profound world teacher, he was determined that Siddhartha would be surrounded with all the comforts and privileges of a king. The entire palace was commanded to ensure that Siddhartha was happy and felt no want. Suddodhana believed that this would ensure that Siddhartha would be completely engaged with the pleasures of the world and its power, and not become introspective or contemplative.
>
> The best teachers were brought from far and near, to school Siddhartha in the arts of kingship. Siddhartha excelled in them, and when he came of age Suddodhana arranged for Siddhartha's marriage to the beautiful and intelligent Yashodhara. Yet, Siddhartha was troubled by the intrigues in the palace and questioned within himself some of the practices and ways of kingship. While he was a very good student, and proficient in all the arts and sciences he learnt, his deepest doubts persisted.

This space where a large part of the community shares a language, and are in harmony with each other, is the living universe of the community. For any group to function on a daily basis, there has to be a steady state, where there is a commonly understood language [group language], and the members depend on each other [security located in the group]. Its qualities are predictability of functions, certainty of action, and stability of the community. This universe provides the necessary platform for community functioning.

This universe is characterised by boundaries and defined roles. What can be seen, said, owned, and acted upon, by each individual, is determined by the paradigms, practices, and norms of the group. The individual has to comply with these norms, and play his appropriate role, and display appropriate competencies. Learning and change are largely from study, advice, programmes, and solutions that fit the group norms and praxis. These are usually incremental, linear processes. Questioning or critiquing the existing practice at fundamental levels is viewed with suspicion.

Each group develops visible conventions of practice and language. Thus, for instance there are clear rules for what can be said to one's superiors. This commonality acts as the binding force of the group; and determines its culture. The pervasiveness of the steady state becomes apparent when one goes into another department or Community. For instance, when a member from R&D goes to the Finance department, much of what is said will sound like Greek and Latin. If each of these departments are insular and inward focused, it will be difficult to understand the terms that they use in their daily practice. The closest parallel to this space is a Petri dish in a laboratory. This dish has a nutrient gel [like the culture in a community] where certain organisms will flourish and others will not. In the same manner, in the steady state of a community, certain roles and behaviours will flourish and others will not. These roles will lie within the boundary of compliance and conformity.

Individual decision-making is limited to the prescribed roles; the area and degrees of freedom are limited. Any changes that a person can make are only adjustments or accommodations within these boundaries. If the person tries to disturb or violate them, reactive authority that is vested with hierarchical control of his behaviour, can be invoked and the individual pays a price for having violated explicit or implicit boundaries of behaviour. Change has to go through a prescribed process, and thus cannot be of a kind that goes far beyond conventional wisdom and acceptability. Transformation is therefore not possible, only adjustments and incremental improvements.

"In a changing world, if the Community continues to remain within the steady state, it will decay and deteriorate. In this universe, foresight and intuition [functions of the individual language] cannot flourish. The individual will feel increasingly frustrated, suffocated, and constrained

[experiences dukha - constricted inner space], within these set boundaries," Sanam exclaimed. "Exactly," AS continued.

When the inner weight of adjustment and accommodation starts exacting a heavy toll on the individual, and distress sets in, he begins to look for alternatives that will relieve him from these constraints.

"This sounds like being in the armed forces!" Ranjan said. "The extreme forms are that of apartheid and the USSR, particularly during the reign of Stalin in the time of the cold war."

"Now back to the story," AS was in his element.

> Siddhartha's father, the king Suddodhana feared that the prince would become a monk, and made sure that the latter was always sheltered within the palace, from the realities of life, while growing up. As a child, and in his youth, Siddhartha only knew about beauty, youth, security and pleasure and nothing of the pathos of life: illness, poverty and death. The enclosed palace and gardens that reflected the concern for wealth, power, and status, within which Siddhartha grew up, is illustrative of the first Space. This world is ordered and secure. During this period of his life, Siddhartha was constantly within the walls [literal and metaphoric], erected by his father.
>
> The King's fear is symbolic of the fear of individuals who live within the given boundaries and paradigms. This fear shows up as 'resistance to change', which is really a form of the unanswered question "What price will I have to pay if I change the way I act, or the context around me changes?" These walls represent the rules of the steady state. Siddhartha's inner disquiet is the reflection of the unanswered question "What price are we paying for remaining within these boundaries of thought, feeling, and action?"

Sanam was enjoying the story interludes, she looked a little unhappy when AS the teacher came forth again at this juncture.

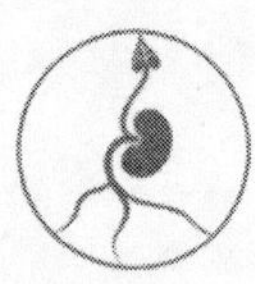

Like a scientist, examine your organisation by evoking the qualities of Arjuna in you. Listen deeply, without judgment and condemnation, but with compassion, with a lot of love for your organisation. What are the underlying rules of engagement? What can be said, seen, owned up to and acted upon? And what is taboo? Here are some statements to trigger your thinking, if you can identify and define 3 or 4 behavioural rules, you would have a good idea of an organisation's DNA:

☺ 😑 ☹ *Be a hero in spite of the system*
☺ 😑 ☹ *Be self sacrificing, work very hard, don't ask questions*
☺ 😑 ☹ *Align with your boss*
☺ 😑 ☹ *Make public agreements but passively hold on to your disagreements*
☺ 😑 ☹ *Adjust, comply and withholding let fragmentation fester*

☺ 😑 ☹ *Only the paranoid survive; stay ahead of the competition*
☺ 😑 ☹ *Get the revenue, get the customer (all will be forgiven)*
☺ 😑 ☹ *We are here to serve the customer, but he is not always right*
☺ 😑 ☹ *Innovate or perish*
☺ 😑 ☹ *Engineering excellence is the key*
☺ 😑 ☹ *Process discipline is paramount*
☺ 😑 ☹ *Satisfactory under-performance*
☺ 😑 ☹ *Difference leads to dissent and danger*
☺ 😑 ☹ *Dissatisfaction and helplessness lead to discharge*
☺ 😑 ☹ *Play the game, humour the management*
☺ 😑 ☹ *Wait, "the management" will tell you what to do*
☺ 😑 ☹ *No risk, no blame*
☺ 😑 ☹ *More of the same and we are safe*
☺ 😑 ☹ *I am only a part of the solution and not part of the problem*

2. DISSATISFACTION AND DISSENT: Individual language and located in the group

> Siddhartha grew increasingly unhappy. He started questioning the practices around him. At first he asked his teachers, and they professed an inability to speak on matters that they were forbidden to, or were unsure of. When Siddhartha emboldened himself and asked his father, the king spoke of 'Raja Nithi and Raja Dharma'(statecraft), which justified the use of force and subterfuge in running the kingdom. Envy and greed were natural to man, and the exercise of justice had to be backed up by power. Siddhartha accepted these explanations and even went along with them, while holding an inner location of doubt and scepticism. On one occasion when his father had Siddhartha sitting beside him at court, Suddodhana asked Siddhartha why he was silent. Siddhartha answered "It is not that I have not pondered over this. While I see the disease of selfish ambition of those in the court, I do not know what the cure is."

This is the Space of attrition. When an individual member begins to find the group language constricting, the person moves to the second Space. He articulates the individual language to himself in certain platforms, but does not act to challenge and change the boundaries and norms of the community culture. It is feared that any such action will result in punitive control, and loss of belonging and security in the community. With each aborted engagement and questioning, he becomes more unhappy and stressed, or submissive and apathetic. This in turn aggravates the controlling tendencies within the group; and sets in motion an eventually destructive cycle. There are five kinds of groups or platforms that he resorts to, in this Space, in response to feelings of attrition.

1. Silent Withdrawal: The individual starts to see the world that is different from the bounded realities of the group. However he is either unable to fully articulate his new understanding to himself, or is afraid to voice it to others. He chooses to withdraw from the group, and brings to the group process the minimum effort that is needed, to ensure membership. He cannot conform to the group boundaries with enthusiasm, nor can he articulate his dissatisfaction.

"Ah yes I understand this," Ranjan sounded excited. "This is why every time I have tried to ask people for ideas or suggestions, so many just keep quiet or say things they think I want to hear. What a waste of talent and energy!" "It is not only they who feel this way MD sahab, I have seen you stuck and caught inside your own cave very often," Sanam reminded Ranjan. "I guess anyone can feel this way from time to time," Ranjan said defensively.

2. Discharge: He expresses his dissatisfaction and agony through temporary catharsis and discharge. This serves to contain the distress, and these discharge sessions act as escape valves for the pressure building inside him. One example of this behaviour is to get drunk and make jokes about one's supervisor in the safety of a group of friends, but then to forget it the next morning and resume the daily routines. While the articulation of dissatisfaction and the new understanding begins to emerge, it is however dominated by

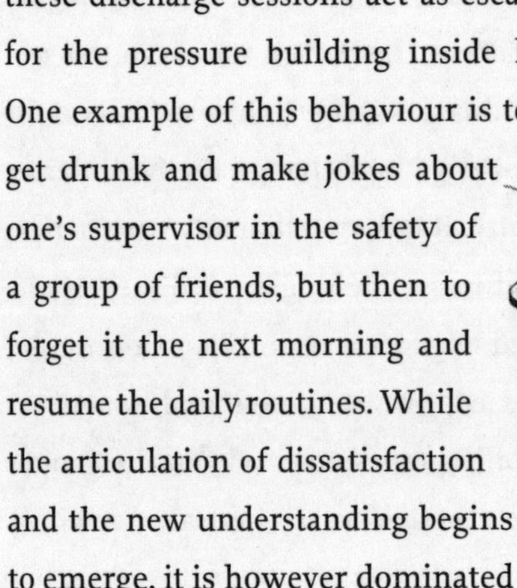

emotional distress. Such discharge does reduce the pressure building up within the Community, but is ultimately wasteful, since the passion and energy generated in the individual, remains unavailable for growth, at the personal and the collective fronts.

"Now I understand why you would suddenly come home and want to just take a long drive, or go to a party where you don't really know too many people, drink just a little too much," Sanam was teasing Ranjan. "At least I don't take it out on you like so many frustrated managers do," Ranjan shot back. "Peace! Let's get back to the professor,"said Sanam.

3. Crib Clubs: These are cliques where members can express their complaints, and disagreements within a private space. This articulation is more cogent than in 'Discharge' sessions. The views expressed in these 'clubs' are usually at odds with the accepted views of the stable group and there is only a weak and helpless critique of the dominant and legitimate discourse of the stable group. However, this critique cannot become public: belonging to these groups is underlined by the rule *'don't sneak or snitch'*. Since these groupings are essentially composed of individuals lacking sufficient self confidence and conviction to stand up for their ideas, they cannot act in alignment to transform group language or boundaries. Most often, they weaken the Community, fragmenting it and dissipating energy.

"I think the founders' club had become one of these," Ranjan said, "no wonder others felt uncomfortable and we were blissfully carrying on with our nostalgia of the past and the complaints about the present. We were part of the stagnation but happily blind to it." AS was happy with these interruptions as they were all on the same wavelength now.

4. Debating Societies: These spaces are an improvement on the 'crib clubs'. Here, different members express their various points of view and discuss them, but take no action. Crib clubs usually centre on a singular critique that is often impressionistic. Debating societies, on the other hand, allow for more varied expressions, and a deeper intellectual consideration. Though they are of higher order than the 'discharge' groups, in that they foster intellectual debate, they still remain largely dissipative, since they do not prompt change in the boundaries of the Community, but remain observations.

"Jagan and I loved our debates even in college," Ranjan was smiling. "We always loved to toss ideas, shoot each other down. In the early days we always came up with something interesting, but of late they are becoming empty of substance." "That's what happens when the organisation is getting exhausted and gets into more of the same kind of answers to problems," AS added.

5. **Kaizen/small improvements:** The fifth is a Kaizen space, where individuals articulate the problem and define solutions within existing boundaries of thought and action. These changes are very important, to improve the living conditions continually. However, they rarely alter the vision of the community or its boundaries at a radical level. Changes are incremental, and community change is minimal. On the other hand, they are a great step forward, since the community now acknowledges a critique, and empowers individuals or groups to act.

These spaces, however, are designed to create only small changes in the status quo. The dissatisfaction and dissonance [agony of the individual], is only marginally alleviated; while the community waste, generated through the adherence to the dominant paradigms is not touched, other wastes are regularly cleaned out. Over a period of time as the discrepancy between the group language and individual language grows, the individual feels increasingly alienated from the group; and his experience of agony becomes intolerable. Small Kaizen changes are not sufficient, and mere intellectual debate only increases the sense of dissatisfaction.

The person then moves into Space 3, beginning the transition into becoming a Hero.

> In the story of the Buddha, it is said that Siddhartha ensured that Channa his charioteer took him outside the palace from time to time. During his few visits outside the royal palace and gardens, he came upon an ill person, an old man, a corpse taken to the *burning ghats* and an ascetic. He encountered the impermanence of life, and was struck by the misery of human existence and felt helpless to alleviate it. He was deeply concerned with the conditions of humankind, and became introspective. No one in the palace even understood, leave alone shared, his concern. Even the wisest of courtiers were driven by politics of power and self-preservation, and could offer him no solutions.
>
> He then decided to leave his sheltered and comfortable life, and his family and kingdom, in search of answers. This was a difficult choice to make, since he was already married to princess Yashodhara, and Rahula was born to them. Yashodhara though, was a deeply intuitive woman, and saw dreams and signs that foretold of Siddhartha's impending journey.
>
> After much thought, Siddhartha came to the conclusion that mere talent and positional power were insufficient to discover a cure for the illness of man that was present everywhere including in the rich and the powerful at court. "I am convinced that I must first liberate myself from the feelings of anger, jealousy, fear, and desire, that lie in my heart, before I can find a way to cleanse the court," Siddhartha had said to his father. "I will not return to *Kapilavastu* if I cannot find the way," he vowed to himself, as he crossed the river that was the

boundary to his kingdom. He gave away all his finery and ornaments to Channa, on the night that he answered the inner call. Siddhartha became the monk Gautama.

Ranjan and Sanam were very reflective when AS was recounting this part of the story. "This is where we were this morning, maybe you were the boatman at the river's edge asking Gautama if he could really cross the river," Ranjan said in a quiet voice.

Now your ability to sense into the various voices across the system will be tested. I suggest two different 'walks' across the system. One, that you as the business head will undertake, and two, you will walk through the spaces as one of the members of the organisation. It is very useful to have a bunch of post-it pads with you. If you can have different coloured ones it will help.

As the head of your system, there will be many times when you feel hurt or withdrawn and find yourself in the space of the 'silent sufferer'. I once heard from a CEO that he was most often loneliest when he had to celebrate an achievement because very few of the team actually knew the path he had to walk. Sit and put down some of the statements about the organisation and its ways that you find cannot be articulated. Now move on to what makes you angry and frustrated. Then look back and think through your favorite cribs and complaints about the system. You would be surprised how many you have! What are the debates you find yourself repeating? How often do you oversee the operations and suggest areas for improvement?

Now, repeat the same walk as though you are a member of the organisation.

Play with the statements. Are there patterns that emerge? Does this make you relook at the DNA statements? How does this link with the story you wrote about the business? We are now ready to help you step into the true Arjuna space, the space where you must 'Undertake the Penance'.

TRANSITION TO SPACE 3 Standing at the threshold

Gautama, the monk, then went to different masters and learnt their techniques. At that time, in ancient India, there were many philosophers, who preached non-attachment and meditation. However, some of these teachers were given to intellectual discourses about enlightenment, or techniques that built on existing practices. Some were great teachers, and Gautama practised the methods and reached mastery, but found them insufficient to answer his quest. The root cause for human suffering remained untouched. After spending a long time practising extreme austerities like fasting, he realised that these methods were no different from the luxurious life he had known earlier; both were extremes. He stopped his rigorous practices and began eating to nourish his health. At that time, he had five other companions with him who criticised him for this, and believed that he was no longer a seeker in the spiritual path and deserted him. In spite of this, Gautama decided to search alone for the answers.

The transition from Space 2 to 3 marks the first step on the journey of the hero. While making the movement, the individual leaves the security of the group behind and seeks to find answers, drawing deeply from his own resources. He has burning questions within him but no guarantee that he will find the answers. This transition is essentially one that is impelled by an enduring *dukha* about the present state, and unwillingness to compromise, collude, and accommodate. In this sense, there are no short cuts or escapes from the alienation as well as sense of isolation on the journey to become a hero. The hero is committed to being brutally honest with himself.

True transition to Space 3 is often the result of an inner call, or because of a great concern for the 'dukha' of others. It is not only a personal seeking, though the awakening to the negatives of the present steady state of the Community or group occurs at a personal level.

"I really understand this," Ranjan said, and AS stopped here for a few moments. He was moved by the fortitude Ranjan and Sanam displayed in their pursuit of the right way forward.

3. REFLECTION AND CREATIVITY:
Located in the self and individual language

> Alone and determined to cleave to the truth, Gautama went into the forest on the banks of the Niranjana river and started to meditate. He was able to discover a mindfulness that was incisive and subtle. By contemplating on the leaf of a *pippala* tree, he came upon the truth of impermanence and dependent origination, of how every part of the universe had played a part in the formation of the seed, the tree and the leaf, that would pass away and become part of the eternal cycle of cause and effect. As he entered a more profound state of meditation he realised that living beings share one common ground of existence with all other beings. Being cut off from this ground and being ignorant of it is the root of anger, arrogance, doubt, fear, jealousy and greed. Through his meditations the *Four Noble Truths, and the Eightfold Path* were revealed to him.

This Space is the private universe of the individual. He retreats into this universe, when all the answers that have been offered so far are insufficient, and the thirst for truth remains unfulfilled. This universe is characterised by an ability to agonise for the truth, a loss of familiar anchors of thought, and the accompanying loneliness. He reflects on the group norms and boundaries; as well as his own contribution in the making and maintaining of these boundaries. While he believes that it is possible to rewrite the paradigm, he is not aware of the mechanics of change. He admits this, and seeks to discover a completely new logic, or radically changed categories and logic to those he used so far. For this, he asks questions beyond what is the presently known, the truth about his own nature and that of the world.

The Bhagavad Gita offers two profound questions to ponder over. "In doing what I am doing what am I really doing?" and "How am I part of the problem and how can I be part of the solution?"

All the great thinkers, scientists and philosophers have talked about their years of search in the wilderness. Insight is often a result of a convergence between intuition, lucid observation, and rational thought. They also talk of entering a 'zone' where there is no self, only the intense quest, and the insight is in the form of a revelation. It is not a personal acquisition.

In the more dramatic versions of the story of his enlightenment, it is said that Gautama sat under the *bodhi* tree, determined that he would get up only when he had attained enlightenment. As he sat under the tree in intense meditation he was first assailed by the monsters of filial duty, then he was assailed by the fierce demons led by Mara, and lastly by beautiful *apsaras.* He gained mastery over each of these obstacles and came to the profound realisation that all of these visions arise out of one's own mind and that there are no external forces to conquer. He is then said to have entered a deep silence and experienced a complete cessation of the self, known as Nirvana.

It is said that the first words that Buddha uttered when he became enlightened were:

Through countless births, I have wandered in *Samsaara*

Seeking but not finding the builder of the house.
I have taken birth, in misery, again and again.
O builder of the house, you are now seen!
You cannot build the house again.
All the rafters and the central pole are shattered.
The mind is free from all *samskaara.*
The craving-free stage is achieved.

In other versions, enlightenment is a more gradual process and a small group of village children are his companions and care takers during this process. He starts teaching them the way and one of them, *Sujatha,* is credited with asking Gautama if she could call him "Buddha, the awakened one."

Dusk was gathering, Ranjan and Sanam sat hand in hand, watching the sun set, AS waited quietly for them to turn back to the discussion. "I guess one must search the desert and the forest before one chances upon one's garden," Ranjan said with a deep sigh.

All the work you have done so far is a preparation for this moment. One of the most difficult things for you to do is to let go of your hopes and fears, desires and doubts about the outcome of this effort. Go into it with a calm, balanced and meditative mind. You have to dig deep and look at those questions and issues that have escaped all your coping mechanisms. Silent withdrawal has not helped, discharge has not, cribbing has been a temporary relief, debates have been useful, but yielded no real action, small improvements were palliatives. What you see are the limitations of your organisation practices. Which paradigms seem to defy change? What does your intuition say are the basic strands of the DNA that keeps the system stuck in the present levels of competence and incompetence? What is your deepest angst about the system? What is the highest potential of your system?

With all these questions in your mind and heart, and no guarantees of finding the answers make a *sankalpa*, a covenant unto yourself, to find the answers. Be prepared for a long search, and enter the space that Arjuna did when he stopped the war and started his dialogue with Krishna! The trick is to ask a question, and listen carefully for your intuition to speak to you, to trust answers that are counter intuitive and flashes of insight that will come to a quiet mind that intensely and lovingly engages with questions of Dharma; an enquiry into how the system can transform into one which is much more enlivening and empowering.

4. EMERGENCE: Located in the self and group language

> The Buddha, it is said, did not immediately decide to go forth into the world, teaching his insights. He realised that his Dharma was profound, tranquil, beyond thought, subtle, and not easily understood, even by the wise. He also foresaw that the world that is dominated by hate and lust, shrouded in darkness and fear, would be deeply disturbed by the truth he would proclaim. He refuted the existence of God and rituals, and recommended mindful living, and meditative enquiry. He was preparing to live a life of silence, and inaction, regarding the teaching of the Dharma. It is said that Brahma implored him to teach, and the Buddha relented.

The individual emerges from Space 3 into Space 4 with new competencies and methodologies and is prepared to offer them to the community. He has clear ideas on transforming the space in the steady state in Space 1. These ideas will change and break old boundaries, old habits of thought, feeling, and action, to allow new elements to enter and take root. While attempting reintegration, the individual exposes himself heroically to the threat of rejection, criticism, and crucifixion by the group: of being accused as an anarchist, villain, rebel, destroyer, and traitor. This is a natural reaction of a people who stay within the given paradigms and ways, since these ways offer a degree of security and predictability.

The hero who locates himself in Space 4 is aware of the resistances that people in the steady state experience to the new. His own insights were achieved through a self-reflexive process of understanding the *'dukha'* in the Space 1, and willingness to pay the price of change. Any steady state reality is a balance between a struggle to survive the dangers of uncertainty inherent in the process of living and the security and predictability promised by the paradigms, social structure and norms that Space 1 imposes. When the Hero proposes the new, he must demonstrate how the new knowledge, new practices, new structure and norms will make life better than before. While impelling the community to change, the individual has to negotiate with the resistance within the community. The hero negotiates with compassion as well as with a conviction, that comes from the knowledge, that while on the one hand, one is adjusting to implement the realities of the present; on the other hand, change involves the payment of a price that will risk the benefits of the present status quo.

The resistance to the New from the Old is a measure of reality. Without this encounter with resistance, the new vision remains a dream. When a new change is proposed, there are two choices that can be made: to either choose to continue with the old or change into the new. This choice has to be wise. It can only arise if all the members are humble enough to dialogue with each other to understand what is best for the community. This dialogue has to be representative, so that the change is real and sustained. Without this dialogue with resistance, if the resistance is simply overcome through brute force, the future growth of the community will be deformed. The harbinger of the new, the hero-in-the-making must encounter and dialogue with the masters and gate keepers of the current reality namely Yudhistra, Bhima, Nakula and Sahadeva.

He has to offer to Yudhistra new laws that create greater happiness and joy; he must offer to Bhima new weapons and technology with which to defend the community and help in its progress; he must offer to Nakula new structures and systems that will ensure greater harmony and ease of working; he must offer to Sahadeva new ways of understanding the world. It is in this process that Arjuna deploys his final astras acquired through his Tapas, he touches the Krishna within.

Gautama the Buddha, went back into the world to teach people about his experience, and guide them to obtaining their own release from the endless cycle of samsaara. His techniques of mindfulness and meditation required no gods and no rituals. It was merely observance of one's own breath and body, emotions and thoughts, fears and desires. This threatened many of the religious teachers of the time, particularly the Brahmins, who emphasised ritualistic worship of various gods, as a way of obtaining *moksha*, and kings who ruled by the use of power. The Buddha was attacked for his teachings, and there were attempts made on his life. However, Buddha found a way of reaching out to the rich and the poor, to the merchants and the priests, and founded a lasting way.

One record of his teaching goes as follows: one old *Brahmin* found that his sons were following the Buddha's meditation techniques, and became very disturbed. He then went to Gautama the Buddha and started shouting at him. Gautama merely listened to him and asked him a question, "What will happen if you refuse a gift from a guest in your house?" The old Brahmin was taken aback by the seeming irrelevance of the question and replied, "He will have to take it back with him." Buddha replied, "I refuse the curses you have showered on me. They originate in your mind and they still belong to you." The old Brahmin was an evolved soul. He immediately realised his error and became a follower of Buddha.

Not all encounters were easy. The story of his great dialogue with Kaashyapa and Sonadanda, both renowned and accomplished teachers of the Vedas, speaks of the intelligence of the Buddha, while the stories of *Angulimala* and *Amrapalli* speak of his compassion. Particularly poignant are his reunion with his wife and son who became part of his Sangha.

Ranjan and Sanam were content to listen and let AS recount the story.

COMPLETING THE LAST STEP ON THE JOURNEY: Return to the group

The Buddha taught for more than four decades before he passed away. During his time he gathered about him many learned and dedicated people and formed a Sangha. These people traveled far and wide to spread the message of the Buddha. It is said that as his influence grew, kings would come to listen to his teachings and there were occasions when he was able to help warring factions come to enduring peace. His Sangha would meet during the monsoons in the bamboo grove, *Venuvana*, which was gifted to the Buddha by *King Bimbisara*. They would learn from each other and discuss the way to conduct themselves and the Sangha. Even during the Buddha's time the Sangha evolved from only male bhikkus to admitting women into the Sangha, as well as working through issues of democratic functioning.

The greatest moment in the history of Buddhism is the adoption of 'the way' by *King Ashoka* 'the great'. Ashoka not only transformed as a person, but members of his family became *bhikkus* (monks). Ashoka proclaimed that the conquest of the heart was superior to the conquest of land. His daughter *Sangamitra* went to Sri Lanka to spread the teachings. He invested his time and his wealth in spreading the teachings and ushered in a wide set of practices of governance and living, based on the Dharma.

The individual returns to this universe as a member who belongs to the community, and who expands the boundaries of what 'can be seen, said, owned and acted upon', based on insights that will empower all the members of the community. When the group transforms on the basis of these insights and dialogues, the group language shifts from being located in the earlier forms of discourse, its technology changes, its paradigms change i.e., its culture is transformed. At this point, the new way is absorbed within the group, and leadership emerges.

We assume that you have found some answers. How do you communicate it? You will now have to risk being seen as a Karna, an outcast or a villain since you will be disturbing the status quo! The fears that have been kept at bay by the present ways of doing things, the coping strategies one is used to, could get disturbed. The key to changing the paradigm, the DNA is to do it one step at a time. Negotiate with the four guardians of the system that Karna had to defeat in face to face combat: The honourable Yudhisthra, the courageous Bhima, the long suffering Nakula and the eternally seeking Sahadeva. These are the pillars of the present system. They keep it alive and well, through their commitment and sacrifice. You have to be able to negotiate with them, walk with them, work with them so that you evolve a

solution that is based on your insights. Work on the dreams and visions they hold and build new dreams together. Help everyone in the system see how their fears and vulnerabilities will be respected and how the new system will offer a larger range of possibilities. Make the system more capable, safer and more fun to be in!

In the Mahaabhaarata war, Bhishma was lying on a bed of arrows waiting for the sun to move northwards, the time he had chosen to die. Yudhistra, the eldest Paandava was filled with futility and sorrow at the losses incurred in the Mahaabhaarata war, he was unsure of how to rebuild society. He went to Bhishma seeking solace and advice. "The war is won but the land is in deep disarray, how do we govern at such a time sire?" Yudhistra said, seeking wise counsel. Bhishma spoke to him about the basics of good governance that Yudhistra could follow after his death:

The nature of a system is 'certainty'. The nature of the structure is 'security'. The nature of beauty is 'order'. These are the 'oughts' of a good society. When the 'oughts' become 'musts', it is a very sad day, since they become tools of oppression and unleash great sorrow.

The way to regenerate the society is

- Not defy or deny but to define;
- Not to resist or desist but to persist;
- Not to denounce or to pronounce but to announce.

Sanam came out of a deep reverie. "My teacher often spoke of the last conversation that Bhishma *had before he died. He would say that all transitions can happen only in the depth of the listening to the new."*

Any change requires that the members of the group, experiencing the reality, face the dissatisfaction in the current reality. However, confronting and questioning the current reality raises fears, and requires the person to let go of dependencies. Some of them are so threatened by this that they accommodate and adjust. Others find tentative ways of articulating their dissatisfaction. Often this takes the form of saying, 'I am the victim, or the recipient of the limitations of the group, or of its leaders'. The step to owning up some responsibility, both for the reasons for the dissatisfaction and the countermeasures, takes some courage. Often the person goes through a 'yes, but ... no, but ...' stage where they reluctantly start to see how they can convert the dissatisfaction into a positive energy. Most people who move through the stages of taking up responsibility for their dissatisfaction, reach a stage of looking at small improvements especially within their areas of control. The step of confronting the group modes and assumptions is disruptive and requires not only courage, but also rationality, rigour, and insight. Only the true hero is willing to confront this challenge. They face the agony of moving from secure contexts, into new areas of search. This search results in a vision that offers a greater truth, relevant to the entire group. This is the hero's journey. When the hero succeeds in bringing back the insight to the group, and transforming the group, he becomes a Leader.

This understanding of a leader or hero as a person on a quest is markedly different from traditional understanding of leadership that focuses on individual competencies, power and status.

It is possible to enforce changes through the use of external force. This external power will deform the structure as long as the force is exerted, but when it is removed, the Community will bounce back to its original form. A cultural change, where the fundamental paradigms and the language of discourse between members are altered, is essential for this transition to be sustainable. This is only possible with the transformation of its members, and the re-creation of new boundaries of existence.

For this shift to occur, individuals within the Community must be evoked to act as heroes in new ways that respond to their inner calling, and the reality outside.

AS brought the framework back to the universe of Arjuna's story now. "Having looked at these movements through the Buddha's story, I could see the parallels to the archetype of Arjuna. The innate drama of the Bhagavat Gita is that of Arjuna at the threshold of Space 3, showing his willingness to question the fundamentals of the known society."

Sanam was really excited. "I can see how Arjuna's Tapas is the great quest," she began, "let me put my understanding of Arjuna and Karna within this perspective."

"The story of Arjuna's journey to discover the Paasupathaasthra is the hero's journey. The dilemma faced by Karna is the leader's dilemma. The hero will be stopped by the guardians of the current reality, namely Yudhistra, Bhima, Nakula and Sahadeva since they are the ones who have dedicated themselves to the good governance and wellbeing of the kingdom. They must not allow the new to enter without a robust enquiry. Also, the new cannot enter anchored in personal ambition. If Karna had owned up to his Paandava-hood, and forsaken Duryodhana through a personal transformation, as the one already in possession of great knowledge he would have transformed the whole society. His position as the integrator and questioner of the present paradigms, as one who sees the shadow of the present paradigms and ways, would get established once he engages in a dialogue with each brother.

"In the Mahaabhaarata, Karna succeeds in defeating each of the four and tells them, 'You will remember this day till you die'. As the battle progresses, Shalya who starts by hating him begins to see the true worth of Karna and his revulsion turns to admiration. This is symbolic of what would happen to a group, confronted with one who brings in a new paradigm, and therefore shows up the inadequacy and limitations of the current ways. However, between Karna and Arjuna, only one can live.

"In order to understand the symbolism of this twist in the story, one must look at the central space between the four heroic guardians in a little more detail. Their four identities represent the four stages of evolution, in the journey of a hero into a leader."

"Saptaparni, the threshold you postulated is like the Abhimanyu *stage of Arjuna's growth. He must confront Karna in the* Dharma Ksetra, *the person who is in every way a hero like his father but has to bear the brunt of society's ugly face. After Karna discovers his true identity, he still has to confront all*

his brothers and win their respect before he can be fully embraced. And then there can only be Arjuna or Karna since both will have merged into Krishna," Sanam said to AS.

"Karna is wise and insightful, but lacks the legitimacy to enter the 'boundary of the known' and transform it. He is consumed by self doubt. Abhimanyu has the knowledge that lets him see the way into the Chakravyuha—the present cycle of existence. In a sense, he has to be able to see its negatives and critique it. However he does not possess the knowledge to show the new way. In the end he is killed by Karna. Arjuna has the legitimacy to enter, he is wise and knowledgeable, he can show the way, but he has not fully overcome self-doubt and cannot comprehend the right time for action. He therefore requires Krishna to guide him. Krishna possesses all that is required of the Leader who can transform the whole group. Arjuna in his fully mature form is merged with Krishna. Krishna is the fully embodied consciousness without any shadow and with the mastery of all five hero archetypes."

Sanam was unstoppable.

"At this juncture the difference in the evolutionary context between the two great Epics, Raamaayana and the Mahaabhaarata, also becomes clear. In each there is a struggle to define Dharma that is appropriate for the emerging times. Thus at every stage of evolution, these five roles become critical. Perhaps the transition from one stage of growth to another always goes hand in hand with strife, a process of creative destruction. The Raamaayana was written at the time when a hunter gatherer way of life was being replaced by more structured and normative kingships. The Mahaabhaarata was written at a time when life was becoming more complex and knowledge was held in teams. The Paandavas who acted from a ground of shared conviction and commitment to Dharma, as well as with an ability to share leadership and work in teams, triumphed over the Kauravas and their reliance on conformity to norms and kinship, that were duties of the earlier age. The war was only the culmination of the inability of the large Kaurava clan to understand and accept the new ways exemplified by the Paandavas. Bhishma is the holder of the Dharma of the yuga. *He therefore becomes the epitome of a great hero, completely dedicated to righteous conduct as laid down in the tradition. He forsakes his youth for his*

father's sake, upholds the honour and dignity of the throne and the symbols of power as regent and heads the Kaurava army, though his heart is heavy with pain. Bhishma as the symbol of tradition has to be confronted, and defeated in battle, before the new can be ushered in. However, in ushering in the new, one needs a deep conviction and 'adhikaar'(inner conviction) in order to act and take on the task of questioning the old, finding the new, and helping people cross the bridge. Karna must transform into Arjuna, and Arjuna into Krishna.

"The Epics explicitly state that they are written at the turn of the Yuga. And each Yuga has what is called a Yuga Dharma, the right way to live and act in that time. Vishnu takes birth at the turn of each Yuga to show the way. Raama and Krishna are both his human form, each a role model of their times. On a smaller scale, a Community is continuously changing, shrinking and enlarging, evolving and regressing, and is not a static entity. The ability to determine the way in which the Community transforms will depend on individual members within it, who are willing to walk the hero's path. Those systems that do not allow for these individual movements with changing times, will become 'sick', and the culture would stagnate. Negative activities would take place, such as creating scapegoats, and insular or ostrich-like behaviours that do not face reality. Those Communities that have been willing to make this shift are able to evolve and grow. Business Organisations that have done this consistently have been studied and written about in the books like 'Built to Last' and 'Firms of Endearment'. Business Organisations are primarily communities in search of security and growth.

"Let's apply all this to how I must lead Mobile Unlimited," Ranjan burst out as soon as AS said he was finished. "Ranjan you must learn to feel the urgency without getting impatient," AS warned. Sanam joined in, "Tapas is a fire and it is very difficult to stay with it, my teacher always warned us. To portray Tapas in dance is very difficult. There are three fires that are being awakened in order that the dross in the body, the emotions and the mind are melted away and the pure golden mind, the Hiranyagarbha *is brought alive. As a dancer, if I cannot bring this bhaavana alive in me, while being perfectly*

still, the depth of meditation required for the transformation cannot be communicated. This is a real test of one's ability to evoke saatvikam.*"*

"That's very interesting," AS came in, while Ranjan was getting fidgety. "Where the status quo is starting to create sickness in an organisation, there are clear inefficiencies that create physical stress, dysfunctions in role playing that cause emotional stress and ineffective decision making that shows up insufficient knowledge and insight into business. One has to stay with the waste of all this literally, before one can convert them into compost. One has to stay with the suffering at all three levels like you say, the physical, the emotional and the mental without moving away."

AS and Sanam noticed Ranjan's discomfiture. Sanam turned to him and said, "Ranjan, you must understand a few very important things before you engage in the Tapas. Firstly the 'heat' is intense, and one can very easily get caught with seemingly important questions which are not central to the search. You remember how I went on and on about the right music and musicians for my new production when my real confrontation was with my own discovery of an authentic style? My teacher had a beautiful spherical crystal that he kept in the puja (home-altar). *To show us what he meant by being mindful in enacting a Rasa he would bring it out and place a red flower next to it. It was amazing how blood red the crystal became. He would remove it, and bring a flame next to it, and the crystal glowed with light. 'Your heart, your mind and your body must be with the bhavana like that, fully reflective of Shringaara (love) at one moment and of roudra (anger) in the next instant. No residue of one emotion should linger in the mind while it is time for the second. Only if you enter fully, and receive fully is the orgasm a complete delight, you transport yourself and your* rasika *(connoisseur) into new realms. If you are not mindful, you will be painful'. I am afraid you will brood and go into your cave, and not stay with the heat mindfully till it burns with insight."*

AS suggested that they take some time off. Sanam decided to play a small musical score and go through some bhaavanas. "You have not seen me dance have you? I have not shown my new piece to Ranjan either. It will help to take your mind off the heavy stuff." She played a piece that described the beauty of

Raama and became completely engrossed in the short piece. She danced seated on a chair all the while!

"I think I understand now the difference between the Raamaayana and the Mahaabhaarata, Sanam, the bravery, the poignancy and the inner struggles of Raama, in being a perfect model of containment, and the exuberance and wisdom of Krishna in awakening multiple potentials." Ranjan was keen on engaging with AS. "Let me understand what you are saying about Karna, Abhimanyu, Arjuna and Krishna a little more clearly," he said turning to AS. "Firstly, we must look at these stories as allegories and symbols of our own inner propensities, if we have to learn inner transformation from them. I am therefore, interpreting the saga from that point of view. Let's go back to Pulin's frame. If we look at the centre where he places Arjuna, on a vertical axis, I am placing Abhimanyu at the bottom. He is the Arjuna full of potential, and like any teenager full of belief in his own potential he enters the Chakravyuha *i.e., the whirlpool of life with great hope. He then confronts a world that has shadows and wheels within wheels. He comes face to face with Karna, that part of him that is deeply cognizant of the negatives and shadows of the world he has entered, with a wish to make a difference. He must experience within himself a sense of* adhikaar, *a sense of deep affirmation, that what he believes to be his potential, his inner belief in himself, and his idea of the world, is indeed real, and not just a fondly held fantasy, reinforced by an indulgent family.*

"Abhimanyu must fully integrate with Karna, who was a person with immense potential but carrying what psychologists refer to as 'narcissistic hurt'. Karna is an orphan, and discovers within himself, abilities and capabilities that mark him out as extraordinary, but ends up being continuously put down. Karna has to not only win external affirmation, he must also develop great conviction that is tested and tempered. When such a person comes to his people offering his gifts and his discoveries, he will be

The inner dialogue Arjuna has at this point in time is not with the mind that has both the questions and the tentative answers, but a mind that transcends the world and is in touch with its own spiritual core, the voice of Krishna.

questioned. When Karna overcomes his self doubt, he settles the inner self-consuming question, 'Who am I to lead change and disturb the present?' Karna therefore experiences the shadow sides of society at every stage of his growth.

"He is now Arjuna, he has no doubts that he is valued for his gifts and his abilities. But, for this very reason, he must proceed with great caution and care. He knows that his questioning of the present ways will be destabilising, it will shake up the present structures and relationships, and there will be periods of uncertainty and suffering before the 'new' takes form. He faces his next demon, the question, 'what is dharmic action? When is the right time?' This question has to be answered in solitude. The inner dialogue Arjuna has at this point in time is not with the mind that has both the questions and the tentative answers, but a mind that transcends the world and is in touch with its own spiritual core, the voice of Krishna. It is only when our actions spring from this spiritual core that we can find within ourselves the lucidity and the energy to bring about real change."

"If I look at my life," Ranjan said after a brief silence, "I trusted myself, acted on the dissatisfaction I had with the way I managed, and created an organisation. I have not really made a lasting difference if I stop with just creating a new product, a new convenience for people to buy. I must ask myself what happened to the dream of discovering a different way to organise, use resources and benefit the world."

AS remained quiet for a long time. "This engagement with you and dialogues between the three of us has stirred something within. There is a lot of work going on today on understanding human evolution that is based on Shri Aurobindo's writings. Many of these ideas closely parallel the yogic idea of chakras. I must put down my thoughts on this," AS said in a very introspective mood.

"I will engage with my team on the question of leadership, and we must continue our explorations with them," Ranjan said as they concluded their short retreat.

From the time he returned from the Mahabalipuram discussion with Ranjan and Sanam, AS was restless. He went back to his library and brought out a well-thumbed edition of 'Life Divine of Shri Aurobindo.' He went over the meticulous notes he had taken when he studied Yoga with Krishnamacharya. His colleague Neetha Nandan was involved in studying organisations and was also deeply involved with a study of philosophy and mythology. AS pulled Neetha into discussions over coffee on the various aspects of the Mahaabhaarata and organisation behaviour. He made notes all the time and after a few weeks, he decided to put his thoughts down. He had promised Ranjan's team that they would have some inputs during his absence. At the end of four days of intense work (and rework) he sent a mail to Ranjan.

"I recommend that you and your team watch some films and discuss them. I will be away for over 12 weeks. Please follow the films in the order I suggest:

1. The Village

2. The Gladiator

3. The Last Samurai

4. The Ten Commandments

5. Apollo 13

6. Gandhi.

7. Ground Hog Day.

"After they watch these films please give them the paper that I am sending you, to read. We will have some intense discussions when I get back. You have challenged me to think deeply on leadership, I am sure our dialogues will lead to a breakthrough for you and your team."

Notes to myself

1. **Composting and tilling again** -The careful reordering of myself has allowed deeper intelligence and insight to emerge. I realise that 'what I am meant to be' is far beyond my imagination. I have released myself from the prison of my limited thought.

2. These dialogues have been intense, they don't let me sleep easily. So many dreams and small insights popping up all the time. Things I have heard long ago. "A beam of light will fill your head and you'll remember what's been said by all the good men this world's ever seen"- the Moody Blues were right. Sanam and I are discovering a whole new world in our relationship; love is taking on a new meaning. Where did I hear these words "neither the warm nostalgia of the womb, nor the fantasy release of the tomb, nor the refuge in a cavernous room, but staying with the seed, in darkness and heat till it blooms". They are haunting me ever since Sanam's dance!

3. I got this mail this morning, and I usually just delete these group mails with sentimental ideas! **The Blessed Buddha once said:** "The Tranquility Link to Awakening (passaddhi-sambojjhanga) has the characteristic of peace, and the function of stilling, which manifests as absence of restless trembling. Stillness of feeling, perception and mental construction is the factor that induces bodily tranquility. Stillness of consciousness itself induces mental tranquility."

4. "Uddaredathmana aathmaanam..." Let a man raise himself by himself, let him not lower himself; for he alone is a friend of himself and he alone is the enemy too! (Bhagavad Gita Ch. 6.5)

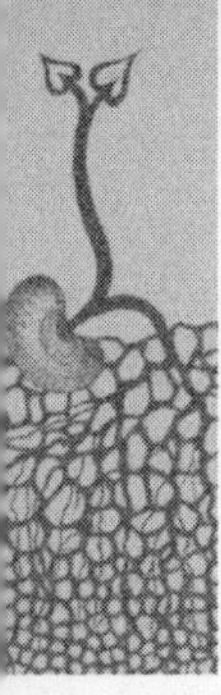

CHAPTER 7
Tending the Garden

"I have been doing my homework like a good student," Ranjan began his mail to AS. "Sanam and I watched the films and discussed the paper you and your colleague are writing. It was great to get back early, sit with a glass of cold beer next to Sanam and watch films! I had to convince myself that that this was critical leadership work!! But getting the romance back into one's life is important for 'tranquility and awakening'. Watching the movies and chatting with Sanam (and her teacher by proxy ☺) has convinced me that I can't go off into a 'vaanaprastha' mode and reenter Mobile Unlimited like a knight on a white steed. I am creating space for myself. I am staying out of ops. I will re-engage when I feel that I have got the insight I am looking for. Till then, I plan to guide my team through some explorations, dialogues and work sharing. Here is what I have done in the last two weeks:

> *›› Firstly, I have asked all my direct reportees to make all their decisions by themselves unless they feel afraid or inadequate. If they do, then they must first seek each other's help before they come to me.*
>
> *›› Secondly, I have given the films to my team and I will give them the paper later. I have decided to ask each one to look at one transition that they have experienced. This must be done in-depth and with a team drawn from the next level of managers. They will come back with an assessment of Mobile Unlimited and their recommendations for change.*

>> *Thirdly, I am off all operations meetings, but I am setting up a 'post ops meet' every Saturday. This is a longish meet based on the way my famous surgeon brother-in-law runs his 'clinicing'. Apparently all good medical establishments do this. Every surgeon comes for the meet with the following: his/her diagnosis, the artefacts of the operation performed (like the removed tumour), pre and post tests etc. The colleagues critique the whole process from the diagnosis to post operative care and examine whether the diagnosis and the artefacts are valid. I sit in on a saturday meet and my team goes through a clinical review: their diagnosis of the situation, the decision and the effects of the decision. All of us comment and I give a final capping statement. The first meeting was great. It allows me to relax and be tranquil through the week!*

More on this as we make progress. I hope your sabattical is not all work, sitting in Sweden. I hope you get to taste the local sights on offer!"

"This is week five since you left, and here is what we did," Ranjan was enjoying his reflective mails it was like his own clinical review.

>> *Jagan, Afsal, Shanti, Rashmi and Raj have watched the films, they are curious about the process. This has got them to come to me and share their ideas on the film and also look for comparisons with Mobile Unlimited.*

>> *I have taken them through the Buddha/ Arjuna story and your framework of the hero's journey.*

>> *They will be reading the introduction of the paper 'Leading Transitions' this week and we will set aside an hour for discussion.*

LEADING TRANSITIONS

Introduction

The choice to work and live in interdependent and interlinked groups was made by human beings a few million years ago. Answering the imperatives of survival and growth in ways other than through sheer

This bedrock of 'the human way' is superimposed with political and social meanings and structures that often go contrary to it

instinct was already a feature of the proto-humans; however, the conscious formation of deeply interdependent groups could well have become the most central feature of being human. This choice allows each individual to transcend his most fundamental limitations. Through communication and language, man transcends **Time** – the learning of all previous generations and contemporaries become available to him. Through tool-making he transcends the limitations of his **Body** – the efforts and energy spent to make 'raw' material into an object with power (for example a drilling tool, a clock, or even a knife) become available instantaneously. Through collective coordinated effort he transcends the limitations of **Space** – a large number of people with differing capabilities and perspectives can converge, take on large tasks across vast spaces, and accomplish planned goals.

Organisations are a result of this choice of collectivity and the positive outcomes that evolved out of this. The great collective adventure of human beings is the struggle to create ways of living and working that provide deep security and meaning to each person, as well as collective systemic energies that create wellbeing along with the struggle to discover *dharma*. This bedrock of 'the human way' is superimposed with political and social meanings and structures that often go contrary to it. Human evolution can be seen from this point of view as the continuing struggle for man to find a meaningful way by which he can overcome his insecurities and fears. Each stable 'way' in which he has learnt to organise himself has simultaneously meant the creation of ideologies, paradigms, political structures, and social mores. This expansion of power and capability of the individual comes at a price. These modes have their positives, in the sense that they allow the individual to transcend his limitations, but, they also have their negatives, in that collective interdependent living demands an adherence to the common agreed norms and ways. Individual preferences, propensities and needs have necessarily to harmonise with the collective agreement or be repressed and managed in ways that do not impact the group. Therefore, each stage has factors that make for stability and convergence, as well as factors that make for dissatisfaction and divergence. Combined with the fact that life conditions are not static, stability and the need for change are in a dynamic equilibrium. Heroes and leaders who question the status quo and bring in insights that create new foundations on which the collective is built bring about transformations from one stage to another. Such changes are never smooth and progressive. Collectives could flounder, digress, regress, just dissipate, or die. Here we present a graceful (i.e. neatly differentiated) unfolding of organisations in order to illustrate the framework.

There have been many systems of classification and explanation of the historical transformation of human collectives. We have found the framework advanced by Clare Graves the most useful. It brings together the context, and the individual response, to explain the stages of evolution of the community. Therefore, the dynamic interaction between the individual meaning-making and choice-making propensities, and the collective consensus, is clear. In a manner of speaking, individual psychology and group sociology can be understood using the same lens. We start this chapter by restating the framework as a set of 'thought-feeling-action-systems'. Ashok Malhotra brought this framework to our notice in the 70s when he was in The Administrative Staff College. He developed a way of working with managerial orientations to values-in-acton based on this frame. Ashok has worked with it subsequently and developed his own version that he calls the 'Existential Universe'. We have worked with thousands of managers and leaders as well as almost a hundred organisations with this framework. While the Existential Universe framework we advance has many similarities to the Clare Graves's frame and Spiral Dynamics[1], we are also influenced by Shri Aurobindo, the chakra theory (both Buddhist and Yogic) and a reading of our own historical processes of change. The shift from the clan to the kingdom during Buddha's times, for example,

[1] Don Beck and Christopher Cowan, *Spiral Dynamics: Mastering Values, Leadership, and Change*, 1996, ISBN 1-4051-3356-2

(as recorded by the social changes brought in by the Buddha) is not a response to a pronounced tribal aggression, as it happened in the west, but due to the tradition becoming rigid. Many of the practices suggested by the Buddha and adopted by the kings he influenced, ushered in a strange mixture of village democracy, community democracy, and State consensus. The structures that became institutionalised during Emperor Ashoka's time are alive today, albeit in an uneasy and corrupted simultaneity with parliamentary democracy, in India.

To make the process easier to understand we will first look at these transitions through the story of Heno, as he agelessly moves through the eons! We will also place the whole process within our earlier frameworks. We will then discuss the process in more formal terms and relate it back to the Hero's Journey. We will be using commonly understood metaphors to describe the thought-feeling-action paradigms that characterise each level of evolution. Spiral Dynamics calls them Value-memes, a term analogous to genes. Value-memes are to the thought-feeling-action paradigms, what genes are to biological evolution. We will then briefly look at the possible similarities with traditions of Indian wisdom and their idea of human evolution.

"Do you want us to be philosophers?" was Afsal's first response, but he did admit that he was deeply triggered by the stuff you have written. The idea that each of us is autonomous and we choose to give up this autonomy in return for a social harmony and efficiency, made him question some of his cherished ideals of obedience. The group warmed up to the idea as they debated and fought. Following this they sat down to examine the basic idea of shared responsibility for creating the kind of organisations we do. Some of the key statements that we agreed on were the following. Firstly, we will have to study how each of us is wielding power. Can we take responsiblity for the 'upward delegation of authority' our reportees have done, almost as though they have no choice? Secondly, all of us are equally responsible for the

culture we create among ourselves and in our teams. And thirdly, the culture can't be static. We have to see how it is relevant to the context and be mindful of the changes required. I am feeling pleased with this dialogue. Jagan (the Sahadeva) will look at the first transition you have described. I am trying to make him appreciate the Bhima and Nakula propensities inherent in a Clan and an Arena universe. I am starting to realise the importance of the stable and predictable Clockwork universe. I have to buckle down and relate positively with this universe before I can create a stable organisation that reflects the Network and the Ecological universes."

The Clan Universe and the Arena Universe

Heno pondered his fate. He had been observing the way the tribe hunted. "This is the way we have been from the days of your great grandfather," he was told by the tribe's Knowledge Holder, "He learned it from the Ancestors". And the Knowledge Holder told Heno the story of how the rabbits had appeared in the Progenitor's dream, and revealed the secret of the hunt. Heno was feeling very unsure, he had by mistake wandered off on a path that the Tribe thought was the land of the Forbidden, it was supposed to be dark and full of red coloured demons. But to Heno's surprise, it seemed like the good tribal lands in many ways. When he thought of the tales and stories of the Forbidden other, he was frightened, but the sense of curiosity and the thrill of new discovery conquered the fear. Heno persisted with his exploration and he found a large grazing ground just outside the dense forest that surrounded the good tribal lands.

Heno was afraid that if he told the Knowledge Holder of his new discovery he would be chastised, but he was thrilled with what he saw, because there were so many plants and so much game to be hunted. Heno knew that crossing the boundaries laid down by the ancestors regarding the places to hunt in, or in the acceptable 'ways' was punished severely. There were many stories of the ones who were taken to the 'end of the world' and given enough food and water for a day and sent away never to return. Sometimes Heno thought to himself, "Perhaps they never returned because they found freedom and chose not to come back to the monotony of the 'ways' ".

It was quite by accident that Heno found a new way to hunt and a new animal too. As he was walking down the new path, partly thrilled and partly scared, this small deer darted across the path. Almost by instinct, Heno picked up a rock and threw it at the deer, and the rock found its mark! "This is so much easier than the old ways of making nets and traps," thought Heno. He thanked the ancestors for showing him a new path and a new way. He picked up the small deer and turned back. Even as he swelled with pride at his new discovery, Heno's mind was filled with foreboding. What would the Protector of the 'ways' say to him? How would Heno convince him that there were no demons in the new lands? What would the great trappers say? Would they feel jealous? Would they feel happy with finding a new 'way'? And what of the Knowledge Holder, would Heno have to invent a story of an ancestor who led him to a new land, across the forbidden boundaries? "Will I be welcomed as a hero or be cast out?" Heno asked himself, as he began his journey back to the tribe. Even as his thoughts grew heavy, Heno said to himself, the old ways are not really helping the tribe, the children go hungry sometimes, and the river is not always full. Let me brave the elders and speak to them of what I have found.

EMERGENCE[1]	**THE STEADY STATE**
◆ **Personified God and belief in one's own gifts and capabilities** ◆ **Prove this personal power by example**	◆ **The entire community as stake holders** ◆ **Resources extracted from a niche** ◆ **Rudimentary set of tools and techniques** ◆ **Belief in magic and adherence to the ancestral ways**
REFLECTION AND CREATIVITY	**DISSENT AND DISSATISFACTION**
◆ **Fear of the magical** ◆ **Own up self interest**	◆ **Scarcity in the niche** ◆ **There are those who toil; what of the free riders? : 'We are' because of 'me'** ◆ **Inadequacy of the magic** ◆ **Helplessness and inadequacy of the tools being used**

The **Universe of Belonging and Protection** or Clan marks the first level, where organising and relating as an interdependent group begins. The Clan Elder emerges under conditions where the community is surrounded by unpredictable forces, has limited information, and seeks stability. Individuals form clannish groups, and are driven by precedence, and blind fear of hostile forces. The individual in a Clan is primarily a member of the group, and the sense of self of the individuals in the group is undifferentiated.

The Patriarch or Matriarch of the Clan or community focuses on the survival of the entire tribe, rather than of the individual. Though the Clan Community emphasises collective action, this action is mediated through the group of semi-elites from whom the Patriarch or Matriarch is drawn. He is an Elder with seniority, one bestowed with special mystical powers [Shaman] or one who is generous in distributing amassed wealth amongst the group. He has to come from within the group or clan.

The individual in a Clan is primarily a member of the group, and the sense of self of the individuals in the group is undifferentiated.

The Patriarch or Matriarch is at once the protector and the progenitor of the system. In fact, most Clans are composed of blood relatives, identical at a very fundamental 'DNA' level. The Clan Patriarch or Matriarch sees the world outside as threatening rather than filled with opportunities. These threats are beyond the individual's comprehension or control. He has to guard and defend his group and its turf, through barricades and fortifications, both actual and psychological.

Though the decision-making is consensual, in that all members can state their opinions, the Patriarch or Matriarch makes the final decision, and this decision has to be followed with obedience. He holds the responsibility of maintaining continuity of tradition, and ensures that all members know the ways and norms of the group. Only he has the legitimacy to interpret reality, act as the keeper of magic to ward off evil, guard the boundaries of the group, officiate in the rituals that are necessary for group maintenance and survival, and dispense justice ruthlessly. He is typically given absolute power to control his group members, and deal with the external reality. This allows for only such roles in the community that reinforce dependency, reception and passivity in choice-making, mechanical and limited technology, and an almost total conformity in thought.

Loyalty to the group and to the Patriarch or Matriarch is the touchstone of one's belonging. An individual group member cannot bring in his subjective reality or his self needs. Since the outside world is seen to be fraught with danger, the Patriarch or Matriarch strictly regulates contact of the members with the world outside. Heroic efforts to strike out are actively suppressed. The member is expected to depend completely on the group, and the Patriarch or Matriarch. Nothing can be done without his express authorisation and he must be in the know of all that goes on. Close proximity, and complete compliance with his dictates are the essential requirements of membership. Disobedience is seen as disloyalty to the ancestors or guardian spirits, and to the group. Difference and rebellion can lead to severe punishments, and to the ultimate excommunication of the individual.

"At this point the group got into an intense debate on the question, 'Are there clans alive today?' It was Raj who pointed out that the founders often behaved like a clan in Mobile Unlimited! We had our own levels of trust and our own 'jargon'. Most people in the organisation treated us as a closed group. We then came to the conclusion that there is a natural pull towards 'father figures and mother figures' in the organisation. If this is not respected a feeling of safety and a sense of 'Us', becomes difficult to maintain in Indian organisations. It then becomes incumbent upon the thought leaders of the organisation to model behaviour so that this initial pull to significant people gets translated into a love for the organisation. The fact that this pull to conformity, uniformity and

seeking affirmation from the elder is opposed by the need to assert one's uniqueness came through as we discussed further."

Dissent and Dissatisfaction

Given the Clan Community's emphasis on precedence, any change becomes difficult, and is also impeded by the nature of the tight-knit group. Individuals learn only under duress, and only that which will help them to perform their tasks better. Individual capacities to explore, satisfy personal curiosity and express themselves are not appreciated, and therefore individual growth is blocked.

Given that the Clan Community sees most events in the environment as consequences of mystical forces, many of which are hostile, an individual in this community often tends to feel threatened, helpless, and frustrated. He also feels hatred and anger. However, these emotions cannot be legitimately acted upon, given the situation that only appropriate and familiar actions are allowed. Hence, this aggression becomes covert and passive.

He also begins to understand the limitations of defining all events through mystical forces; and begins to question their power. Sacrifice and individual scapegoating no longer provide solutions to personal misfortunes. The individual increasingly confronts the limitations of the technology that he possesses to control the environment. This questioning also includes the nepotistic Patriarch or Matriarch's power, derived from representation of precedence and tradition.

Since Clan Communities believe in sharing everything equally, individuals find the denial of their own self-interests increasingly difficult, and begin to resent the demands of the group on their personal resources. This becomes even more acute with the perception of scarcity in a limited context, and the need to survive in a chaotic environment.

Reflection and Creativity

In this quadrant, the potential hero confronts the control exerted on his life by mysterious forces. He faces his fear of the magical demonic forces, and of the unknown. With this, he begins to question the importance of precedence and tradition that control his actions within the community and outside. Curiosity is given space, and not suppressed. Exploration is also fuelled by the fear of dwindling resources, in the limited niche.

The hero-in-the-making also contends with the discovery of personal power that the process of individuation brings

The hero-in-the-making also contends with the discovery of personal power that the process of individuation brings. He owns up to the price he pays in belonging to the **community.** He faces the impulses of his own self-interest; and begins to come to terms with his loneliness. He begins to learn about the outside world in fresh terms, and confronts his fear of survival. Dependency on the group is replaced by a counter dependent, "If I am not for myself who will be for me," stance. His fears, when overcome, and conquests, when achieved, are not attributed to the Clan gods, but to personal gods, for whom he is the uniquely chosen one. With this confrontation, the hero-in-the-making begins to look for means to expand his arena of action beyond the group, and enters into the unknown external environment.

Emergence

The exit from the Clan, and the entry into the Arena, marks a shift in authority, from the group to an individual, who has both power and charisma. The leader begins to prove his personal power by example, and goes beyond the boundaries of the group praxis to bring back greater good. Maintaining tradition and internal norms become subordinate in importance, and the individual begins to shift to the acts of mastering and controlling the world outside. The hero shows the way. Compliance is replaced by rebellion, courage and bravado. In shifting from Clan to Arena, the leader retains his authority for as long as he can promise the consummation of the self-interest of his followers, rather than collective well-being.

Summary

If we look at the clan, it seems to be the first level where the human organism realises and recognises the fact of life and death. The system map that is generated in the mind, and therefore the Value-meme it holds, can be summarised as, 'I must live'. The action choices however remain instinct driven, while the consequences of the choices on 'life and death' are recognised post facto. Some of the speculations one makes on the discovery of early fossils with 'decorative beads' on them, suggest a form of self-worth born of a greater ability to survive than ones neighbour.

The clan level could be characterised by the V-meme, 'We must live in order that I live', and the 'we' here is defined by the gene content of the others in the tribe that constitute 'us'. The value meme therefore would include recognition of the 'us' based on an identicality of features, and proximity of relationships. Many of the descriptions of the 'gifts trails' among the Polynesian islanders, seem to reveal memory of the lineage, kept alive through the conventions of 'gift protocols'. The map of the 'system' is therefore an undifferentiated 'us' and the 'other', a magical set of helpful and harmful spirits.

Since the self and the system that one is part of, are not differentiated, a self-system interface does not arise. The unconscious assertion is, "I and the system are a continuum". This V-Meme creates Clans that are Congealed-Monoclonal Systems.

We have described this strand of the DNA of an organisation's culture in stark manner so that the underlying ideas are clear. This universe of belonging and protection is fundamental to all groupings. Without this, the glue that binds a group together is lost. How do you apply this understanding to your organisation?

Ask yourself whether the members of your organisation have a coherent idea of 'US/WE'. Do they feel a sense of an unspoken and a taken-for-granted-bonding when the word 'us or we' is used? What are the institutions of celebration and togetherness that energise the organisation? I don't mean the year galas and melas, but the spontaneous expression of joy, the spontaneous sharing of sadness. When one sees group belonging in the same way as with a trust-worthy friend, then this sharing takes place. But, this sense of 'us' must also be cultivated. Are there seniors who are treated as mentors and coaches without creating a formal system? Are there seniors who are sought out by the members of the organisation for advice on personal issues and other help that is not official? Do members of the organisation befriend each other easily? Is there a sense of fun in the working climate? A sense of ease in bringing up difficult issues without feeling fragile?

Now let us look at the dysfunctionalities. If the 'clannishness' is deeply entrenched then you see the following: small cliques that share a homogeneity (either language or class or religion); lateral entrants to the organisation feeling like a fish out of water; change of any kind becomes very difficult; every policy or strategy has to be reiterated by specific people to their trusted followers in face-to-face settings. If there is insufficient cohesiveness you will see the following: very few spontaneous celebratory events and formal stiff participation in the offical ones; individuals feel like islands or orphans and seek friends and mentors outside the organisation; very little confrontation; very little participation in improvement initiatives.

Study the organisation through this lens for a few weeks. Cultures are deep and enduring. Don't be in a hurry to unravel it!

"OK Saptaparni, here goes," Ranjan began his review of the new week. "I was anxious to see how the experiment will turn out, but I must say I was impressed by Jagan's presentation.

"Jagan began by stating that there were important positives in a clan. 'Friendliness and trust are the key. It is only when these become exclusive that we create oppressiveness. Have we done this in Mobile Unlimited? My team says yes! There is the founders' club, and other small clans all over. Some are crib clubs, others are functional.'

"He then presented his recommendations: 'Ranjan, we kept in mind what you said, that you can add to the core and change the pattern, you can't take away or crop. The core word we need to enliven is being'innovative'. We are going to study 3M and their practices of creating 'Skunk works'. We recommend the policy and practices for this technique after each of us in our group leads one small 'In-group'. (By the way that's what we want to call them). We are not going to say technology only, but look at some creative experimenting within any chosen area of interest. We don't want any expectations of results, we are sure the creation of trust and the openness to discuss various issues will create friendliness and bonding'

"Shanti wanted to know how a 'free for all' would be avoided. Jagan has asked her to work with the group to see how an element of fun and freedom can be brought in without any sense of control. Others were happy to let the groups be self-managing.

"We will continue after the break, don't go anywhere AS!"

THE ARENA UNIVERSE AND THE CLOCKWORK UNIVERSE

Heno was a warrior, bold and brave. He had won the biggest trophy of the land-between-the-rivers. The tribes in these lands lived in an uneasy truce. They banded together under the Mighty Maricha, and came together twice a year to celebrate the day of the War God, and the day of the Mother. It was customary at the celebration of the War Gods that the young men fought each other. Many champions would battle, each representing a War Lord, or a village. The rules were few and victory was all that counted. The ones who lost the early bouts were condemned to humiliation, and would become those who waited upon the War Lord. The winner

got much praise and many anxious parents offered him their daughters in marriage.

Heno had just won the highest trophy, but he was troubled. He had learned the brave and cunning tricks from the Master and his uncle Rana. He was made to face his tears even as a teenager. "You must make your pain your friend, and your fear your motivation" the Master would say. His uncle Rana took him for hunts; made him track wild animals, and helped in skinning them after the kill. Heno learnt fast, and was intelligent. "Boy, you think too much," the Master would often say. "What is there to think about? Learn the skills with sword and the shield; learn to use the spear and the net, learn the ways of cunning, and the wiles of women. Never fear death, be ready to embrace it."

Even as he grew into the champion of the land-between-the-rivers, Heno saw much that troubled him. There was suspicion in the air between the tribes, and every now and again there were squabbles - "The rogues from Mapla came here to steal our cattle" or "My daughter is a girl of virtue and never goes beyond my word, how dare the upstart Nemo ask for her hand, she is worthy of a great champion". Often, Heno saw in the spectators of the games, both fear and fascination. What confused him though, was that the tribes between the rivers were much more powerful than those across the rivers. Every now and again, raids would be organised, sometimes with the guidance of the elders, and sometimes by impetuous youth. The villages across the rivers dreaded these raids, and though some were well-prepared, they often gave in, and offered grain or dried meat or cattle in return for peace. Young men were encouraged to go on adventures, and there was a custom that if a young man wanted glory, he either was a champion and a great hunter, or he went away for a year and returned with riches and exotica that would be a bride price.

"Is life just an endless vigilance against the other and an extraction of riches?" thought Heno. "I have so few real friends that I can trust. Though we make merry together every once in a while, so many of my companions look at me with envy or with fear. This year on the day of the Mother, I will take a bride. Already Tara is betrothed to me, I will have brave sons, but she will live in fear that one day I will fall in battle, even though she is proud of me as a

champion. I must be ever ready for battle, that is the honour of the champion, but sometimes I wonder if my bravery is only the other side of fear. Often, I have seen the proud warrior in front of me look at me in fear, as I start to dominate him. I wonder if he is only a reflection of who I will be tomorrow, as I lose my strength and youthfulness. I can't bear to see the way the losers are treated; they often become the victims of the village elders' wrath and live in humiliation. Maybe I hate that so much that I train harder to become fit and strong.

"What if there is a way to end this constant vigilance and strife? Can we agree on ways to prove our powers that do not mean brutal battle? We lose so many young men who could be good fighters. Can we find ways to fight together, just as many sticks bound together are harder to break? What of the tomorrows? Can we learn to plan for a tomorrow, and not live only for the day? Can the Master teach many of us to be competent, rather than just a few to be champions? What is more useful to the tribes, many who can fight as one, or one who fights the best? Why can't Acharya just be the best sword maker, why does he have to fight too? Does the Mighty Maricha have to hoard all the riches, to give as he pleases to his women and his sycophants?" Troubled by all these thoughts that came in a rush, Heno decided to go away into the forests for a time, and seek the answers from the Gods.

With the emergence of the **Universe of Strength and Desire,** the Arena, the locus of control shifts from the one who interprets mystical forces to the one with personal power. The Arena emerges in times of uncertainty, risk, or crisis, when the context undergoes rapid changes. The hero emerges as a powerful and immediate response to a hostile environment. He is not a person with a vision to control and therefore defend the group from danger; he is charismatic, aggressive, and tactical. The others in the Arena respond to their own fears and risks, as well as danger to the survival of the group, because they see him as the one to have relevant answers, they become the followers of the hero.

4. EMERGENCE	**1. THE STEADY STATE**
• Supremacy of discipline • Security of predictability • Safety of collective compliance to law • The power of obedience.	**• Extract and maximise for progress • Be on the look-out for the prey; be a master of trapping, hunting and fighting • Be opportunistic, understand risk and reward, bargain hard**
3. REFLECTION AND CREATIVITY	**2. DISSENT AND DISSATISFACTION**
• Awakening to the consequences of self reliance and antagonism at the cost of interdependence • Importance of investment over plunder • Value of time and postponement • Self-control over self- indulgence • Confronting the mystery of death	**• Inequity and domination • Humiliation of the many by the few • Inadequacy of sharing and teaching of technology • Lack of mercy, constant vigilance • Fear of betrayal, stress and fatigue.**

"Saptaparni, at this point we stopped and asked ourselves where the five hero archetypes are in this picture. It became clear that the four brothers Yudhistra, Bhima, Nakula and Sahadeva keep the present alive and functional. Arjuna is the one who is called to enter the 'reflection and creativity space'. He critiques the present from a location of great concern and love. He risks everything, goes into the unknown and agonises for the group. We also saw how at this point, Arjuna has to resonate deeply with Karna. Karna is a hero equal to him in every way but is constantly de-legitimised by the present social context and character. Many of us were touched by the pathos of taking a voluntary step into this space, and the courage it calls for to stay the course."

The Hero in the Arena is a courageous adventurer who inspires faith and loyalty in his followers. He runs ahead of the pack, letting it be known that he is in charge. He, for the first time in the spiral of evolution, demonstrates the importance of individual autonomy beyond group imperatives, and through this, brings his individual life force into the community. He believes that fortune favours the brave and mighty, and this 'dare' becomes his hallmark, as he energises himself and his group. His purpose is grandiose, suffused with expansion. For this, he confronts danger with courage. This quality enables him to undertake many pioneering efforts. He infuses a 'can do, will do' mindset into his followers. Often, the characterisation of heroes in movies and books is modelled on the Arena.

This emphasis on individual might and capacity, results in self-absorption. The Chief or Champion believes that the world is full of the means, [people and objects] to fulfil his self-interest. The recurring question behind any action of his is, "What do I get out of it? What's in it for me?" Payoffs for the Arena-hero include wealth, power over others, as well as excitement, and sensual gratification.

The Chief or Champion is opportunistic in his responses. He is concerned with immediate rewards and is unconcerned about the future. Hence, characteristically, he consumes lustily, and acts expediently, rather than invest in the future. He is unconcerned about the waste generated by his actions, as long as it does not affect his needs for personal gratification.

Within the group, the Chief or Champion's primary concern is to increase his personal power and control. For this, he is capable of exploiting a large number of people, if he cannot inspire them to follow him. He directs the efforts of his inferiors through a well-designed set of provocations and evocations. He keeps the group on the move to look for greener pastures within stringent boundaries laid down by him. His power can be challenged only through a display of superior strength, sometimes in actual combat. The followers in turn gain by cutting bargains, and balancing off their usefulness and continued allegiance. Acquisition and distribution of largesse becomes a key to the maintenance of the community.

The 'magic of Clan' are the personal gods who protect and grace the person, depending upon how one honours and pleases the gods. Conquest is also proof that 'my god is more powerful than your god'.

Some common characterestics of the Chief or Champion are: great dynamism, curiosity and exploration, courage in the face of danger, a will to succeed no matter the consequences, impatience and dissatisfaction with the status quo.

"Saptaparni, this was the point at which the group started to see how important it was for them to release me from the unconscious hero-worship that they held me in. For Jagan and Afsal, it was a moment of fear to articulate this reality and to consciously let go of me. It also meant that they owned up to all the unique contributions they had made. They saw that looking for my affirmation would keep them from becoming authors of their own journey and co-creators of Mobile Unlimited."

Dissent and Dissatisfaction

Change in the Arena is constant and often only at the activity level, and not in fundamental ways. The motto is, 'the next challenge is always calling'. Curiosity given free reign seems to prevent any consolidation or savouring of what has been gained. The Chief or Champion also tends to closely control these forays so that the people stay within their power-knowledge.

Given the emphasis on personal power and instant gratification, the Chief or Champion's world along with the excitement of expansion and power, is also filled with isolation, pain, and chaos. In the opportunistic Arena, his allies are only useful as long as he continues to play the game of power, and it serves their self-interest. He has to continuously defend himself, and take revenge for hurt, to maintain his position in the hierarchy. This constant vigilance and suspicion about his allies and followers, leaves him feeling fatigued, burnt out and fragmented. His relations with others are

This constant vigilance and suspicion about his allies and followers, leaves him feeling fatigued, burnt out and fragmented.

characterised by pain, betrayal, oppression, exploitation and revenge. Under the pressure of constantly having to find out who the real friend is and who the real enemy is, he might regress to clannishness, characterised by parochial belonging.

Living with the constant anxiety for survival, he begins to confront his own mortality, inadequacy, and boundaries, for the exertion of his personal power. At the same time, he is pushed by the need to manage the resources that he has hoarded, as a consequence of his expansion. However, he remains unable to change his actions, since admission of these feelings of anxiety and exhaustion results in the risk of being displaced by his enemies.

Dissent is usually not expressed directly, and is apparent only in the increase of chaos. Divergence and striking out on one's own is the preferred way. Collusions and compromises are frequent, and they fall apart easily too. The rebel-dissenter might indulge in discharge sessions with drinking buddies, or form crib clubs, constituted by parochial belonging, or tightly knit clans, bound by loyalty. These act as safety valves where the stress of constant vigilance can be released. However, since the Arena is not a stable and enduring community, this is of very little value. The unstable nature of the community and its nomadic nature are in themselves a source of stress, and relationships tend to be transitory. Therefore the hero often hides his feelings of victimhood and humiliation through discharge, pretensions and posturing. These discharges are also modes for venting his feelings.

Reflection and Creativity

In this universe the Chief or Champion, with his continuous impulse to expand personal power, confronts the idea that reality is not merely sensory impressions. He sees it as functions of underlying laws. Discovery of these laws awakens a higher purpose than the self. He becomes aware of the consequences of his restless actions, his relations with people and the system. He confronts the accompanying fear of betrayal, and loss of status due to the inevitables of life, such as ageing and disease. He begins to explore the complexities of planning for a future.

The Chief or Champion in this space also begins to place value on methods that help conserve the wealth that he has hoarded. He begins to emphasise investment over plunder and order over chaos in his community. He starts to pay attention to stability, predictability and security.

The exploration extends to the realm of the mysterious and God is redefined. God is not only present at a personal and punishing/rewarding level, but is also the King of a heaven, the Designer and architect, the ultimate arbiter of good and bad; a hero of superhuman proportion but also a holder of the 'dhwaja/sceptre' symbolising law. There is a return to the virtues of the group, but not the constricted view of a clan. Death is explored and defined as a movement into a hereafter that is conditional to how one has lived and dealt with others. Joseph Campbell describes the story of corn, that the Native American traditions recount, as the archetypical story of this transformation of a paradigm. The Raamaayana is also set in this transition, where tribes and fearsome heroes have to be brought into the fold of a society with laws and rules, and a divinely inspired '*dharma*'.

He understands the need to demarcate boundaries of self-control, and postpone self-gratification

Emergence

As the Chief or Champion of the Arena transforms into the King or Controller in the Clockwork Universe, he is willing to accept non-negotiable boundaries to his personal power, laid down by a Higher Authority. His focus shifts from continuous expansion, to administering discipline; from functioning individualistically in a chaotic environment, to creating order for stability and security of the group. For establishing this order, he obeys a higher authority, and displays devotion to the 'right way' and action. The Champion willingly bows his head to an unseen God, and therefore all the followers accept the new dispensation. He also begins to feel a sense of accountability for his actions. Dynamism and autonomy are modulated by a sense of accountability, and lust is now controlled by guilt.

This does not mean that the transforming Leader loses his authority, but now the leader is directed by a greater power. The Clockwork Controller's ego remains strong. He retains the right to interpret the Writ, and the power to ensure that all members of the group follow it. Therefore personal charisma and self-righteous or revolutionary zeal still remain important, in becoming a leader. The Follower retains a measure of autonomy within prescribed boundaries and rules, in return for security and predictability.

Summary

This V-meme can be characterised by the statement, "I must live and I must live well". The self is counterposed with the two parts of the system that negate the self. The self is asserting itself with respect to the undifferentiated 'us'. The functional aspect of this self-assertion lies in the dynamism this value meme brings in. It motivates the individual to go beyond the boundaries laid down by the clan (or the group) that the individual belongs to. Psychological fears of the 'dragons spirits' that lie outside these boundaries are challenged. However, an unbridled red also seeks to invoke power for self-aggrandisement or self-protection. The self-preservation aspect of the 'selfish gene' dominates over the 'reciprocal altruism' aspect, as the key survival strategy.

The self-system interface is characterised by, "If I am not for myself who will be for me?" and "I versus the other". This V-meme creates Arenas that are Chaotic-Multivalent Systems.

This is an important strand of the organisation's DNA. When it harmonises with the universe of belonging, it creates a great momentum for growth. The key question to ask oneself is, 'Does each member of the organisation have a clear idea of what heroism means for us?' In the absence of this shared idea, you will find individuals who shoot off in various directions, do what they think are great things and come back to you seeking to be embraced and honoured. When they shoot off and get into frenzy, you are sitting wondering what they are up to and why? A healthy sense of belonging gives the member a feeling of peace, and a healthy arena culture gives the person a sense of honour and pride.

What are the indicators of an unhealthy Universe of strength and desire? Overemphasis of this universe will lead to unhealthy internal competetion. Each person is entrenched in the, 'what is in this for me,' question. Personal ambition and acquisitiveness will defeat all organisational efforts to create synergy and collaboration. Every discussion will seem like a bargaining platform. Unbridled conflicts will erupt and you as the leader will feel like the proverbial 'monkey between the cats'! When there is insufficient fostering of this unverse, there will be a great reluctance in people to take up challenges, there will be a sense of apathy, and you as the leader will feel like a rabble-rouser each time you have to instill dynamism in the group.

Do you have a well-understood way by which heroism is rewarded and self-centeredness is punished? Is this reinforcement immediate and do all your direct reportees act coherently? Are you consistent and enthusiastic in your praise? When the annual recognition happens is it looking like a ritual? Does it leave a lot of heartburn? Do many see the rewarded and recognised people as deserving?

"This is the part I asked Afsal and Shanti to work on. Afsal is a Nakula and Shanti is a Yudhistra if you recall. I think they struggled with the assignment. Here is my take on what they presented.

"Afsal started by talking about the difficulty that Shanti and he had in seeing the positives of the Arena. 'We see this level as creating chaos, and since we face the unexamined brunt of this in Mobile Unlimited, we struggled to see what to retain of this' 'We did find the key word,' Shanti added. 'Dynamism we will retain, we want to add 'responsiveness' as an action word that brings others into one's action. 'Mobile Unlimited has a lot of this characteristic and the fact that the idea of an innovative products company attracts many people makes them look for dynamism. We see this at once as an asset and a liability. The average person does not distinguish between freedom and license, between self-expression and responsiveness.'

"Afsal and Shanti have come up with an interesting idea of defining people's work, based on 'customer contracts' and not based on goals. This will create some order in the present apparent confusion between departments. The idea of departments will be diluted. We have to see how this can be taken forward but all of us see immense possibilities here.

"AS, I must confess to you that hearing Jagan and now Afsal and Shanti come up with such novel ideas made me a bit defensive and envious. I caught myself thinking 'Hey, I am the leader here. I ought to come up with the ideas.' Thanks to all our dialogues and reflective work, it immediately struck me that I (primarily, and others in collusion) have created a Tribe. I have become its chief precisely because of my need to get excited, pick up ideas and run with them. I was often insensitive to the way I was grabbing another's idea and making it my own. You would say I was undermining their psychological ownership of Mobile Unlimited. I see this very clearly now. Both Afsal and Shanti kept asking me for my opinion, my thoughts. I waited till a consensus was reached and closed the meeting without adding anything. I know Afsal will be very tentative, but, I am hoping Shanti will feel a greater sense of belonging, more legitimate since the idea has a HR flavour to it."

THE CLOCKWORK UNIVERSE AND THE NETWORK UNIVERSE

"How can you even dare to say that the Book may be wrong," the Judge thundered. "You are the son of an iron smith and you have no right to question the Book". Heno was silent for a while. He was being accused of having transgressed the law. Heno had always been fascinated with metals. The colours that they changed into when heated, how they changed quality if they were hammered well, how the heating and cooling and the packing in the different muds made strong swords or brittle ones. Heno's father had warned him, "You learn quickly my son and one day you will make the best swords in the land, but don't ask too many questions and don't try new tricks. The Fire Gods and the Iron Gods are good to us because we are obedient, just as the King rewards us because we are obedient." But Heno became very interested in understanding the 'whys' of his work. The books told him how to do things and how if he obeyed, there were rewards waiting in this life, and in the next. But his curiosity always won over the fear of punishment, and the guilt of not following the law.

One day he met the old Alchemist. Some called him a trickster, others called him a wizard, but they kept a safe distance from him. The Alchemist did not look dangerous to Heno, only a little strange, distracted, and very preoccupied. Heno picked up his courage and followed the alchemist to his home next to the forest. He waited a while and then knocked on the door. The old man came to the door after a few knocks, and was surprised to see a visitor. "Go away," he said, "If you are seen here you will lose your position and privilege, why you might even be called a devil worshipper and thrown into jail". Heno was disappointed. He heard strange sounds and saw many flasks and trays with colourful substances. The old man was writing on a large notebook when he had been disturbed! Heno had been warned not to read anything that was not the right books, but the hunger for knowing the secrets of the metals drew him.

He went again and again till the old man relented. "I will teach you about the metals and the salts," he said, "but first you must learn the methods. If you don't follow the method, you will not know what you found or why you failed. In fact you might even hurt yourself. It is similar to the way you practise your craft, but here, you follow the method to discover the new, not to be imprisoned in the old!" he said with a hint of laughter in his eyes. So Heno started to be the Alchemist's assistant. He always came in after dark and went home in the dead of night.

At first the Alchemist made him practise very simple things: How to make a fire of the right temperature; how to pour the right amount of liquid and measure it and when to add the new liquid. Heno had to learn how to make the same coloured liquid every time by adding just the right things at the right time and the right temperature. After a year of this, the Alchemist had taught Heno about the many salts he had, and the metals. Slowly, he began to ask other questions. "Do you believe in after-life?" Heno was a little shocked and surprised by this question. At first he was anxious even to ask the question, but the Alchemist probed, "you hear the elders read from the books, or the priests preach the scriptures, but none of them have any direct evidence". "Look at what we do here, we start with a question, we find ways of testing and measuring, and accept the answer only if we can test and measure the outcome. We love the question, we love the doubt and the curiosity, and we are always sceptical of the answer, even the ones we give!" Heno started to listen and as he did, many other answers about the 'ordained truths' started to unravel.

"I was not born as an iron smith, nor the other a teacher, we are sons of fathers trained and conditioned in a particular way. Why am I interested in the new thought that the Alchemist talks about, while the teacher's son is an utterly indifferent student? The last king was a dull man, given to indulgence and court intrigue, as they say was his father, but the new prince is brave and bright, and we hear that he gives wise counsel to his father. So how can we take all this as divine dispensation?"

The Alchemist also introduced Heno to the deeper secrets of the search. "As is the world outside, so is the world within. We cannot discover the truth of the metals if we do not probe the truth of ourselves," the Alchemist would say as he introduced Heno into the ways of contemplation and self-enquiry. "The practice of devotion, driven by a fear of God and death dulls the mind, we must search for the roots of fear," he would often say.

However, when Heno saw his father, a whole different tune played in his mind. He saw an old man, who had sacrificed a lot to do his duty as the eldest male child. Heno had seen that some of his uncles had been very mean to his father, but his father always said, "It is my destiny to be the first born, my duty and my privilege to offer without regrets. The pain helps me become a better person, and God is the true Judge of all this". Heno saw in his father a man of great contentment and honour, one who bore his burdens without question. For his father, Heno was the hope and delight. "One day you will be the best sword maker in the land, and everyone will say to me, 'What a great craftsman Heno is. You have brought him up well'. And that's the day when all that I have lived for, will bear fruit".

But, this was not the whole story. Heno's sister was very sensitive and intelligent, but not a day went by when the mother was not reminding her, "Learn well, Zara, you must bring honour to us, by being a good wife". When plaiting Zara's hair, the mother would plait it tight and Zara would cry out in pain. "Learn to hold your pain little one, that's the lot of women". Every time the rumours of a husband who was cruel or unfaithful came through the cracks and walls of their home, the mother would grow pale and anxious, but would put up a brave face and say, "We are doing so many good acts and gaining merit. God will smile on us, and bring a worthy man for Zara to wed and love".

The intellectual freedom of questioning and experimenting with the salts and the metals drew Heno deep into the fold of the Alchemist. One day he discovered that cooling a red hot iron with a solution of salts made the iron resist rusting. When this iron was worked with and hammered thin, it had the whippy strength of a spring. So when Heno fashioned a sword by heating and quenching, beating and folding, he could make the sharpest and hardest sword ever made, but with an elastic spring at its core.

Heno thought long and hard before he took the salts to his father's yard and secretly started using his new method. He had just made two magnificent swords, when a jealous neighbour complained to the officials, that Heno was learning dangerous tricks from the Alchemist, and making swords using magic.

As he now stood in the court, accused of breaking the law and learning from the Alchemist, Heno wondered what his defence should be. Should he claim with pride the great knowledge he had discovered? Should he bow to his father's anguish and beg forgiveness, so that his family would not be held in shame? Should he question the books that the Judge made him promise upon, and question the Gods that were conjured up by the priests? Should he conform and comply, or should he respect the search for truth?

4. EMERGENCE	**1. THE STEADY STATE**
◆ Exemplify the value of risk taking ◆ Compete and collaborate; Differentiate from tradition, question the given, innovate through the application of hypothesis and method	◆ Act now for rewards in the hereafter ◆ Inherit own and control. Status and power come from position. ◆ The Value for the craft is fixed; the market is protected ◆ Master the craft of your birth ◆ Stability and security are paramount, being respectable is everything
3. REFLECTION AND CREATIVITY ◆ Rationality over the writ of higher authority ◆ Trusting one's own evocations ◆ Conquer the fear of breaking boundaries ◆ Honour the purpose and the goal ◆ Commitment over duty and role boundaries	**2. DISSENT AND DISSATISFACTION** ◆ Stagnation and boredom ◆ Silencing of dissent ◆ Blindness to the new ◆ Rewarding of obedience ◆ Oppression through hierarchy ◆ Inequity

The **Universe of Roles and Boundaries** or the Clockwork is the space of predictability. The source of power for the Controller or Manager is not his individual might but his representation of the rule of law, policy, and procedures, and the adherence of all the members of the group to these rules. His authority is usually derived from the absolute truth encoded in the Higher Authority or the Book; or dictated by precedence. He cannot add to this law that is laid down. His primary purpose is to standardise and commoditise the daily running of the system. In this, he is constrained and in turn constrains the group, to procedural boundaries. His power is derived from being the maintainer of the order.

In this position, he has the right to interpret the law and represent the Higher Authority in the system

This is not to say that the Controller is not powerful. In the world of boundaries that characterise Clockwork, people are divided into hierarchies and ranks. The power of the Controller comes from his 'better' rank; and he acts *in loco parentis* to the rest of the group. In this position, he has the right to interpret the law and represent the Higher Authority in the system. He not only interprets the events in the work life in general, but also those out of it. Hence, an individual's respect and reputation is always on the line.

He ensures compliance to dictates of the system; and regulates the conduct of his subordinates through morals and prescriptions. If they remain within the boundaries that are set, he takes care of them through patronage–*noblesse oblige.* He fulfils their needs and motivates them to perform their task. He judges their performance by cherishing efficiency; and rewards those who believe, serve and work hard to uphold the system. He also protects them from extreme danger, so that they can perform their tasks and remain focused. This graciousness and protection increases his worthiness before the greater Authority. His willingness to conform to the dictates of the Higher Authority is rewarded in a handsome manner at some future time [in heaven, or upon retiring].

The Controller does not tolerate initiative, dissent, or innovation from his subordinates. He is essentially blind to diversity. The unfaithful, undisciplined, and the rebellious are swiftly brought to order. This is usually through training and indoctrination, imprisonment and correction. However, in contrast to the Chief or Champion, the controller allows his members to have some responsibility for themselves; and demands allegiance to the task, rather than to himself. This allows for some elasticity in individual decision-making, compared to the absolutism of the Clan and Arena leaders.

Dissent and Dissatisfaction

The Controller creates change through adaptation of the Writ of the Higher Authority, by fine-tuning the existing order. He takes care that the security and regulation of the systems remains intact during times of change.

The Clockwork Controller is forced to maintain the boundaries of the system. This can result in an experience of oppressiveness in the members. A member cannot show dissent against the Writ because he can lose his status in the well-ordered hierarchy and can face the consequences of undergoing indoctrination, and loss of personal freedom.

Since he does not have authority to change the Truth, he can only adapt and adjust, he cannot innovate

With the need for obedience and repetitiveness in Clockwork, the Clockwork Controller becomes an automaton. Since he does not have authority to change the Truth, he can only adapt and adjust, he cannot innovate. He has to be obedient and continuously repetitive. His choice of action and profession are limited and prescribed by birth. Thus when the natural gifts the person is born with are not appropriate to the given 'box', there is great suffering and personal loss.

He sees new and contradictory experiences as threatening, and is forced to blind himself actively to them. This includes the evocations of his personal experiences, especially when they contradict authority. His individual potential remains unused and he begins to feel stagnant in his personal growth.

In the face of continuous pressure, he may regress to an Arena kind of personal power, and might become rebellious, and use violence for the 'legitimate' purpose of creating a new order. The forums for discharge and crib often take on the quality of opposition and conspiracy, against the given order.

"We had to stop here and share our reflections. It became very obvious to us how very important this stage of evolution of the human mind was. Raj spoke about how the Pyramids were built, and how the idea of an all-powerful god and the extensive organisation of people into work groups with specialised skills had made the enormous structures possible. We also saw how deeply our thinking of organisations is stuck in this mode. Though each of us is very dissatisfied and angry about the control and conformity this level brings in, the fact of the stability it provides is a huge force in its favour. No wonder we keep feeling anxious when we have to grow out of this mode. In Mobile Unlimited, we have used technology, not become a technological organisation! For some of us, it put our ambivalent relationship with religion in perspective too. We took a break here Saptaparni, each of us needed to reconcile a lot of our assumptions about our worlds. We needed some time."

Reflection and Creativity

The Conformist or Controller who enters this space confronts the alternate realities and begins to examine their validity. As a result he begins to question the Writ, and begins to experiment with reality, using his rational mind to arrive upon his own truths.

He also begins to accept and confront his own inner evocations, even though they might seem wrong and illegitimate, as seen from the pedestal of the 'Divine Writ'. After all, he has been trained to own up only what he must feel, what he must think, what he must do, as ordained by the Great Designer. He must now venture into the fearful space of questioning his conscience, and weighing it against rationality, nature, and truth. The Good, the True, and the Beautiful are not the givens anymore; they have to be discovered and exemplified. He questions his own self-worth within the system, and begins to aspire for more than what is promised by the Clockwork order. In the process of this discovery of rational truths, and his own inner world, he risks reprisal for disobedience, as he begins to assert his individuality. While his swing back into individuality is similar to the Arena level he does not express himself in an ad hoc manner. He uses rationale, and evokes the substantiveness of shared purpose. He therefore begins to seek systematic and logical methods through which he, and his world, can improve.

Emergence

As the Controller transforms into the Network Coordinator, individual competencies become more important than Higher Authority. The Leader begins to question the purpose and effectiveness of the Writ. He is enterprising and begins to take risks. He moves in the Clockwork hierarchy in unconventional ways and leverages the resources consolidated by the Clockwork order, as capital for his enterprise.

His expressions are now purposive and aimed to promote his individual capacity to lead a committed group, to a set of shared goals rather than uphold the ordained truth. He builds this capacity through scientific and technological innovations. He no longer places importance in fulfilling duty, so as to get rewards in the distant future. Instead, he values ambition, to seize opportunities in the present moment, so that he can derive rewards in the near future, and build capabilities that are strategic. While this might be similar to the Arena in its dynamism and energy, what differentiates the Network Coordinator, is his willingness to strategise, create powerful teams, and share rewards arising from the accomplishment of goals. He builds on the role boundedness and procedural rigidity of the Clockwork, by defining methods through which the present is questioned, enquired into, and changed. While change and innovation are greatly valued, they are balanced against wide dissemination, and rational rigour.

Summary

The clockwork value meme can be characterised by the statement, "I must live within the ordained system". The self is recognised as independent and the organisation outside of the self is also recognised as existing independently. However, there is a relationship between the two, characterised by the submission of the self to the rules and norms of the organisation (be it religion, organisation or nation, work group or civic society). A degree of separation is recognised, between the self, and the system that is outside the self. The inner self is shaped and restrained through the deployment of religious control. Self-sacrifice and self-mortification are the evidences of its practice. The outer self is trained into compliance through authority vested in individuals, by the rules of the organisation; legitimacy and status in the hierarchy become key issues, uniformity replaces identicality. The system map in a clockwork V-meme comprises a self as separate from, but located within, and embracing the monolithic system. The clockwork V-meme is probably very important in that it is only in this level of evolution, that survival choices get strongly mediated by logic and reason (though this logic is largely dogma and ideology based).

The self-system interface can be characterised by the assertion, "I am in and for the system". This V-meme creates Clockworks that are Structured-Hierarchical Systems.

Organisations are built on secure foundations and secure foundations need predictability and certainty. They must create a sense of solidity without being imposing. How are you defining and energising this strand of an organisation's DNA? At the very explicit level this has to do with policies, rules, norms and the bureaucracy.

At the cultural level it has to do with discipline. Without a healthy sense of belonging and an enthusiasm to respond to challenges, discipline becomes dry and without any power. Where the team spirit is high and the heroic self is awakened, it becomes a potent force, the stuff of history and legend.

How disciplined are you? Do you skip procedure and pull rank when you feel constrained by the policies and practices you legitimise? Do you hide behind structural constraints when you have to confront difficult dilemmas, and decisions? Are there clear practices for regular communication? Is the work-year punctuated by planned events that bring the whole organisation together? What are the symbols and reinforcers of unity? Do you have standards and operating procedures that ensure efficiency?

When this universe is over emphasised, the organisation will feel mechanical and the work will be a routine. Boredom will set in and mediocrity will reign. Discussions about strategy will be rare; review of actions will yield no learning. People with ambition will leave the organisation and the clock-watchers will remain. When it is insufficient, efficiency will suffer, mistakes will recur, there will be a lot of blaming, planning will be toothless and a cover for inaction, roles will neither be well defined nor respected.

"I wondered initially about your making the story of Heno symbolic, but I see how it triggers imagination without raising immediate parallels and associations. Raj our quintessential Bhima, and Rashmi, the Sahadeva were my choice for this assignment," Ranjan began writing. 'Raj found it just as difficult to work with this aspect as Shanti and Afsal had. 'I hate fixity, I rebel against convention,' is how he started. 'I see now that if we have to take 'scalability and repeatability' seriously, I can be an agent of disruption'. It took the group some effort to help Raj look at the global phenomenon and not just get caught with the personal. (I guess all of us action-heroes have this difficulty AS ☺). Rashmi was quiet, but she came in with her reflection 'I was

forced to look at the whole process of producing something for a customer and how a customer looks at value. We can't be innovative for our own sakes'. Hard to swallow, but all of us had to admit that our start-up days and blindness to our organisation building responsibilities had to end. It will be a couple of weeks before we continue. This has been a difficult reflection to digest.

"The suggestion that Rashmi and Raj came up with was very simple and clear.'Let's learn and apply Dr Riyuji Fukuda's method called SEDAC (Systematic Enhancement of Daily Activity through Creativity). He calls it a 'method to develop reliable methods'. It seems to balance scalability and improvement. Fukuda san started this method in an R&D lab that he mentions in his book " Managerial Engineering: Techniques For Improving Quality And Productivity In The Workplace". Maybe Jagan's 'In-groups' can also harmonise with SEDAC'.

"I am excited and anxious. Let's see how I manage the transition and hold my nerve. I remember you saying that a new mode will go through a period of learning, and that doesn't mean that it's a failure. Rahul Dravid did not become a good one-day player overnight. Sanam is a real gem; she is so cool when I speak about my doubts. She calls me Abhimanyu or Karna depending on what I am getting caught with. That's funny but....

"We have decided to take a couple of weeks off from this process, do some small pilots and review them before we go forward. We may want an 'off-site' when you get back. The action part is fine, I also see an inner churn that each of us is going through, a relearning with its 'adult' issues like you had said. Bye for now AS."

Notes to myself. May 1st

1. Most of the gods and the heroes in our tradition are sculpted in a seated posture, while very few heroes from other cultures are shown in this posture. Shri Ganapathy Sthapati, a traditional sculptor and temple designer, has said long ago that our heroes are acting from Satva gunam, while other cultures see the heroism only in the Rajasic. I am starting to comprehend what he meant... It is so difficult to be aware of the reality unfolding and remain patient, to be the backdrop while others act. To see them act and fail and learn!

2. Dharma, creating the ground, doing the right thing, is subtle, lasting and difficult. Karma is the act of taking full responsibility for one's actions and the world one creates, Dharma Sankata, or choice making in the face of competing demands and remaining true to one's values. These are probably the most important words for me to keep in mind.

3. All change and growth have to be 'inside out'. The team has responded to the tasks. They have been impacted, I don't know if this is leading to introspection and inner search, or it is leading to disturbance. Am I rocking the boat or am I turning up the soil to allow the weeds to become compost?

4. "Shruthiviprathipanna te yada ....." when your intellect is tossed

about by conflict of opinions, and has become poised and firmly fixed in equilibrium, then you shall get into a state of yoga.

(Bhagavad Gita ch 2.53)

CHAPTER 8

Offering Flowers

"It's been a fruitful two weeks. Letting the teams regroup and get back into action has somehow got the operational differences under control. Raj is referring to Jagan and bringing his team into the problem solving effort. Many issues that were simmering have been articulated in the 'In-groups' and the team is enthusiastically taking up the question, 'How am I part of the problem and how can I be part of the solution?' They seem to find some starting points for action. Next week we start with the more contemporary transition. Waiting to see what Rashmi and Afsal will have to say. The two are so reticent ordinarily I hope I have done the right thing.

"When do you get back? I can't wait to hold another retreat. The need to go inward and look at ourselves is becoming urgent. I need this to be anchored and facilitated by you."

THE NETWORK UNIVERSE AND THE ECOLOGICAL UNIVERSE

Heno had a sudden vision. He saw circles interlocked, circles large and small, spinning in an orderly rhythm. Vertical and horizontal circles, triggering hundreds of smaller ones, and he wondered, "What does it all mean?" The reason was very simple, Heno had witnessed two events at first hand that he could not reconcile with, and for days he had been deeply disturbed. The first was a ceremony he was covering in the outskirts of Sydney.

In a small dusty village, before the commencement of a 'body, mind and spirit' conference, two aboriginals had been invited to perform a space clearing ritual. They were an old couple, in their 60's, neatly dressed in colourful western clothes. They started their chanting, after asking the group that had assembled there to form a large circle. The chanting was accompanied by a dance and the two of them seemed to go into a trance. After more than an hour of this rhythmic mesmeric chanting and dancing, they came out of the trance and told the group, "There will be rain tomorrow as the sun rises, this space will be cleansed, and then you can start your conference". It was the height of summer, not a cloud in the sky. It had not rained for more than eight weeks, nor was rain predicted. Heno went to bed very sceptical. But, almost at the stroke of dawn he was awakened by a peal of thunder! There was a heavy downpour for an hour, a thunderstorm appearing out of nowhere to drench the little town. "This is unbelievable," Heno thought aloud, shaking his head. "These guys are so sure of their method that it seems to be a perfect balance of the inner and outer spaces. The scientific method can never adequately explain this, but that does not mean that what I saw is not true".

The next week Heno was covering a UN conference on environment and issues of CO_2 concentration in the atmosphere. He watched in disbelief as the US representative took the stage, and proceeded to question the wisdom of all the scientists who had spoken that day. In the end, the substance of his statement was clear, "The US way of life cannot be jeopardised. Yes we create the highest amounts of CO_2 and other pollutants, but if we were to cap it, there is a huge sacrifice that the President has to ask of his people, and that is going to be very difficult". Heno had known this was coming, but, hearing this message at the end of a series of dire warnings from eminent scientists and a very poignant plea from a group of teenaged school children almost in tears as they said, "All that you took for granted as a future for you and us–the gardens, rivers and sea side resorts, are endangered by the way you elders live and the way you exploit nature and the way you fight". The refusal to take a world-centric view of the future, the refusal to value scientific evidence was stark.

As the vision of 'circles in spirals and circles within circles' settled down, Heno started to unravel the meaning of the vision. "Everything in this world

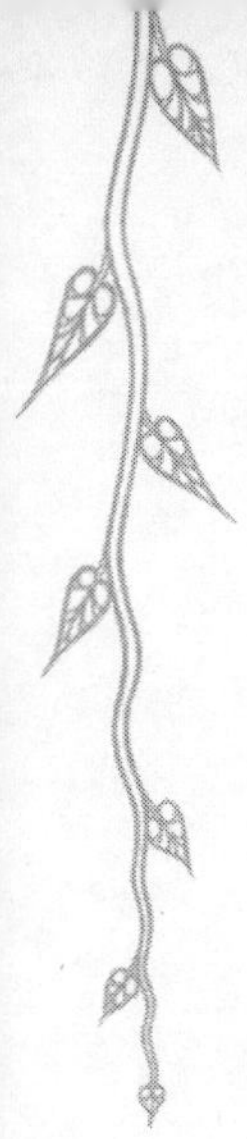

is connected and interdependent. Nations are rich or poor not only because of themselves, but also because of how the world economy is regulated. The monsoons in India are dependent upon sea temperatures in the South American Pacific Ocean. And even as we claim the success of science, we are confronted with the smallness of its view, and the limitations of an analytical view.

"How can we justify the destruction and devaluing of indigenous knowledge, based on the powerful but narrow view of science? Even physics today admits to the fact that the hypothesis and the method influence the observation, and the inference. The rainmakers were precise, but they found a way by which the mind acted, not dead technology. How will science meet and work with this knowledge and the knowledge-holder?"

When Heno asked the rainmakers, "Can you teach me your technique?" they squinted their eyes, moved their hands over Heno's head and said, "You come from a family of spiritual teachers, some of them knew the secrets, we could teach you, but can you go through the rigour and discipline of years of training with us?" How is this different from a professor who told Heno, when he applied for his Ph.D., 'Your uncles are into research, you probably have a background that values study, your college grades are good, and your IQ scores are high? Yes, you can work with me, but can you stay with the rigour needed to do sustained research?'

"What is the mind space that will hold these two worlds together? What collective governance can make nations act for the future of mankind? Can metaphor and measurement, technology and spirituality, the inner and the outer, progress and ecology, find a space in which to rest together and dialogue?" Heno was introspecting on these questions when he heard the words of his yoga teacher, "Gati, Sanghatna, Niyati – that's the nature of this world". (Continuous movement and change at the most microscopic levels, deep and total interdependence of parts, order and rhythm in the movement and interdependence – that is the nature of this world).

"Perhaps I must look at the convergence and coherence of the inner and the outer, science and spirituality," said Heno to himself.

4. EMERGENCE ◆ Value of collaboration and relatedness ◆ Ecological interdependence ◆ The whole and the part ◆ Sustainability	1. THE STEADY STATE [mechanical] ◆ Strategic Investment; shareholder's voice; economic measures ◆ Sustained competitive advantage ◆ Planned obsolescence ◆ Continuous innovation and improvement, Scalability ◆ Value for merit, purposive effort
3. REFLECTION AND CREATIVITY ◆ Fear of the mystic realms ◆ Relinquishing the profit motive ◆ Re-examining the meaning of money and power ◆ Questioning the purpose, examining interdependence	2. DISSENT AND DISSATISFACTION ◆ Speed of obsolescence ◆ Pressures of competing, Isolation and lack of touch ◆ Instrumentality of self, destruction of the environment and the basis of life

The **Universe of Purpose and Aspirations** or the Network ushers in the features of the technological world. The Orchestrator or Coordinator of the Network Universe is purposive, focused on completing tasks to ensure competitiveness of the community in the midst of flux. He shapes collective purpose, and determines goals. The Orchestrator has similar drives as the Arena-Chief: he is acquisitive, and looks at profit through present effort. He models individual success and exudes confidence. He drives the group for efficiency and results, using carrots and sticks. Network leadership is marked by the ability to 'play the game well'.

However, the methods used by the Orchestrator to fulfil his leadership agenda, are tempered by Clockwork sensibilities such as accountability and respect for the law. He is not driven by the satisfaction of immediate personal gratification, and therefore, he is capable of enabling strategy. He is not impressionistic in his actions, and relies on objective data to achieve the purpose: deciding, planning, monitoring, steering, and evaluating the outcomes.

To him, the world and people are resources and competencies are meant to be perfected. They must then be deployed, in roles that are task-centred, so as to increase the effectiveness in achieving the purpose of the

Network leadership is marked by the ability to 'play the game well'

community. These tasks are linked activities, impacting each other, and the entire system. He continuously sharpens the technological edge, to design the systemic interconnectedness and convergence between the technologies. The rigour of the scientific method underpins all his efforts, and thus ensures repeatability, measurability, and predictability.

The Orchestrator balances innovation, autonomy and control, thus creating a bounded system, where dependability and order is ensured. He maintains a stable environment within which individual members can perform their tasks in a secure space and advance to higher authority.

Finally, the Orchestrator recognises that he does not have all the solutions needed to achieve success in a complex environment, and appreciates member contributions unlike the omnipotent Chief or Patriarch. He begins to understand the importance of teams. For the first time in the evolutionary spiral, tasks, roles, positions, seniority and status are not synonymous as in the Clockwork. Knowledge can get obsolete quickly and one can be a member of many teams and organisations simultaneously. Each task requires deep knowledge of the domain, and young generalists could orchestrate experts in various specialisations! And leadership must change depending on circumstance and contingency.

Transactions and task relatedness last as long as the primary purpose remains meaningful. The leadership agendas are collectively negotiated. Discussion and persuasion are the ways of the Orchestrator. While the individual has a lot of influence, only the thought-action reality is brought to the table. Humanism and the 'feeling' world are kept out of the equation.

He seeks to inspire and evoke the members so as to ensure the achievement of his agenda. In the absence of control, the group stays together through the tension of interdependencies and shared purpose. The orchestrator is responsive and resourceful in determining roles, internal norms and processes. Given the larger, ambiguous context, his ability to read trends and relate them to the group's goals and capabilities is critical to the success of the group. He sharpens ownership of link responsibilities, and creates mature interdependence. Differences are accepted and worked through. In this sense, he shares power rather than control it and yields authority when needed. People led by an Orchestrator are likely to feel involved and responsible for the group and its purpose.

"I must be honest AS, it struck all of us that we only know parts of this universe. We really need to immerse ourselves in the underlying assumptions, modes and practices of this level of inner growth before we become truly scientific people, respecting the gifts of science. Many of us felt that at the level of Nations we are tribes using science! Most of us are using and playing with technology as if we were children playing with our toys. Our thought-feeling-action frames have not caught up."

Dissent and Dissatisfaction

Individuals in the Network continuously seek new opportunities for achievement and compete with each other to get a share of the rewards. The Network methods used are scientific and rely on empirical enquiry and testing.

The members of the Network Community become aware of the dangerous consequence of their singular focus on efficiency, profits and returns on investment. People and the environment are rarely brought into the equations and as a consequence they get degraded. Is the member feeling trapped in the continuous drive to compete for a larger piece of the pie? When carried to extremes, the means becomes the end. The mechanical processes that are adopted lead to the members feeling that they are being treated as instruments. This is a result of their roles being seen as a set of tasks, where the emotional reality is absent. The member contends with his continuous fear of being discarded or made serviceable at lower worth, like a worn-out tool in the

People and the environment are rarely brought into the equations and as a consequence they get degraded wake of 'progress', 'necessity', or 'the bottom line'. As knowledge gets obsolete, so do the carriers of the knowledge!

The member of such communities feels resentful and unhappy at being treated more often as a 'consumer' rather than as a person and citizen of a country. He feels isolated, and is forced to categorise all his relationships into competitors and collaborators, with some being both simultaneously. Finally, the weakening of the Clockwork and its institutional relationships further aggravates the feelings of alienation. Hence the Orchestrators also often feel lonely and deprived of human relatedness and touch.

Members also become aware of the consequences of the technology that they have spawned upon the environment around them and the dangerous draining of natural capital. They also realise the limitations of this technology in solving critical human issues. This calls into account ownership and accountability for their actions. In a regression to Clockwork, they might resist this change by calling for 'values', but these values remain a nostalgic return to the predictability and safety of the Clockwork, where values and norms are seen to be interchangeable.

Reflection and Creativity

Individuals in this universe are forced to reflect deeply on the purpose of their existence; and the sustainability of their actions. The fact that the measurable world is a small part of the entirety of existence, dawns on them. They confront the limited meanings of wealth, money and power, and the hollowness of such meanings that are obtained at the cost of the sustainability of the earth. They become aware of the costs that are paid, because of their bounded definitions of economic viability and the colonial attitude of exploitation of natural resources. They list the dysfunctions caused by using technology exploitatively and indiscriminately, especially on human relatedness and on the environment.

Poeple also awaken to the importance of human values and re-examine their work in the context of the wellbeing of the larger system.

Their priorities shift from only material acquisition to include intangible, personal aspirations. Their understanding of subjective and objective truths converge, giving rise to an understanding of underlying patterns and ecological realities.

"We gave up trying to understand and apply the learning to ourselves at this point. We must dialogue this at length when you get back."

Emergence

With Ecological awakening, the hero-in-the-making is no longer content with opportunism, self-gratification, and consumption, and therefore he drops out of the competitive 'rat race'. The emerging Institution Builder begins to sense the need for integration between people, the work world and the inner spirit. He moves deeper into self-discovery, balance and equality. No longer content with instrumental knowledge, he begins to integrate a spiritual imagination into his strategies. He begins to express his evocations as a human being, rather than rely on his role appropriate expressions. He begins to take responsibility for more than his own wellbeing, and relatedness with others becomes important to him. He begins to take account of human and environmental effort and waste, in his understanding of success.

Summary

The network V-meme can be characterised by the statement, "My survival and growth depend upon personal competence and the ability to compete, which leads collectively to organisational efficiency and effectiveness". The self is independent of the system, and therefore has a choice of belonging to different systems. But, this belonging has a 'bargain/negotiability' built into it. The network V-meme recognises that there is an environment that is separate from the organised system that one is part of. However, the relationship with the environment is exploitative.

The growth of the organisation that one is part of is dependent upon its ability to compete advantageously with other organisations in exploiting the shared environment. The systems map now consists of three elements – the self, the organised system and the environment. Rationality and practicality gain over instinctive or ideological choice-making. The organised group's membership is based on a mutuality of purpose that its members share. The purpose is fed by self-interest.

The self- system interface is, "I, and the system that I am part of". This V-Meme creates Networks that are Rational-Purposive Systems.

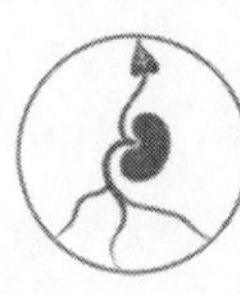

While many modern organisations use science and technology, this universe of rational purposive thought and action is not well understood. The key indicator of the absense of this universe is lack of organisational learning. When the excitement of innovation rests on a discipline of roles, which in its turn is energised by the dynamism of desire and nurtured by a strong sense of belonging, you have the great entrepreneurial organisation.

Examine your organisation and see if these processes are present: there are effective methods by which tasks are done and there is a method by which these methods are examined, analysed and replaced by more powerful and reliable methods; data gathering precedes strategy and the effects of planned action are measured; the frequency of measurement and the choice of measures leads to effective review, learning and insight; these learnings and insight become the starting point for the next cycle of meaning-making, decision-making and action.

An excessive focus on this universe leads to a tyranny of purpose and a celebration of achievement without regard to social and ecological impact. Greed rears its ugly head! It also leads to analysis paralysis and a pursuit of innovation without regard to applicability and use. Science and technology become the new religion and measures like GDP become the mantra. Insufficiency leads to lack of learning; lack of preparation leads to

insufficient capacity creation. Use of meaningless measures leads to stultifying and wrong use of statistics.

Is your organisation really scientific in its temper? Do key individuals understand the importance of doubt and testing, or is data used to reinforce dogma? Is there a healthy practice of debate and critique? Do differences lead to deeper examination of the reality? Are people excited by knowledge and discovery? How are issues presented to you? How well do you study data presented to you? Are you learning all the time? How do you share your learning with others?

"Rashmi and Afsal were at a loss where to start. We were unsure too, so we decided to let the two of them make a few reflective statements to get the ball rolling. 'We have always seen ourselves as technological and professional, we are seeing how Mobile Unlimited has been a tribe that is technologically capable and not an organisation acting from a network culture,' Rashmi said. 'I think we have remained inside our competency areas to avoid confrontations. Problems that can only be solved through collaboration have been allowed to fester; we then fight or wait for you Ranjan, to get in and solve it for us. This is one of the reasons we are on a treadmill of sorts.'

"'Many of us dislike the market battles and the kind of aggression it takes to capture markets,' that was Jagan. 'I for one love the thrill of technology, but not the co-ordination and orchestration that strategy requires.'" Surprisingly even Raj came up short, 'I guess I have not moved away from being the lone-wolf salesman.' he said.

"Surprisingly the team was sombre and introspective without getting disheartened. They were unanimous that the steps each of the group members had taken so far may be small but they are right and they will move us forward. The team however joined in with great enthusiasm when Rashmi and Afsal proposed the key word we need to look at - 'impact'. This too led to soul searching. We agreed that our success had taken us by surprise and we had not planned for the impact we ended up making in the market palce and indeed in the fledgling industry segment. 'Innovation with impact,' is the tentative theme for the next few years. We will discuss this again.

"We have all decided that we will read and discuss the next transition you have discussed in your paper. Until we find stability in bringing the elements of the network that we think are important, we will not have the prerequisites. We will be talking in the air.

THE ECOLOGICAL UNIVERSE AND THE HOLARCHICAL UNIVERSE

Heno had been a great critic of the world of technology and he loved to read Foucault and Derrida. Even if he did not really understand them, postmodernist art and intellectual virtuosity held a fascination for him. Heno had felt violated at the idea of the wars fought in Vietnam, Afghanistan and in other places in the name of ideologies. Chomsky was a hero in Heno's eyes.

For a time Heno experimented with the ideas of the 'flower children', ideas of love and freedom. But, soon he saw that this movement too lacked substance. While the Post Modern critique was intellectually stimulating, it had no foundation of its own. "Foucault lived with prostitutes, but he taught at the university," Heno said to himself. "Maybe the world of capitalists found a purpose in supporting dissent, so long as it remained intellectual and kept up the façade of democracy". The humanists did not seem capable of really unseating the technologists. "Maybe we are in the early days," Heno thought. His mind then went to the lives of Che Guevara, Gandhiji and Mandela. "They lived lives of great personal integrity, and they probably touched spiritual depths within themselves, but the revolutions they fostered have all regressed into political quagmires or thinly disguised dictatorships."

This was when Heno decided that he must enquire deeply into the spiritual path. The life of the Buddha fascinated him, the practice of Yoga called to him. Heno took up discipleship at a very reputed Yoga school and spent a few years in intense study. He met many on this path. Some were eminent thinkers and genuine seekers and many were on a 'trip of self discovery'. The difference between the two was immense. The serious seekers were agonised by the state of human beings, the blindness with which people lived their lives, manipulated by politicians and corporations, getting more and more deeply sucked into a paradigm of ecological disaster. Yet, beyond finding a personal peace, they were still struggling to craft a meaningful alternative. "The next step will be a mutation in the consciousness," J Krishnamurti had once said. Many believed that the days of individual heroes were gone.

As Heno went deeper into the practice of meditation he started to confront the shadows and demons of his mind. "Learn to surrender," his teacher told him as Heno confided his difficulties. "Every time I come close to surrender, I face a wall of fear. All that I have become, all that I have acquired, in my search for security and substantiveness, I have to give up. I see that I grasp them with a deep fear, yet letting go would mean facing an emptiness and void that is simultaneously enticing and terrorising". "That Heno, is Nirvaana! Where 'you' end and true living in the here and now begins. It is learning to stay with the utter transitoriness and vulnerability of life."

4. EMERGENCE • **Transcendence and insight** • **Vessel of grace**	**1. THE STEADY STATE [mechanical]** • **Sustainability; shared growth** • **Quality of life; Inner wellbeing** • **Ecological impact** • **Meaningfulness; spiritual growth**
3. REFLECTION AND CREATIVITY • **Fear of loss of self; Fear of power** • **Surrender to the flow of the here and now**	**2. DISSENT AND DISSATISFACTION** • **Helplessness and limitations of knowledge** • **Celebration of the subjective and resultant loss of reality** • **Space for unique self expression** • **Space for pragmatism and the 'in-evitables' of living**

The **Universe of Meaningfulness and Intimacy**, the Ecological value-set is the world we are hoping to establish. The Institution Builder is devoted to the mission that furthers collective purpose and well-being, rather than only on the task focus and leadership purpose of the Network Orchestrator. He is also committed to translating it into sustained action. The collective power of 'Reciprocal Altruism' triumphs over 'Self-Preservation'. However, the Institution Builder differs from the controller in that he is proactive in mobilising potential for the greater good, rather than reactively proving himself to the Higher Authority.

The Ecological Institution Builder begins to envision the future for the members and the community. For him, 'time is a vector into the future'. Therefore, he moves from the narrow time focus of present action evident in the previous rungs of the spiral, and stops acting for a fantasised heaven. He is no longer taught in expedience and opportunism. Instead, he energises other members to seize opportunities in the present, to prepare for a shared future. He is urgent in this, since for him any waste is ultimately one of loss of potential.

The collective power of 'Reciprocal Altruism' triumphs over 'Self-Preservation'

The Institution Builder understands holistic perspectives. He finds balance between community growth and individual aspirations and potential. He recognises and satisfies basic economic (Network) and security needs (Clockwork) of group members and places them in a larger ecological perspective. His Humanism helps him to find space for touch and bonding, as well as for self-expression. In his ideal world, expression and relatedness would be simultaneous and mutual.

The Institution Builder does not see members as resources that can be counted and deployed, like the Orchestrator. Instead he sees individuals as part of a collective, having diverse attributes and potentials: positive, friendly, considerate, responsive, and generous. He trusts them to perform their roles rather than drive them with carrots and sticks. He places importance on the feelings of acceptance, consideration and affection and acts to increase the individual's sensitivity to the consequences of their actions.

The Institution Builder forges collective commitment, so that each member derives his/her identity from the group. For this, he sets up open discussions to decide together on the shared vision and goals, norms of conduct, systems and roles, and link responsibilities. Dialogue and consensus are his methods. People under the Institution

Builder's stewardship experience space, nurturance and a challenge to better their earlier achievements.

The Institution Builder does not just direct, but facilitates and enables the community. Since he values reciprocal participation, he is merely first amongst equals. He is more of a colleague and friend in a flat structure, than a superior in a hierarchy. He only exercises his authority to maintain the discipline needed for proficiency, so that the greater good can be promoted.

Leadership in the ecological community can be like herding cats. When members do not fulfil expectations of self-discipline and mutual consideration, he can be at a loss. He cannot stand above or apart from the collective and wield authority at ease. Often, he might err on the side of niceness and avoid the use of power to retain acceptance in the group.

Some key words associated with the Institution Builder are accountability, autonomy, humanism, harmony and health.

Dissent and Dissatisfaction

The Institution Builder in his celebration of the subjective, might sacrifice intellectual rigour for emotion. His perception of reality can be poor and he often feels helpless with the limitations of his knowledge.

The Ecological level can become a loving trap. While the members of the community might experience nurturing, security and acceptance, their creativity might be stifled. The pressure on altruism and sensitivity to others comes in the way of self-expression. The member often has to underplay his individuality and aggression, to ensure inclusion. The Institution Builder is unable to re-draw the boundaries of the group without the consent of the entire group, and individuals who are not on the same paradigm of thought take advantage. The Institution Builder is caught in a

The pressure on altruism and sensitivity to others comes in the way of self-expression double bind. “If I exercise authority, I go against my values, if I don’t, I let the group down”. The attempts to educate and evoke the goodness of the members often result in loss of valuable time and resources. Though he celebrates diversity, it begins to have narcissistic undertones.

Since he has to equalise with the members of the group (often irrationally) to ensure self-acceptance, the Institution Builder cannot be stringent in his task demands. Neither can he regulate permissive relations, or demand accountability. Over time, this lack of rigour and discipline can lead to complacency that can threaten the community and make it dysfunctional. Under pressure, the Institution Builder can regress to the authoritarianism of the lower levels, fulfilling buried individual power from the Arena or to parochial Clan leadership.

Reflection and Creativity

The Hero-in-the-making in this universe is acutely aware of the inequities in human relatedness, and the steady aggravation of environmental crises. He is aware that current solutions are limited and that more radical ones are required for sustainable transformation.

He is also acutely conscious of losing himself in the collective and begins to differentiate his own individuality. He confronts his fear of wielding personal power and authority and begins to reflect on ways of using it for enhancing life and potential. He is no longer satisfied with the blurring of all differences and hierarchies. He begins to differentiate between experiences, while discovering coherence and simultaneity. He therefore remains an actor in the present while surrendering to the flow of time. He explores the transcience of the self and consciousness, realising that neither rational thought and technology, nor organised religion with its dogma and hierarchy, can succeed. He sees that they are the cause of the human predicament.

Facing the inner roots of his drive to seek refuges, shields and saviours, is a terrorising experience. The spiritual path he has chosen demands that he should introspect and end the roots of fear and desire within himself. The outer expressions of man are but the reflections of inner drives and chaos. Letting go of Narcissistic strivings and the seeking of refuges, is an act of courage, unlike any of the thresholds crossed by the earlier heroes. However this might be the one where individual transformation will simultaneously impact all of consciousness.

Emergence

The Hero-in-the-making, now moves forward as today's Leader, with a presence in the here and now that is simultaneously powerful and vulnerable. He also has a sense of his place in the larger flow of life and the unfolding evolution; retaining his Ecological sensitivity while flowing with collective will and the human processes. The Leader shows the way to simultaneity of many kinds. Primarily he understands how to integrate individual aspiration and collective wellbeing without sacrificing either. His thinking increases exponentially in complexity as a result of this simultaneity, and he is aware of and uses the best that each individual offers, at their level of evolution and growth. He is spiritual and pragmatic at the same time.

We have yet to see such leaders in our midst, but we can speculate and wish for such a person to emerge. In all likelihood, this will be a collective phenomenon, where the behaviour is manifest by many, and no one person is anointed as 'the Leader'. But for our present discussion we will refer to this phenomenon as the Leader.

The Leader helps in the emergence of meaningful goals for the individual, for families, for the organization and society, nested in a vision that continuously **expands boundaries** and seeks new frontiers. He transcends the need for personal glory, benefits and security, and is not acquisitive. He finds meanings larger than the self; in creating and redefining milestones for himself and the collective that continuously challenge human ingenuity.

The leader is frequently on the cutting edge and is truly strategic, harmonising future vision with current realities. He is an actor-participant deeply anchored in the present day complex realities, knows the variables involved and remains versatile so that he can act appropriately. He designs, develops and transforms the organisation so that it is in harmony with the current reality that it is embedded in. What is needed now is tending, mending and seeding.

Simultaneously, the leader resides in the realm of vision and is committed to 'creating the future', where the available means are of little help. He observes the horizon of the unknown and the unfamiliar. His beacon here is his own values and faith in the self and in humanity and the power of discovery. He challenges prevailing wisdom, reformulating the purpose, so as to elevate, energise and retain the group's relevance.

The Leader lives the values he espouses and leads his group by example. He is inspirational, evocative and creative. He engages with members with dignity, spontaneity, potency, abundance and poise. He has deep faith in his self and humanity and stakes his trust in other members and the future growth of the system. He commits to nurture each member so that they can discover and harness their potential. For this, he challenges the team and for this too he may be seen as demanding, hard-nosed and tough.

He commits to nurture each member so that they can discover and harness their potential.

The Leader empowers, enables, facilitates and inspires members when required. For the most part he serves group members. He shares his expertise, experience and insight with other members of the group, to educate, teach or coach individuals or work teams. He ensures that members get necessary resources, such as knowledge and material, to fulfil their tasks. He also anchors different management methods that are friendly to the group members, like flexitime, alternative working hours, remote working and job interchange.

The Leader inspires the members to seek new forms of being human and discovers and understands reality with them. He actively and openly involves them in the creation and growth of the community through dialogue. He celebrates diversity, as a display of creative potential, and an opportunity to forge mutuality, and to experience communion. Engagements in the collectives he leads invoke introspection and insight, a renewed flow and refreshed relevance.

The authority of the leader is accompanied by competence. He does not use status symbols to impress. Fools are not tolerated for long. Threats, coercion, competition, authoritarianism and material incentives do not drive performance. For most part, members are self-motivated and set goals for themselves that are bound together by shared visions and purpose. The Leader ushers in a **Universe of Duality and Simultaniety**, a world of Holarchy.

Summary

The ecological V-meme is characterised by the statement, 'We grow if our community and its environment grows'. The ecology of systems and the deep inter-dependence between various elements of the 'system' are understood. The world therefore comprises many communities that inhabit the larger ecology. Network has a strong component of instrumentality in the interdependence and purposiveness, with respect to one's own abilities. Ecological sees interdependence primarily as belonging to the larger ecology. The particular system one belongs to is seen as a part of a larger level of interdependence and as a sub-system of a larger whole.

The individual appreciates the importance of values that are humanistic, and also accepts a relativistic position with regard to other value systems. The value systems are not dogmatically held, but on the contrary could be held with an overly sympathetic point of view. Subjective meaning is valued above objective purpose.

Environmental impact is a major consideration in choice making. The humanness of the individual could become an overriding principle, blurring all the differences that are embodied in the individual. The values of the holarchy transcending the weak relativism and pluralism of the ecological,are essential to assertive action. The holarchy's ability to embrace and include, allows not just an appreciation of the other in their own terms, nor just a post-modern critique, but an ability to act from each of the value memes/paradigms appropriately. One enters a spiritual space individually and acts with inclusivity in the world.

The self-system interface is, "I, my system, and many systems". This V-meme creates Ecologies that are Complex-Adaptive Systems.

This is a strand of organisational DNA that is just emerging. Its importance is becoming clear. The impact of using technology without regard to its larger impacts and without regard to issues of sustainability is staring at us. Yet we seem to be so caught in the grip of the systems of technology and economics that have evolved in recent times with no real solution in sight. Any organisation that enters this space and is willing to incorporate the Universe of meaningfulness and intimacy into it is willingly experimenting with itself. Those that are still asking only about scalability and profitability are playing with our future, though blissfully unaware! Sustainability can be built only through good science that values the heart.

Are you as a leader really willing to ask yourself and the organisation hard questions about the larger purpose of living? Are you willing to redefine the good life? Are you willing to pioneer a way of leading organisations and walk a relatively lonely path? Are you willing to temper your smartness and talent with wisdom and compassion?

Where can you start? Firstly, look at the diversity within your organisation and ask how this diversity is valued? Is mutual respect and dignity evident in the way people interact with each other? Do people with different backgrounds of language, religion, lineage, educational backgrounds dip into their subjective wisdom when discussing issues? Do questions of effectiveness and efficiency override questions of evocation? Do members of your organisation come up with surprising solutions that converge varied capabilities and expertise? Do people bargain for more personal benefits and acquisition or do they voluntarily seek ways of deploying their wealth and capability to engage with collective issues? Do they read a lot, watch concerts, show an interest in the arts?

"So what happened in your last discussion? I am eager to know," said AS even before he took his seat and sipped his cup of tea. Sanam was also looking forward to this meeting.

After watching the films suggested AS, Ranjan and Sanam had read through the paper. Sanam was following Ranjan's dialogues with the group with great interest. She went back and looked up her notes from her theoretical lessons with her Guru. She felt that there were some parallels with her field of study. "There are many frameworks in Indian thought that talk about the evolution of an individual's psyche. One of the explanations of the chakra theory comes close to this framework," she said, impatient to begin a discussion with AS and Ranjan on the subject.

"Let's begin with the reality at Mobile Unlimited. Let's not forget why we are doing this study and exploration," Ranjan insisted. They agreed that Ranjan's need was high priority.

"Well," Ranjan began, "it was a strange discussion we had last week. Reading about the universe you have called 'Ecological' asked everyone of us what our purpose ought to be as human beings." "Did they understand that Ecological is not the going green kind of stuff but a much more basic quest of finding harmony among many peoples, many minds, many ideologies so that we may live with a sense of respect towards others, and the earth?"

"Yes, we *did. That's why we came up with some basic questions. It became obvious very soon that we had more than met our early dreams of success in our professions. We are very proud of Mobile Unlimited. We have exhausted our purpose, but we have not really explored what living means beyond purpose and achievement. In any case the word 'impact' had caught our imagination and we quickly went back to it. I think we need time before we look at the question of a larger meaning."* Ranjan laughed, *"It is a scary thought to discover that one has been so caught with what Maslov has described as the early steps of his motivational ladder that one has not woken up to this area of the self. A strange sense of emptiness did creep into me. I was glad to stay with 'impact'. We now have three streams of customer impacts. One is to be the leader in Mobile Unlimited's transactions. We started this business, but we have not focussed enough here. We are going to call this initiative 'Lightning'. The second is to be like the ESPN of mobile sports information. Add trivia, quick polls, link to twitter chats and the like." "I hope it won't just be cricket," Sanam quipped. "No, all sports, especially the Olympic sports. Give information on aspiring sportspersons and the like. We will call this 'Owens'. The third will be to resemble Hallmark cards. Create beautiful greetings; offer information on the hundreds of celebrations we have in India. For example how many people know that Holika is the goddess for 'offering and seeking forgiveness' so we reach out to dear ones we might have hurt unwittingly, burn off the old and celebrate a new future of care and love. We will call this 'Dew Drops'." "Nice ideas, but not great names," Sanam commented. "These are internal identifiers for the 'in-groups'" Rajan clarified. "Most exciting will be the 'Zapp', our foray into developing new apps for hand held phones. This will take us into the next level of technology too."*

"How do you feel Ranjan?" AS *enquired, "You do look like you are still searching." "Let's come back to it," Ranjan said after a while. "Let's look at what Sanam has to say, I need time to figure out what is bothering me."*

"I have been waiting for this discussion, and preparing for it, so give me some air- time guys," Sanam said as a prelude to her sharing. "Your introduction

to this essay says that you and Ashok Malhotra have been influenced by Shri Aurobindo, as well as Yoga and Buddhist ideas. That helped me a lot.

"It is important to keep in mind that the interdependence between the individual and society is taken for granted in Indian thought. Ideas such as 'dependent origination' of the Buddhist tradition as well as the idea of 'Gati (continuous change), Samghatana (interdependence of all parts of the universe) Niyati (order and rhythm in the change process)' enunciated in the Saankhya *tradition, underpin all the traditions of Indian wisdom. Therefore, the individual is a microcosm of the macrocosm and any change within his consciousness impacts the whole, just as the individual is a continuum of society and is impacted by changes in any part of society. Also, mind and body are a continuum and are two aspects of a single phenomenon.*

"The Tantric *formulation explains the chakras in the body in a unique way, using the analogy of the union between man and woman. The* Moolaadhaara *(at the base of the spine) is seen as the space where the man and woman are in total merger and the Sahasraara (at the top of the head), is the space where they are separate, alone, and acutely aware. There are six steps that lead from the Moolaadhaara to the Sahasrara. In some versions, there is a stage that preceeds the Moolaadhaara* Chakra. *This is a space halfway between the base of the spine and the feet, where the energy that makes a man stand up, and realise that he is alive (and can therefore die), resides.*

The Tantric formulation explains the chakras in the body in a unique way, using the analogy of the union between man and woman

"When the person's consciousness resides in the Moolaadhaara Chakra, the person is like a child, who cannot differentiate between himself and his surroundings. Everything seems to be an extension of himself and his emotions get reflected off everything in his space. Life is a movement between heaven and hell. When the child is sated, and his wishes fulfilled, the world is joyous. However, this joyousness could turn into a hell, of fear and pain, if the world is not experienced in total harmony with his inner wishes. There is the world of the 'self' and the world of the 'other'. The world of the self is undifferentiated life and everything within this is identical to the self. The world of the other is

undifferentiatedly demonic, everything outside the self is an agent of death. This space seeks solid earth-like and substantive experience of the world, to feel alive. The man and the woman are in tight embrace and totally involved in the union. The identity of the individual is completely merged with the context of his life. The identity goes through the heaven of merger, and the hell of dissolution.

"The next evolution of consciousness takes one to the Swaadishtaana *Chakra, approximately at the level of the navel. The pair in total embrace and merger begin to realise that the man and woman are different, but in each other's hold. This is a world that is characterised by a wish for intimacy and a fear of possession. The most powerful emotions that rule this space are hunger and sexuality. The person is ruled by a need to conquer and dominate the other. It is as though they are saying, 'If I am not dominant and holding the other captive in my space, the other will attack me or escape, leaving me alone and anxious'. This is also the energy of self-expression and dynamism. This is the space of vitality and the movement of the praana.*

"The Manipooraka Chakra comes next, and is situated approximately at the solar plexus. The man and the woman have drawn away from each other, but are still holding each other's hands. This world is characterised by the awakening of thought and planning. The emotions that rule this space are those of anxiety, unpredictability, and inadequacy. The other must be held within the framework of 'dos and don'ts', so that the other remains within one's control. The other can be shaped and made to conform. There is also the realisation that both the man and the woman can stand independent of each other on a common ground. This is the space of the planning, thinking, worrying and defining mind.

"Consciousness then evolves into the Anaahata *Chakra, situated in the chest. The man and the woman are now separate and can see each other clearly. This is a Chakra where self-absorption gives way to an ability to appreciate and offer the self to others. Freedom is valued and observation and learning are practised. However a feeling of emptiness is also experienced in one's separateness and the experience of loss is feared. The other is given freedom to be, but is also enticed by love. The other is free to move but is held gently*

within the boundary of the interaction. This is the space of the 'discovering and discriminating mind'.

"The Vishuddhi *Chakra is situated at one's throat, and is the space where the man and the woman stand alone, each aware of the separateness of the other, completely calm and self-contained. However, if this aloneness is not held in balance, this separation can lead to feelings of loneliness and craving, specifically referred to as a thirst that is difficult to quench. In this space one can be spontaneously joyful; the mind is transcended. There is an immense experience of the power of creativity and the person who sees this creativity as originating within the self can get caught in feelings of grandiosity and megalomania. This is the realm of the Titans or the Devas and the Asuras, both of whom have great gifts and powers. The Asuras are caught in an egoistic belief that these powers belong to the individual to do with as they wish. The Devas realise that these powers are gifts with which to serve others. If the Asura does not realise his folly and recognise the divine as it reveals itself to him, he is condemned to regress and work for his evolution all over again!*

This is the realm of the Titans or the Devas and the Asuras, both of whom have great gifts and powers

"Aagnya *is the chakra situated between the eyebrows. In this place there is only the self and a realisation that the many worlds one experiences, are actually created by the self. When one awakens to this mind; surrender to the Divine and becoming completely open to the wishes and directions of the Divine become possible. The Daivic or Asuric deployment of the self are determined by the depth of one's surrender.*

"The consciousness beyond this is situated in the Sahsraara, *at the crown of the head. Self is transcended and the divine play is experienced in a space that is luminous and forever nascent. This is the space of the merger of one's individual consciousness, with the universal consciousness".*

AS listened to all this with deep concentration; he then began where he felt he could tie in Sanam's inputs with his own framework. "In this framework, how does evolution take place?" he asked. "Each chakra is a universe in which consciousness is trapped. This conciousness is manifested as thought, feeling and action, appropriate to each level. This impacts the body and the senses. However, *there is also a 'suffering' peculiar to each level. Dukha, which can be understood as 'suffering or pain due to a constriction of space', describes this suffering more comprehensively. The common reaction to the Dukha is to seek Sukha, a release from pain into pleasure. This seeking is within the same universe. Therefore, one goes into a vicious cycle of pleasure seeking and avoidance of pain. The three symbols of the hub of the Dharma wheel are experienced as real and enduring the false self, desire and hate. Dukha has another vector, the urge to transcend suffering. One releases oneself from the vicious cycle through Tapas i.e., a process of using the heat of suffering to generate insight. This is the heart of yogic practice. Consciousness or Atma desires intensely to evolve through each level and reach the Sahasrara, where it unites with the Paramatma or primal consciousness. Once a chakra of a particular level is truly transcended, one seeks the '*Bhooman*', or the deeper ground on which this universe rests. The mastery of the previous level is enduring. This process is discussed in depth in the* Chandogya Upanishad *in the chapter 'Bhooma Vidya'. The questioner is asked to go into a more fundamental space of the self, walk backward in a sense so that he can see where the current consciousness is arising from. The enquiry and inner journey ends with the discovery that praana, and the primal consciousness, are the ultimate foundations of all the universes."*

"The parallels between this scheme and the frame-work we are proposing, is striking," AS was animated now, Sanam nodded and AS continued, "The movement from each level of consciousness to the next is likened to a new birth in our texts is it not? If the person carries unresolved issues from the earlier 'birth', they inevitably surface and the person has to encounter them before the passage to the next is completed. Therefore, a consciousness can take many births before it truly transcends the cycle of birth and death. Also, the mythologies are full of analogous stories that warn the seeker, that if the energies of each level are not 'propitiated' they turn into demanding demons. The story of Arjuna's penance is the allegory of the journey each of us must undertake, to encounter each level fully, internalise its wisdom and its gifts, and move on to the next confrontation with the evolving self.

"At each level of evolution of the thought/feeling/action paradigm, the negatives of the previous levels can be overcome and the positives garnered.

However, this transition and transformation has all the drama of Arjuna's penance. The reactivity to the dysfunctional aspects symbolised by Perundi have to be forsaken. The attachment to the functional aspects symbolised by Mohini have to be given up. And the realisation of the gifts that come with the evolution of the mind cannot be treated as a personal acquisition".

Sanam and Ranjan were deep in thought. The parallels that could be drawn between such seemingly differing fameworks amazed them. Sanam felt she could contribute further here and drew in a strand from the field of yoga. "The fourth chapter in the Yoga Sutra *says that with the ripening of meditative inquiry there is an ending of all thought, of the type, 'What does this mean to me?', that arises spontaneously with any experience that one has. We are all born with Vaasanas (subtle seeds) that carry forward the essential algorithms of the consciousness of the previous birth. Out of this seed, an 'I' is constructed and the 'I' creates relationhips of desire and hate with the external world. This combination of a false self, desire and hate, are the driving force of the wheel of samsaara. The Budhist Mandalas represent this concept at the hub of the wheel, in the form of the hog, the rooster, and the snake. The ending of this driving force is the ending of the repeated process of creating false selves in the hope of ending sorrow. This is called* Kaivalya *in Yoga,* Moksha *in Hindu thought and Nirvaana in Buddhist thought. This state is not a state of death but a release from all the veils that hide and cloud perception; to the accurate perception of 'what is'. In this state, the 'true' is seen as true and the 'false' is seen as false. Choice making is 'Sensation, perception, action', Intelligence mediates this process and choices are therefore 'right choices'. All the gifts of nature and of oneself become accessible and these are deployed by the awakened person in a way that causes the increase of dharma".*

The Budhist Mandalas represent this concept at the hub of the wheel, in the form of the hog, the rooster, and the snake.

AS responded immediately, "according to Pulin Garg the crossing over to the creative realms implies an ending of fear as the motivator of action. There is an intense awareness of being alive and an intense experi-

ence of flow. The self is not an objective, separate individual. It is composed of holons and every level of existence is a holon composed of subsystems that are holons in their own right. The relationship between these holons has both tangible and intangible aspects and the interdependence is deep and subtle. Each part of the ecology is to be valued for itself on its own terms. Human knowledge is also viewed in these terms and several knowledge systems are valued simultaneously, each within their own structure. The systems map now becomes complex and multi-dimensional. At this level it now comprises the self, organised systems and ecology, in a constant rhythmic dance. Time becomes the new dimension in the ecological map and because the self is not experienced as being caught in the inexorable vector of time as it moves from the past into the future. Flow becomes the basic systems map".

"Transcending from the Survival, Clan and Arena V-meme set is a huge paradigm shift. Instinct driven choices between self preservation and reciprocal altruism, give way to laws and rules that are collectively agreed upon and legitimised in the Clockwork level. Instinct is sought to be controlled by the new paradigm of order and divine design. However, the world is experienced through the senses as solid and permanent, change is seen as ordained. The 'other' is believed to be external and therefore controlling and directing anxiety and fear become relatively easy. Transcending Clockwork, Network and Ecology, is probably a more difficult paradigm shift. The world that one is responding to, becomes more and more invisible, the interdependencies are too numerous to comprehend and the transitoriness of the world creates ennui and alienation more readily than enquiry and introspection. The 'other' lies within the self! Consequently the type of courage required for the confrontation and transformation is entirely different from the earlier journey. Our picture of heroism though is still very much entrenched in a 'Rambo' ideal! The consequence has been that the use of technology by minds that do not work in a scientific and rational paradigm has brought great destruction to our world. The mitigation of these negative effects calls for an evolution of the mind to be truly ecological in thinking (not just environmental and green). What seems to be happening is, that confronted with the destruction and danger wrought by the misuse

of technology, large groups of people are becoming atavistic in thought, feeling and action, while using the powerful tools provided by science and technology".

At this point AS felt it was time for a break from all this excited discussion. "I often wonder whether these beautiful formulations are so enticing because we project a kind of heaven into them," Sanam agreed, "it is only in flashes that I realise these ideas in concrete ways. Sometimes in my dance, sometimes when I am cooking, singing or just sitting quietly with Ranjan. I wonder if I live beyond the level of my Manipooraka Chakra for a significant length of time" (this is the chakra that can be related to the Clockwork paradigm).

"I think it was a good idea that your team paused at the Clockwork transition," AS returned to the issues at Mobile Unlimited. "Without a good grounding at this level, one does not have the platform to reach higher." Ranjan felt that he had a great deal to ponder over both about his understanding of his own role in his present situation and that of the other key players. The trio decided to mull over all this and meet again later. "Let's plan an off-site, Saptaparni. I feel that there is a need for me to reflect and introspect with my team. I see all of us pulled forward by our hope and pulled back by our fears. We are taking small steps, but without a convergent future picture. I would not be surprised if all of us are secretly hoping that Ashok Natarajan, our friendly Angel Investor, makes an 'offer we can't refuse' and we cash out. If we don't have a compelling purpose that aligns with our own sense of a larger meaning in life that may be the best solution. I also think that we want to take the next step and one day become a giant among giants." AS agreed and said "Let's set this up".

"I can see how I have built an arena", Ranjan launched off into his reflection. "Bhima loves the arena where he can wrestle and prove his powers". "Don't knock yourself," AS cautioned. "All good entrepreneurs must create the context around them where they can be their best. In the early years of a king's rule, he is a hero who attracts followers. He builds loyalty and people love him. Why else would they risk their lives and future? The problem is that after the battles

are won, the land must be governed. Way back in history we have the tales of many heroes who never built on their victories. Alexander was a prime example of a hero who was invincible in battle, but it is Ghenghis Khan who created the greatest and longest-lived empire. His fury in battle was matched by his ability to foster good governance. Ashoka too was such a ruler."

"Can we then see Ghenghis Khan as a combination of Bhima as the external face and Yudhistra as the steward of his people?" Ranjan asked.

"Creating the laws to be followed; the rule book to ensure fairness; the courts to judge and establish reward and punishment are all important. Recall Bhishma's advice to Yudhistra, 'Certainty and order are the foundations you have to create'. You have to really work with your aversion to machine-like precision and predictability," AS said in reply.

"Let us work with these reflections to see how we transform ourselves and the company," Ranjan said, as they finished up for the day. The next reflective session was set for the following weekend.

Ranjan could hardly wait for the off-site. He was excited, restless and constantly making notes. He too found that he could draw parallels to Indian thought based on his knowledge, even though it was not as deep as Sanam's. He found himself discussing this with her over the next few days. "The raaga and tala[1] *that each hero likes will be different," Ranjan began as he and Sanam sat for their morning tea. "The tribal music and dance is so simple and repetitive that everyone joins in, like with the case of the* Dandia Raas. *The arena calls for more strident notes and a sharp 4 x 4 rhythm. I can see now how the background music is used in films to create a range of feelings and moods in the audience. Without it, the screen images and the actors' emotions would not engage the viewer as much. Old films lack this sophistication and seem so much more stilted, Sanam."*

"I found it very difficult to get musicians to reflect the rasas in their voices and in the way they rendered the songs," Sanam added. "When they do, it becomes so much easier to get the bhava just right."

The next couple of evenings were spent in listening to music. The Beatles, followed by Kumar Gandharva *singing* Kabir, *round to Simon and Garfunkel.*

[1]Raaga and Tala are an intrinsic part of Indian Classical music. Raaga is the specific scale of notes that the artists explore through music while Tala is the system of rhythm within which they operate.

"The Beatles definitely get you aroused, it is arena music," Ranjan concluded. "But Simon and Garfunkel are not in that space. It is much more reflective and lyrical poetry. I wonder where you could place them?" Ranjan then concluded that a lot of Indian classical and jazz fell into the area AS had called ecological-holistic, and Beethoven was clockwork or network with a somber respect for the spiritual. "I think there is a lot to orchestrating a piece of music, that I need to learn," Ranjan said at the end of a long session of comparing western and eastern classical music. "Just solos and jugal bandhis and a few jazz riffs are not enough anymore," he said to himself.

Ranjan came back very late on Saturday, tired but satisfied with the off-site. It was late in the day on Sunday when Sanam was able to get Ranjan to have a chat with her.

"Lots of changes to make in our way of operating," Ranjan began, "many of the changes have to start with me. But, the good news is that we will work together and go global. Wow!!" Ranjan jumped off his chair and did a wild dance before he sat down. "A lot of serious work too," he continued. "Discovering the Arjuna in me and developing the 'dancer-warrior' within will be really some adventure. And what is more, I need to understand choreography and orchestration as well". Ranjan was clearly torn between his excitement and his anxiety. "We will understand each other a lot better at the end of this journey," he said to Sanam. Ranjan then turned to his notes, "By converting every challenge we faced into a problem, we have created a culture that is leaving half-built walls and rooms, sometimes undoing what we have built too. So we have not built lasting infrastructures".

"I don't understand, what do you mean by infrastructures of work-style?" Sanam asked.

"I am rushing this. Do you remember, AS saying that understanding the Dharma Sankatas, the dilemmas and polarities in decision-making, is the mark of a leader, while heroes rise up to the challenge in front and don't see the invisible realities around the challenge? As a group, we have not been systematic in balancing the short term and long term dilemmas. We have built many 'technology heroes', but very few good middle managers who will solve a problem, study

the methods that are replicable and create procedures. Sure, we celebrate these heroes, but today celebrating them is not the right thing to do! We must learn to reward the people who ensure no crisis, no surprise and seamless delivery! These are the new heroes. The way we manage now, does not help our people plan a career, so they don't really bother to teach others either."

"I understand now," Sanam said, "I found myself exploring new areas the moment I took on teaching at my guru's school".

"On the more visible end, our sales people do not cultivate relationships, they go from one opportunity to another and that is one of the reasons we have so many 'small additions' to do on a base product. We have not created a pipeline and predictability, so the orders tend to have a short lead-time. The more time we spend on these discreet orders, the less time we have for R&D and there is an absence of standard operations". After a few minutes Ranjan turned to his notes and said, "The other major aspect of our present culture is that the founders spend a lot of time on the ground, face-to-face with each other, and with the 'crisis heroes'. Much as I dislike owning up to this, we have unwittingly created clannish groups. We can't rely on face-to-face communications anymore. Shanti is trying really hard, but there are no forums for dialogue, or communication, no routines for looking at 'people' issues. No wonder the more passive and rule-bound people complain of favouritism. I am a Bhima and I like the personal touch, but I can see how this breeds a coterie and dependency. Each of the leaders of our specialist areas is imitating me! So we now have four tribes, the creative guys, the nerds, the hunters, and the drones! This is where I must create a clockwork culture and really foster the Yudhistra and Nakula type heroes. They now feel used, unrecognised and either leave or hang on because they have found a comfort zone. We really have to think this through. Shanti and Afsal have done the right thing with the 'customer contract' idea. They will take it further, create a CFT that focuses on creating 'cultural pillars', observable behaviours that will result in a culture of error prevention, throughput focus, knowledge creation and real friendliness. They will also work out how the new heroes will be recognised and fostered. I think our entire recruitment and performance system will have to be reworked," he said with a sigh. "I hope we can do this fast enough".

"There goes the Bhima again!" Sanam said "I thought you were learning to balance the short and the long term, why bring in the issue of urgency for such a critical change in culture? Go step by step, but don't hassle them with deadlines and the urgency that comes from your restlessness".

"You are right Sanam, AS also pointed this out. I often catch the problem end and the crisis-end of a dilemma and forget the real Dharma Sankata of organisation building. I also realised that my fascination with heroism has blinded me to the individual/team polarity that is always present in organisations. We guys at the top ended up engaging with delivery/quality polarities that belong to the shop floor and even there, converted them into problems!"

"Ranjan, my guru taught me a game to play by myself whenever I get caught with these dilemmas. He said he learnt it from a Korean martial arts expert who was also a Tai-chi teacher. It goes like this," Sanam opened her palm and touched the point under the little finger and said, "This" and then touched the point under the thumb and said "That". Then she went "This-That, This-That," a few times. "You must really jump from feeling how good 'this' is and how good 'that' can be," she said.

Ranjan interrupted, "What is this and that?". "Ah!'This' is one option and 'That' is the other opposing option. You go 'this-that' a few times and then you switch to 'neither this-nor that'," and she touched the palm under the forefinger, "Both 'this and that'," and touched the opposite point. "You play with all these four and then sit back, meditate and the best answer will come". Ranjan was fascinated. "AS taught us a method that is very similar, to help us understand the pulls and pushes, the price to be paid and the up–side of these dilemmas, before looking at the whole pattern and making a choice. 'You can never take the subjective out of this choice-making as you can with a problem, nor can you take away the unintended consequences' he said. 'That's why perceptiveness, mindfulness and meditation are recommended by Kautilya as essential practices for a king'. This is all very fascinating".

"We really got to look at what we have done so far, because AS helped us to practise what he called 'listening without judgement and absolving shame and guilt' as we went deeper into reflection and dialogue. This really

helped Jagan and me. As the founders we were getting into a guilt trip as we talked about the organisation. It took a bit of prodding and pushing by AS to help us through this one. It helped us greatly as we realised that one person or a small group does not create a culture. The entire membership collaborates and colludes to create a culture and to maintain it. As we examined the dynamics of the top management group it became clear that the Nakulas and Yudhistras in this group chose to be 'silent sufferers', or 'cribbed and complained' in twos and threes rather than confront us. 'We did not want to rock the boat,' they said. As we examined both Rashmi's and my stance it became clear that while we became restless with procedures and building relationships, Raj Peter and Afsal became nervous when they had to take a stance and fight through an issue. So all of us had our areas of dissatisfactions with the organisation, but we had found adjustments and accommodations and ways of working together. We called this a 'great team' but it was a pattern that hid a lot of negatives. Jagan's idea of the 'in-groups' was a great intuitive step. As a top management team we have all decided to do some introspection and look for ways to awaken our latent sides. I am going to learn music, Afsal and Shanti want to learn karate and Raj wants to do photography, especially wildlife. We are also going to anchor these activities for the whole organisation, so we get to meet people completely outside of work roles. AS told us about how in the design principles of Vaastu *the idea of creating spaces in homes and towns where people meet without roles and differences was very important.*

Listening without judgement and absolving shame and guilt

"Every temple has a space that people congregate in, after having a darshan in the sanctum, where they listen to stories from the Raamaayana and Mahaabhaarata, music concerts, or watch dances or drama. When they go to the sanctum, all ego and external rank is dropped. In the crowd that mingles to listen to the stories they become equal, as humble human beings, understanding how their heroes had to deal with the dilemmas of living. Apparently old homes also had a space like this called the koodam, *a central courtyard with a* tulasi *growing in the centre. We have decided to create such 'koodams', not only for music and yoga or Zen meditation, but also as forums for dialogue".*

Sanam was thrilled. "This was the practice all over India," she said, "we lost these spaces over the years. The Buddhist practice of the Sangha *had these aspects, as did the Ashwamedha yagnyas".*

"We also found a lot of issues that are basically operational. They may not interest you, but let me just recapitulate for my understanding," Ranjan continued. "The good news here is that the SEDAC process that Rashmi and Raj have initiated will suit this focus perfectly. What is more, it will allow the top management to look at many strategic questions in a systematic way. Our revenue model was a reflection of the arena culture, and did not have the strategic perspective and depth measures of a 'network' culture. Our earnings are tied too closely with the service providers' billings and our positioning is not clear. We need to ask ourselves a very important question here. Are we a service focussed company or a product company? We realise that this lack of clarity on the revenue model is preventing the back-end operations from becoming a predictable and stable 'clockwork'. 'Small innovations, big immediate billing, huge back-end stress, lots of volatile activity, short-term profitability, with no sustained building for the future' is what Ashok told us when he first saw us. 'I like your energy but, you guys must become strategic' is how he put it. Then we came to Jagan's issues and realised how far we have come without realising it! Sanam, we have created a whole new industry and we are behaving like a start up! There are many small operators that have become our vendors, many copycats who wait for our innovations. We are a benchmark of technology. This was such a revelation. Owning up to this was great, but scary. How do we discover a 'complete and collaborative' way of working with the business ecology we have created? This is a really 'big egg' and Jagan will work with Raj and Afsal to look at how we 'co-create' with our service providers and create a reliable 'supply chain' to minimise routine tasks at our site. Ashok Naaraayanan, the VC you remember, has helped us realise that we must actualise the identity that is waiting for us; we have created 'Thought leaders and industry leaders'. We are not 'Warriors in a start-up' anymore.

"What is most exciting, Sanam, is that we invited Ashok over to dinner, to share our new design for Mobile Unlimited as we go forward. We needed to re-examine the timing of the IPO. It appears that he has been talking to his

directors in California about my new interest in looking at the Mahaabhaarata and using the metaphors and insights from our tradition to revitalise ourselves. One of them is part of a new group of people who have come together to create 'Conscious Capitalism Institute'. This group is igniting a movement towards ecologically responsible and socially responsible businesses. Many of them are actively into meditative and self-transformational practices. This director has asked Arun to support this process. The Angel investors now want to encourage innovation in technology as well as governance; they feel that India is the best place for this. The way forward according to Arun is 'American Entrepreneurship, Japanese Management techniques and Dharma-Wisdom traditions of India.'

"I am going to be really busy over the next few months Sanam," Ranjan went on to say. "With each dialogue on the culture and behaviour, we have seen the connections between the 'practices' we follow, in creating our products and services. These visible actions are the outcome of the ways each of us has related to each other through work. We now have a whole set of new practices to put in place, HR and Finance policies to evolve, and daily management and review to be instituted. AS is excited with the way his engagement with us has turned out. He is inviting me to spend a semester with him to document some of the work, as well as to examine new perspectives on leadership."

Notes to myself

1. Good to rest after working hard! It is incredible to see the joy in the team once the tensions within and between us have been resolved. Friction and frozenness giving way to flow! Each of us is becoming self -reflective and proactive as a result. We challenge more and support each other too, and all this without Saptaparni to help. I was anxious, but the struggle has been worth it.

2. In being the best that I can be, I seem to trigger the same intent in others around me and we are exceeding our own expectations of ourselves as a team.

3. "Karmanyevaadhikaarasthe...." Let your concern stay with the action alone and not with its fruits, let not an attachment to the fruits be thy motive, nor be drawn by inaction. (Bhagavad Gita Ch 2.47)

4. Now Back to my map:

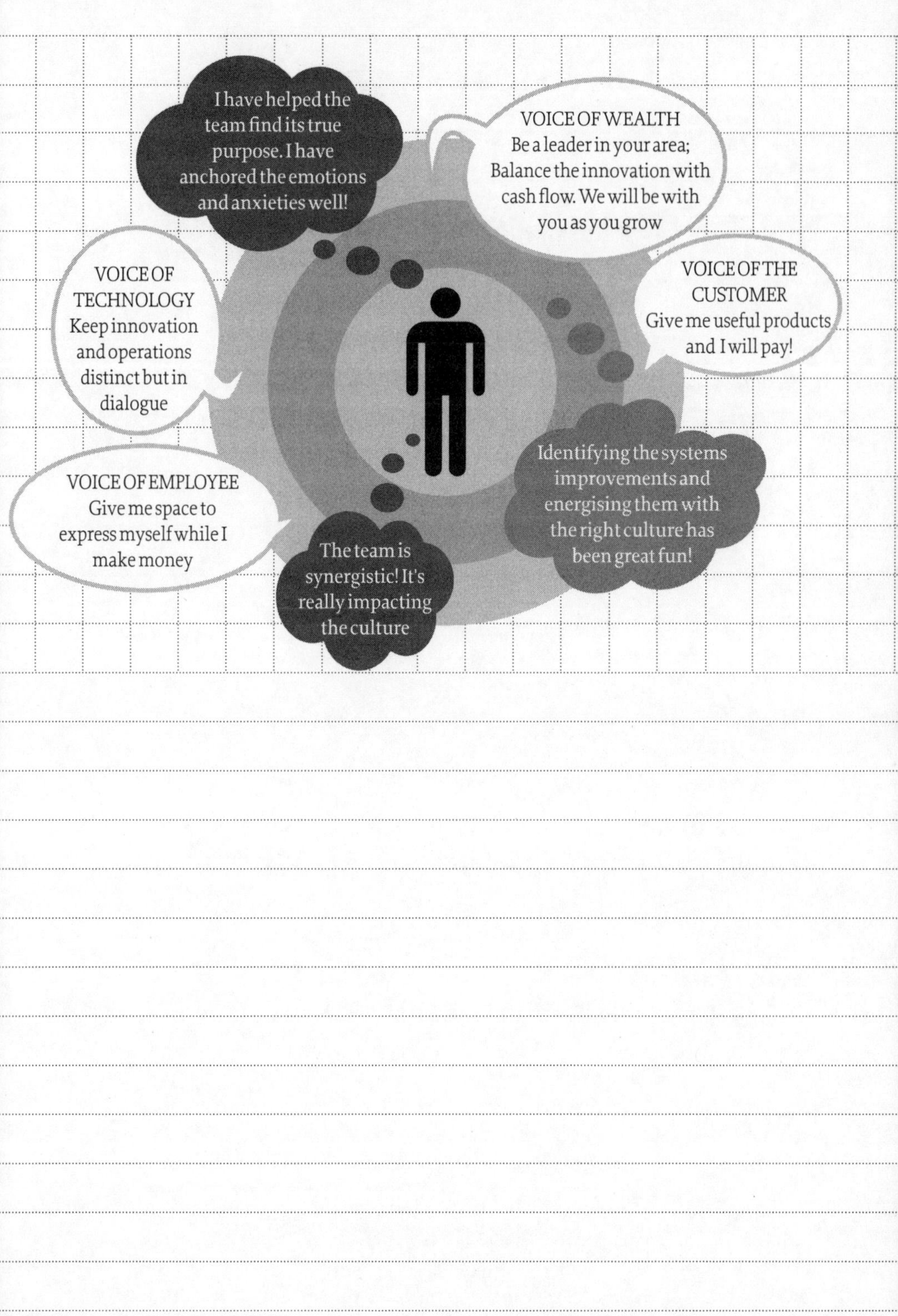
I have helped the team find its true purpose. I have anchored the emotions and anxieties well!
VOICE OF WEALTH
Be a leader in your area; Balance the innovation with cash flow. We will be with you as you grow
VOICE OF TECHNOLOGY
Keep innovation and operations distinct but in dialogue
VOICE OF THE CUSTOMER
Give me useful products and I will pay!
Identifying the systems improvements and energising them with the right culture has been great fun!
VOICE OF EMPLOYEE
Give me space to express myself while I make money
The team is synergistic! It's really impacting the culture

CHAPTER 9
Inspiring a thousand Gardeners

"Einstein said that scientific problems that are created at one level could be solved only if they are approached from a higher level. This seems to be true of human problems also. When leadership brings in a new paradigm it helps the organisation evolve and grow. Even if the efficiency is high in an organisation, when the existing paradigm is inadequate, then the introduction of a new paradigm of thinking helps the organisation in this evolutionary process." Ranjan began to write this as his introduction and soon found that his thoughts flowed easily on to the paper.

It was more than 6 months after the discussions when Ranjan was able to take up AS's invitation to take a sabbatical and document the ideas on the leadership process that had emerged, through their experience with Mobile Unlimited. The Angel Investors decided to go for a limited IPO since they were interested in being part of what they called 'Entrepreneurial Experiments in India'. The whole top management team became even more cohesive after the IPO, none of them wanted to 'rest in peace'. A new dream was igniting the organisation. The series of dialogues that each team member had with his reportees, not only galvanised the managers, it created deep conviction in each of them.

Ranjan spent the six weeks he promised himself in doing things he had never dreamt of doing. Going to the library, meeting CEOs, visiting craft groups and development agencies and having long discussions with AS and Ashok on a range of subjects and issues. Academic writing was not a favourite activity of Ranjan; however, Ashok and AS convinced him that his way of conceptualising the leadership issues was valuable. Reluctantly, Ranjan wrote the paper. He found it immensely absorbing. Being able to create a cogent conceptual narrative of his thoughts and insights gave Ranjan great confidence in being able to lead Mobile Unlimited on its new journey.

THE LEADERSHIP CHALLENGE IN ORGANISATIONS

We will examine some of the struggles of leadership within organisations, to map the journey of an Arjuna-in-the-making. Then we shall go on to speculate on what this journey might imply in a larger context. The critical aspects of the journey are the two thresholds Arjuna must cross when he hears the inner call for awakening. Firstly, the lonely quest of self-discovery that is like a walk in the 'desert' and secondly, the offering of the gifts he has discovered, back to the community. We will focus here on the second, since it is more explicit, and through this try to understand the inner aspects of the transformation.

The Indian Business scenario is replete with examples of the small enterprise that has been entrepreneurial and dynamic. In fact there are examples of whole communities that devote themselves to trade and business. There are also communities that expressly value the emigration of at least one son in every family to a foreign land and the repatriation of wealth to the family at home. Many of the trading communities benefited from the British colonial practice of dealing with the local populace, through local money lending and banking institutions. This created a peculiar situation of an entrepreneurial form that was encouraged and valued in the traditional context. This drive hit a barrier and had to evolve in a 'foreign' paradigm of business at a certain stage. Therefore, each of these entrepreneurial efforts grows to a certain level and then faces a huge challenge in evolving to the next paradigm. Some of

Tolstoy has said that all successful families succeed in the same way, but those that fail do so in their own (many interesting) ways these businesses find a stable way of remaining in business. Some go through the fluctuations of making progress, hitting a wall, dissipating energy, falling back on the old dharma and regaining health only to repeat these fluctuations around their respective limits, for growth and evolution. Tolstoy has said that all successful families succeed in the same way, but those that fail do so in their own (many interesting) ways. We will look at a few cases of Indian enterprise that have not flourished the way they initially promised to, but have not failed either.

The Craft Enterprise

We can see the struggle to grow and evolve clearly demonstrated in craft groups, as they seek to get integrated into the larger markets. Typically the story starts from a Master Craftsperson, who retains the traditional knowledge of the community. When India gained Independence the commitment to ensure that village communities grow and get assimilated into the larger nation was very strong. It was the continuation of the Gandhian dream. Many committed persons like Nelli Sethana, Kamaladevi Chatopadhyaya, and Pupul Jayakar went about looking for such crafts-persons. With their exquisite eye for aesthetics and their knowledge of the indigenous practices they were able to forge partnerships with these holders of the tradition. Let us examine one such attempt that is fairly typical: The Kalamkari art of the state of Andhra Pradesh that was revived by Kamaladevi. A training school had been set up with government aid and one of the families from the weaver community that held the tradition came forward to participate in this progressive attempt. Other families refused to co-operate. This training centre not only revived the craft, but also, the Kalamkari art from the area of Kalahasthi regained its stature. The traditional practice of making screens for temples was expanded to the designing of wall hangings and large murals.

The movement from a Clan to a Clockwork V-meme had begun and flourished for a time. When it came to the time when the leadership of the enterprise had to be handed over to the next generation, the fragility of the new form began to show up. At the helm, Kamaladevi had handed over the charge of the agency setup to a Master Craftsman to foster these small enterprises. He not only shared Kamaladevi's vision of a craft revival but also commanded a lot of respect from the community. However, the shaping of the new organisation and community was very demanding. It required great wisdom as well as a personal charisma to lead the crafts persons through a transition from the Clan V-meme to the Clockwork-Network V-memes.

The V-meme of the group had not evolved to the extent that its leaders had.

The followership that had grown around the Master Craftsman came from two sources. Firstly, traditional weavers entrenched in the clan who nevertheless respected their leader and hoped to gain stature and wealth through his adventure into modernity, rather than forsake their heritage. And secondly, the newly trained crafts persons who came from varied backgrounds and saw themselves as possessing an artistic skill. As the control of the old man waned, a fight ensued. His son claimed the authority as his right. Others who had grown in the new mould and saw themselves as more competent made their claims.

The government-appointed-head of the training centre, watched helplessly as the cohesive enterprise deteriorated into an arena fighting for power. The V-meme of the group had not evolved to the extent that its leaders had. Though the innate nature of being role-bound as is the traditional Indian way, had worked very well in the structured hierarchy set up by the ' Master Craftsman and Kamaladevi partnership', the real evolution through a confrontation of beliefs and conditioning had not happened. All was not lost however and rival groups were set up, each following the new practices of the entrepreneur leader. Many years later, when the Crafts Council of India went back to Kalahasti, they were able to pick up the strings, set up a co-operative that re-established the quality focus and oversaw the business processes. The Master Craftsman's son was given a respectable place as a teacher, which he reluctantly took up. His leadership was not respected as much, since he could not get over the feeling that his family had lost its pre-eminence! The craft is growing slowly and stable practices of training and conducting business have since been set up.

Some of the recent successes in bringing the craft enterprises into the market are Fab India, Dakshina Chitra and Hidesign. These organisations are hybrid and they are modern organisations run on fairly mature Clockwork and Network principles that provide the platform for the clannish small craft enterprises to trade with. The design suggestions are offered and products are traded, however, the clan production unit is not disturbed. The Saravana Bhavan, a global hotel chain seems to show how clannish organisation can be successful in the contemporary context. The average employee sees the head of the organisation as a father figure, who in turn has a 'guru' as an advisor. This relationship is explicit. The employee is not paid very highly but all his life space requirements, like the education of the children and conducting the marriage of daughters is taken care of by the organisation. In Tamil Nadu the term 'pangaali' referred to a set of people intertwined with each other sharing joys and sorrows as well as profits and losses. This organisation seems to marry several aspects of a group of 'pangaalis' within modern forms.

THE FAMILY BUSINESS

The Family Business in India has an interesting history. The spread of indigenous business families has long extended on both sides of the Indian coast. In the east, for example, Chettiar families had set up trading houses and had evolved a method of conducting business that extended to the whole of South East Asia. The *Partha systems* of the Marwari families, was a very sophisticated system of operational control over widely distributed manufacturing and trading centres. When the British Colonisers set up business in India, these were their natural partners. The Colonisers were wary of transacting business with the mass of the Indian population directly. The traditional business families and their commercial practices were a very dependable bridge. They found that the mercantile network, set up by the Chettiars for example, was a robust and reliable organisation spread all across South East Asia. A natural partnership was established between the two groups. Some of the earliest banks created in South India like the Indian Bank were an outcome of this partnership.

Two types of Indian entrepreneurship emerged at this juncture. Some of the established families opportunistically jumped on the new bandwagon and in many ways betrayed the trust-based older system. The business guilds that oversaw these traditional families were not able to enforce their control and going to the newly formed courts did not help either. It is an interesting footnote that these families have not gained a positive reputation, nor have they really prospered in the emerging business reality.

The more 'disciplined' families though, set up ways of internalising the new reality. The patriarch of the family (called the *Kartha*) would select individuals from among his wards, who would learn the 'foreign ways'. Practices were set up so that when these people returned to the fold, they shared the practice without disrupting the established stability of relationships and authority. The entire interrelated set of textile businesses in Coimbatore have come up in this way. This is very similar to the ways in which the Japanese families approached modernisation. The Japanese Keiretsu is a vast and interconnected set of small and large manufacturing companies. The most visible part of the Value chain is the final product, but behind this is a vast network. The Toyota Manufacturing Company is the visible end of a Keiretsu that allows the famous 'just in time' system to function flawlessly.

Let us examine the struggles of one of these families. We take up the story of a fairly respected and flourishing family enterprise. The initiator of the process of modernising was triggered into the process by the efforts of Jawaharlal Nehru, the first Prime Minister of Independent India. He had invited many such families to create Modern Industrial Organisations. As was common at that time, the entrepreneur invested in the new business by entering into collaborations with western industry leaders. The sons were made the heads of various businesses. However, all decision making was through a process of consensus. One of the prominent Chettiar families in Tamil Nadu took up the invitation to create Modern Industry. The patriarch of the family became the promoter of what is now a billion dollar group of companies.

Under the leadership of the patriarch the business grew and became a large enterprise, with many lines of business. When he died the reigns were taken over by his brother. By this time, not only had the width of management expertise expanded, many of the next generation had been educated in elite boarding schools in India and later in Universities abroad. The family was one of the first to recognise the need for inducting professional managers and engineers into the organisation. Two changes seem to have hit the family simultaneously, the death of the patriarch and the induction of professionals into decision-making levels. Meanwhile, the business context was also moving away from the early protected green-field, to a more competitive and mature field. At the helm, the decisions became more conservative and the new patriarch was not always seen as *dharmic*. However, the rest of the family held on to its commitment to the ways and found forums to air and contain differences. As the professionals grew, and the business grew with them, they began to voice their insights and perspectives. Obviously, competence is not made to order in families! The older agrarian practices of dividing the field among the sons, was proving to be dysfunctional. Some businesses run by more competent family members flourished, and others languished. The family found a way of dealing with this by identifying the Bhimas, the Nakulas, the Sahadevas, and the Yudhishtras, among themselves and placing them strategically. This strategy worked, but the group as a whole started fluctuating across its capability boundary.

Two changes seem to have hit the family simultaneously, the death of the patriarch and the induction of professionals into decision-making levels.

The family had identified the need to manage growth. It had learned to deploy differential capabilities appropriately. The family was at a threshold between Clockwork and Network Systems. It had grown and was managing its growth adequately, but it had not evolved! The insight into the need to embrace a new paradigm was apparent to some of the members of the family but the ability to discover the new, as a collective, eluded the family. It had moved into the phase of relinquishing managerial control over specific companies, to professionals. It had understood the use of metrics and operational control but the strategic decisions remained with the family. Its brief experiment with having professionals act as the Executive Chairpersons has not worked well.

The tension that has not yet been resolved in an energy releasing way lies in the space between the top management professionals and the members of the family at the very top levels of decision-making. The Network systems and values coexist with a Clockwork / Clan system and values in an uneasy dance. This is a struggle within the family, within each member of the family (some of whom have been successful professional managers in their own right) as well as within the highly educated professionals, individually and as a group.

If we look at two examples namely the Murugappa group and the Birla Group we see how they have resolved the tension in contrasting ways. The Murugappa Group has decided to retain the centrality of a united family and formulated ways of working together. The choice of containing their adventurousness and risk-taking processes within a broad conservative frame has worked for them. Most of their business remains agriculture-based and therefore they have inherent controls as well as support from governmental policy. Their growth has been steady. Their management teams have been stable and the governance of the group has gone back to the family after a stint of having professional Chairpersons. The Birla Group however, decided to work with a lot more flexibility and a degree of independence was given to its members. The Aditya Birla group found a lot of energy in being unfettered by the need to conform to a tradition and has grown fast. It has inducted many professionals into its ranks and emphasises the network aspects of its culture. In a recent bid to bring multiple perspectives into the managing and leading process, the Shinganias are experimenting with the concept of a co-held leadership in Raymond.

(These interpretations are based on the several reports published in Business India and Business World in the last few years about these business houses.)

THE NEW BREED OF ENTREPRENEURS

There is a new trend in Indian business today: Engineers and Management professionals who come from middle class families, striking out on their own as entrepreneurs. For many of them the role models are Narayanamurthy and his colleagues who promoted Infosys, Technocrats like Promod Chaudhari who created PRAJ Industries Ltd., people like Vinod Khosla and Venky Harinarayan who created successful start-ups in America. Many of them decide to venture out on their own, after achieving success in their careers in large multinationals like GE and IBM. They have nurtured a dream of being entrepreneurs, and keep searching for the idea and the opportunity that they can capitalise on. Others like them are spotted by the top management of professionally run companies like the Tata Group and given entrepreneurial challenges.

We pick up the story of a group of technocrats in their mid thirties who have created a mid-sized business in the area of Medical equipment. The promoters were either colleagues in their earlier (respected multinational) organisation, or classmates from their Engineering College. An Angel Investor, who made his millions in the software boom of the 80's, and had come back to India to 'help India become a global player', was funding the start-up. The promoter group was very competent. They not only had technical people of proven track record, they had six 'Sigma' black belts, as well as aggressive marketing professionals in the group. Each of them had taken charge of a key area. The company was working on an immediate strategy and had lined up a product pipeline. In fact it was this perspective that helped them weather the first few years of aborted attempts to enter the market. The product they had zeroed in on and were about to launch became unviable when a competing product was launched by an industry major.

The CEO of the fledgling company was troubled by the fact that, in spite of having such a fine team and one that had worked together in the earlier organisation and been very successful, the speed and precision with which they worked did not compare with their proven capability. The marketing whiz was coming up with new ideas, creating excellent PR, but not bagging enough deals. On paper the company was very strong. It was in the right niche market, namely small and medium hospitals in India, South East Asia and Africa. Its product out-performed costlier competing products and yet they were not able to raise their levels of performance and dominate the market. They were hovering around success, a bit too long.

The company had been employing process rigour but not getting consistent quality; courting the market, but not getting the orders. Every time they sat and examined the root causes, they came up with what looked like a well-analysed picture. When they went to the work spot and started attacking the problems, they invariably became ad hoc and had to run behind vendors and suppliers, manage attrition and keep encountering surprises. Some of the original promoters became restive. They could not reconcile with what they called the yo-yo between mature analysis and immature crisis management. The CEO was experienced but inconsistent: sometimes he was the old and much loved team leader and at other times he was like the orchestrator of a one-man-band having to do all the thinking, directing and execution, thus leaving all the others feeling like his errand boys. His charisma and the belief that the others had in his capabilities, kept the team together. However, the resilience was wearing thin. Some of the promoters were nostalgic for the 'earlier days', some were torn by the insecurity their families were subjected to, and some were finding it hard to admit their failures and went into 'doing more of the same', but with more careful planning and energetic execution, only to return empty handed. The team displayed bonhomie on the surface, but lacked the resilience to have robust and well-directed dialogues that could look at the dangerous truth squarely.

> They could not reconcile with what they called the yo-yo between mature analysis and immature crisis management.

It was only after the CEO and the Investor decided that they had to own up to the reality that they were in a war mode (resources would dry up if there was no top line growth) that they sat down to re-evaluate their working methods, with the help of an OD consultant. It was obvious that the team was approaching a green field start-up, with the style relevant to a mature organisation with a powerful brand and deep pockets. The CEO had to unlearn, go to the battleground and lead the team like a commando unit. Their analysis was based on the assumption of the availability of infrastructure that had been built over many years. Work practices and culture that they could take for granted were entirely missing. Worse, many of the company employees had grown up in very different organisations, with incompatible cultures. The products had to be made and designs tested, before the six sigma methods could be used.

When this realisation hit the group, and they found the resilience to accept that they had to act in ways that they had earlier held in disrespect, namely to rally behind a chief who would direct the operations and call the shots, by being on the work spot, (no meetings and discussions anymore!). There were too many unknowns and resource constraints, for the possibility to work on the 'discussion, autonomy and metrics-driven review' model they were schooled in and had become adept at. Some of the promoters who saw that they could not make the change, opted out. Three of the key members of the team, the CEO, the product designer and the operations head, decided to continue. The work style was changed into a more opportunistic and responsive style, with the CEO calling the shots. The

Investor weighed in by deferring the idea of an IPO. He decided to 'get back into the game' by deploying his brand image and connections, to open doors in the market place. A war room was created for shared information and the more elaborate Management Information System was abandoned. The company turned the corner. Since the promoters were deeply ingrained in mature process methodologies, they were able to bring in processes step-by-step and create a reliable manufacturing base, as they confronted and conquered each barrier that they encountered.

SUCCESSFUL NEW-TECHNOLOGY ORGANISATIONS

If we contrast Tata Consultancy Services (TCS) and Infosys, we see two different faces of organisations that are very successful start-ups. Though TCS is part of the Tata Group, Mr F. C. Kohli ran it like a start-up. We see the organisation being built up from a pioneering IT services organization into the Largest IT consulting organisation in Asia by the time Mr S. Ramadorai took over the reins. He then built it to a multi billion dollar giant before handing it over to his successor. There is a strong theme of pride in being Indian and basing oneself on the positives of the Indian psyche in 'The TCS Story', written by Mr Ramadorai. The sense of belonging is high, the inherent 'role discipline' of the average TCS employee provides a container where the aggression required to compete in a new sunrise industry is contained. A subtle sense of faith in oneself and the context pervades the organisation.

A subtle sense of faith in oneself and the context pervades the organisation.

The Tata values are the base that integrates all of these invaluable features of the culture. It is on this platform that the Network-Ecology is built: The alacrity, with which new knowledge and abilities and skills are internalised and mastered, is a key ability that translates into excellent project management. Hundreds of small to large project teams spread all over the world and working in partnership with different industries and businesses cohere in TCS.

Infosys reflects many of these capabilities, but with one crucial difference. It has emphasised its entrepreneurial core. This may be the reason why many start-ups have been spun off by Infosys like OnMobile and Progeon Ltd. This emphasis on entrepreneurship, anchored in middle class values, has been the bedrock of its founders. However, the average Infosys role may be drawn more by its Arena-Network profile and less by the value-base. The problems faced by Infosys in retaining its speed of growth while it becomes a mammoth multinational could arise from a lack of coherence in the base. A question that arises is, "do the rank and file have the sense of belonging and the discipline to stay the course or are they caught with their own Arena selves and the need to become millionaires?" The latter without the former would lead to discontent especially among the middle management. They will 'cash in' on the Infosys brand and jump ship rather than emulate the founders in their early efforts to build the organisation.

THE PATTERNS

On the face of it, these cases look very different. But the leadership challenge they faced has a similar pattern. All of them were poised for growth, but held in suspended animation. At the threshold of growth, they are held in tension across a debate that is unresolved. This unresolved debate wastes energy that could propel them into the next stage of growth, provided the energies could be made to converge.

Two sides that seem to take counter positions articulate these issues. On closer observation, these positions are V-memes articulated through the problem set. In the first case, the Craft Enterprise, the Clan value of holding the knowledge close, of respecting and protecting the heritage, of an automatic passing over of authority to the descendants, is articulated by one group. The other articulates the Arena V-meme of the authority being held by the champion, of opportunistically cashing in on the brand and the like. While the initiator of the 'new way' found an answer to this '*Dharma Sankata*', the fears and hopes of the followership had merely been held in abeyance. They surfaced when his control waned. However, the group was engaged in the debate because the articulated arguments represented the wished-for reality of the two groups, that held on to the two ends of the polarity. The ambivalence with which they held the two V-memes was played out in the drama of the debate.

The only way the debate can be resolved, and both sides discover the common ground they stand on, is when each of them undertakes the hero's journey i.e., Arjuna's Penance. Individually, each of the members must go into the desert and confront the three symbols of the penance: The aversion and fascination of Perundi, the magnetism and pleasure promised by Mohini, and the acquisitive self vanquished by Shiva. The journey of the followers is not the same as that of the pioneer. The follower now has guideposts and mentors. He knows that a successful role model has shown the way. But he must walk the path, in order that both the leader and the follower energetically act from the more evolved V-Meme. Acting from the V-meme under the shadow of the hero leaves behind unresolved feelings and fears. These ambivalences play up when the person has to make authentically self-reliant choices.

The other cases are very similar. The members of the family in the Family Owned Organisations hold the heritage and its continuity in ambivalence. The pull of the freedom to make one's own choices and be one's own master is voiced by the professionals, who speak from an apparent base of rational logic and study (the Network). The security of a trusted group to belong to, and to be able fall back upon, is voiced by the family (Clan/ Clockwork). In the case of the professionals in the start-up, the dominant voice is that of the rational and analytical networked team. The action that spontaneously emerges recognises the reality of the Arena that is dynamic, unpredictable and potentially dissipative. The habits and conditioning that predisposed the promoters to think-feel in the network mode, was at variance with the visceral action response to the context, yet they blamed each other for the chaos, unable to either recognise it, or resolve the *Dharma Sankata*, and act appropriately.

It is important to keep in mind that the decision to emphasise certain aspects of the culture is not an internal decision. It is a choice that is appropriate for the business context. The Murugappa Group probably read the stability of the markets and businesses it was in before emphasising the more Clockwork and Clan aspects of its culture. The Birla Group needed to differentiate between the businesses that needed aggression and the ones that were in more stable and mature business ecosystems. TCS for example has to balance the fact of its being part of the larger Tata Group. It will attract people who value stability and professional freedom. Infosys will attract the more enterprising and less conservative. Fab India and Dastakar cannot destabilise the intimacy of the craft group while introducing new designs!

EXAMINING 'FAILURES'

Some of the failures in making the transition are very informative too. It has become a growing trend these days for bright young technologists to create start-ups in India. Using a combination of technical innovativeness and intelligence gathering through friends, they often make the first breakthrough and enter the market with a great product or service. This has happened in the Pharma Industry and in the IT and Telecom sector more easily than in Industries that require complex manufacturing techniques. After the breakthrough phase, the organisation is beset with many issues of converging growth with evolution. Growth is easily measured in terms of the top line; however evolution requires the insight and courage of an Arjuna. Questions that are uncomfortable have to be confronted; Technology Models, Revenue Models and Organisation Models have to undergo transformation, often simultaneously. The giant among dwarfs wakes up into the world of global business and is a dwarf among giants. To make the first breakthrough in Pharma for example, many organisations got into formulating and marketing supplements and 'tonics'. Some went into areas that required technical expertise and quality control like 'IV' solutions. In the local markets with their combination of rapport based setting up of distribution channels, and rough and ready tactics like appointment of distributors, they make a break-through. They are cost competitive and have the 'juggad' (native inventiveness) to see them through. This is classical Bhima behaviour. Soon the need for a systematised and strategised Organisation Building and Knowledge Building becomes essential.

Two kinds of 'failures' seem to be a trend at these thresholds. In some cases, it has taken about a decade to reach the state of readiness for the organisation to announce itself to the world through an IPO. Now the organisation gets a new lease of funds, either through the IPO or an angel investor. A new board is constituted. This board often comprises people who have run 'Big' companies, mostly senior leaders of Multi-Nationals. At this point in the transition a peculiar phenomenon takes place. The entrepreneur who has relied on his 'native' intelligence suddenly feels inadequate. The ones who come in 'know' how to run a company. When these 'ones who know' are Indians from the 'big' companies abroad, the problem is compounded. A strange kind of imposition of new practices starts. The young company goes into the mode of 'being taught'; the Bhima-Arjuna who took the lead in initiating enquiry, encouraging risk taking and orchestrating the organisational learning becomes a follower. This process of being taught is often a Yudhishtra mode where 'best practices' of various organisations (that some of the board members have served in) are introduced. Strategic calendars are set up for the top management and presentations are made to the board. Where the Non Resident Indian takes control, a strange brand of ill-founded Bhima mode takes over. Nothing less than a billion is worth looking at as a 'Vision' (with no real understanding or respect either of the adventure that this fledgling organisation has gone through so far or of the ground conditions). In both, the appropriateness of the practices in the present phase of the organisation's evolution and its business ecology are not examined.

The giant among dwarfs wakes up into the world of global business and is a dwarf among giants.

The set of explorers and entrepreneurs who went forth on an adventure get cowed down or seduced into a set of processes that robs them of the raw risk-taking ability and the hunger for learning that defined them so far. The transition gradually becomes a polarisation between the new dispensation and the disaffected creators of the business. The former is vocal and articulate; the latter are overwhelmed and sulking. Many started working not for the lure of large pay packets and sweet deals after the IPO, but because they were not capable of being Yudhishtras and Nakulas serving the Organisation. They were originators and innovators, the rebels in the larger system. At least where the new board comprises managers from Indian Organisations, the tension has a chance of getting resolved. A form of mentoring takes over and a dialogue emerges between the entrepreneurs and the knowledgeable board members. The 'Arjuna' quality of the early promoter often comes to the fore. The dialogue also allows the Nakula and Yudhishtra tendencies of the early team to surface and be respected. Issues of Dharma and Dharma Sankata get voiced and dealt with. Where the stage is not set for 'version two' of the organisation to emerge through dialogue the organisation flounders.

When the newly funded organisation also gets a new head from abroad, often a conflict is set up. An obsession with numbers and a race to succeed (in terms very different from the original motivations) gets articulated, nay insisted upon. The excitement of adventure, discovery and exploration gets converted into a predatory attitude towards business. Initially the team is excited their years of toil will bear fruit. Soon however, subtle battles for control and domination start. The basic character of the organisation is sought to be changed, not through enquiry into 'what is right for us now' but from a state of high where the new head 'knows what is right' and he 'knows' that the present organisation and its ways are inadequate. The 'plundering and harvesting' coloniser replaces the five hero archetypes and the members of the organisation who came together initially for the excitement and love of the new challenge. They are seen as replaceable and the resistors to the new ways. Soon the organisation gets hollowed out, new loyalists replace the top management that broke brown earth and seeded new seeds. The Kauravas have won the day!

THE AVERAGE INDIVIDUAL

The average person has the potential to appreciate and act from any of these V-memes. However, many conditions of the person's nature, and the person's propensities, predispose the individual to feel comfortable in certain V-memes. In our experience, most Indians have a leaning towards the Clan and the Clockwork. The dynamism and assertiveness of the Arena are repressed and often played out through passive aggression. Aspirations are high and the need to act from the Network is understood. However, the difficulty with self-assertion and competition prevent self-reliant action. The person suffers from a syndrome of wishing for great things without evoking the will to act. The Ecological V meme is held in a lot of ambivalence. On the one hand there is a natural ease to be inclusive and friendly, on the other hand there is fear of being exploited. The ideals of the so-called spiritual, are held on to strongly, however, the ways in which the spiritual is practised are traditional. The inability to contextualise deeply held urges has made the average Indian withdraw into a personal space.

This portrayal of the value dilemmas of the average Indian fall in line with many of the observations made about the Indians being pliable and role-bound. The few who have a strong Arena propensity therefore, are able to take on entrepreneurial roles. They find disciples and followers to act in ways that are directed by them. Sustaining the momentum and leaving behind a vibrant Institution becomes a challenge. This happens at the small business level, where many shops and trading houses and small-scale industries are run successfully. They flounder when the growth requires a change from, say a Clan orientation to a Clockwork orientation, and the entrepreneur finds it difficult to trust non-family players and no one from the family is competent to take charge. Individual entrepreneurs have difficulties when they have to trust other professionals and mentor them through the difficult process of becoming leaders. The transition is probably made more difficult by the fact that in India the manifest and public face of the Clockwork and Network memes is that of British Colonialism, and lately, of Globalisation. The familial and the social mores of the tradition have to make the jump to the modern world where the underlying assumptions of man and the world are very different. A study of the ways in which the *Naadar* communities of the Virudunagar area have encountered modernity, and engaged with it on their terms, to overcome the negatives of the caste-system as well as to grow and evolve, gives credence to this line of thinking. In the space between the two polarities, it is expedient to choose whichever is convenient at that point in time, rather than go through the journey of enquiry and resolution; therefore, the proliferation of Yudhishtra, Sahadeva and Nakula managers in Indian organisations and the lack of Bhima-Arjuna Managers.

We find this reality reflected in the Political stage of India also. Great individuals like Mahatma Gandhi who created powerful organisations in their lifetime, were unable to find credible successors. Political opportunists using the Clan V-meme to exploit their followers and amass power and wealth have managed to leave behind fragmented political parties. India has seen the birth and flowering of great people at all levels of the V-meme. However, as a nation, we are still grappling with deep fragmentation and we have not discovered a way of integrating the imperatives of the four quadrants we spoke about in Chapter 1. We therefore have great individuals as examples who are our icons of each quadrant, but no person or process or institution that balances all four.

LEADERSHIP IN THE LARGER CONTEXT

What then is Leadership in today's global context? The crisis is there for all of us to see. The most glaring one is the ecological crisis, brought about by unrestrained use of technology and market fundamentalism. The most anxiety-provoking crisis we face today is the religious atavism. Terrorism is its ugly visible face, but the cynical competition for harvesting souls, that goes on insidiously, is just as abhorrent. If one uses the framework of evolution that we have outlined in the last chapter, the ecological crisis is the unwelcome effect of the 'Network' mode of thought and action. This can be solved only when a critical mass of leaders, with a truly holistic vision, help raise the consciousness of man, to act with ecological responsibility.

However, the value frames of the 'Network' are at odds with the ideological and hierarchical modes represented by religion. Organised religion is putting up a fierce battle! It attacks the 'godlessness' of the 'Network', and the strict rationality of the scientific approach to knowledge. Religious ideology and orthodoxy, does not see its own dogma and belief as pre-rational and at times irrational. The post-modernist critique of both the ideological and the so-called technological world-views lacks the vibrancy and energy of Gandhiji, and does not result in relevant action. Ken Wilber argues eloquently for a trans-rational, world centric, spiritual orientation to life that echoes and builds upon many of the ideas of Shri Aurobindo. J Krishnamurti in his dialogues, talks and writings, has emphasised the nature of the crisis faced by mankind and the need for a complete break with the past. He calls for a mutation in the mind, a radical change that comes about when a rational, unconditioned mind faces the crisis directly, without any movement away from the fact; no theory, no method, only incisive profound observation.

Only when a critical mass of leaders, with a truly holistic vision, help raise the consciousness of man

Let us look at a few propositions and explore what Leadership in the emerging global context may be based upon:

- Today wealth and attention flow to the 'idea' that will ensure the individual feeling of security and power (in terms of wealth creation); Ideas that can generate personal / organisational wealth.
- Attention does not flow to ideas that can ensure collective well-being.

- Network System leaders will probably take the world towards a technological zenith, while promising a sensuous paradise.
- The unintended consequence of each paradigm is a waste of human energy. One easy measure of this is the estimate of the total cost of war, of reversing climate change, wastes in production, wastes in goods produced and not sold, bought and not used etc. Yet, the military industrial complex and the technology of consumerism, drives the use of human thought and resource utilisation today, in a way that produces enormous waste of all non-renewable resources. The intended consequence however, is individual security, well being and growth.
- Each paradigm hides a global collusion:
  - Ecological – collusion of celebrating empathy without discrimination
  - Network – collusion of celebrating individual consumption and greed
  - Clockwork – collusion of celebrating the domination of race and ideology
  - Arena – collusion of celebrating personal power
  - Clan – collusion of celebrating collective delusion
- The role of a leader is to explore the myths and beliefs of the current paradigm, and lead people to a more holistic way of living. Since fear and desire and all its manifestations hide under these collusions, it becomes an onerous task. With the collusion becoming more deeply enmeshed, the collective power invested in the collusion is also enormous.

Let us now look at some of the so-called acts of leadership of the last few years. We look at George W. Bush to start with. Issues of integrity clouded his ascension to the Presidency. His plank was 'protecting the American way of life', and in obviously pandering to the right wing neo-con-mind-set, he was playing upon the negatives of the arena and clockwork paradigms. Obviously, the USA can be secure only when the world feels secure, yet 9-11 was an excuse to unleash a horrendous 'war on terror', and pound Iraq into submission. The fear caused across the globe and in the US of A, was then played upon expertly, to further a clear Clockwork paradigm agenda of Imperialism, justified by 'resource security for the US'. Al Gore and his championing of the Ecological paradigm had no chance against this resurgence of Clockwork - Arena. Supporting 'tin-pot dictators' in the search for resources has been the norm of US foreign policy paradoxically calling it 'creating a free world'. The real agenda has been 'energy / resource security' for the USA. The processes whereby a small minority of the world uses up a large proportion of world resources in the name of free market forces are sustained by a peculiar combination of Arena, Clockwork and Network collusions. World forums like the UN, WTO, Kyoto protocols, all get subverted by this combination of political processes within the USA, its foreign policy and the Arena / Clockwork processes across the globe. Mankind seems to be held in thrall by Arena / Clockwork, while having learnt how to use the techno-economic tools of Network. The AK47 wielding terrorist is the visible symbol of this reality. A President, who speaks of the crusades, claims to have conversations with his god and engages in an unjustified war, is presented as the counterpoint of this symbol! The estimates for meeting the Millennium goals ran to about a hundred Billion Dollars, but the G8 never found the will to back up these goals with investments. Not only did the war in Iraq cost many times this amount, the moment the economic crisis hit the world, trillions of dollars were found to bail out Banks!! Obviously this form of leadership cannot solve the crisis faced by mankind today.

The Gandhian model advanced a powerful form of the Ecological system.

Let us critique the Gandhian model. The Gandhian model advanced a powerful form of the Ecological system. Gandhiji asserted that "*Swaraj* (self rule) is my birth right, I am born free" and fought for independence from a colonising British Imperialism. His form of resistance was satyagraha (truth – force), and non-violence. He did not look at the colonising British as an enemy. It was not 'India vs. Britain', but interdependence based on the recognition of the rights of a nation to be independent. He definitely did not voice Arena values – 'promoting personal power/ personal acquisition and tribal domination'. He definitely did not voice Clockwork values – 'the other as evil/devilish and 'us' as victimised but angelic', and himself as the great saviour. He spoke of religion, but clearly articulated a trans-rational spiritual view of religion, condemning pre-rational superstition. He attempted to redefine business in terms of trusteeship of wealth, and development from the point of view of the poorest in society and not in GDP and consumerist terms. Personally, he was an ascetic seeker, who documented and published his journey in the paper he edited and in his book – 'My Experiments with Truth'. Nelson Mandela has taken much from this model. Both have probably lived at a personal level that is truly spiritual but were leading the world into an Ecological reality. Mature interdependence and pragmatism at a national level, combined with transcending social differences, and acting from compassion at a social level, seem to be the hallmark of their way.

Though India rallied behind the Mahatma as it asserted itself and gained independence, the carnage of partition and the path India has taken to become what it is today, has betrayed the leadership values Gandhiji represented. Clan-communal forces, Arena-corruption, Clockwork-revivalism, and Network-economics and occasional Ecological voices are all active and dancing to a weird cacophony in the country. South Africa is betraying the Mandela vision in its own way.

Is it possible for Network organisational leadership to show the way? One does come across a few examples of business organisations that started with a Network paradigm that act from Ecological concerns. Patagonia for instance has pioneered a whole range of organic cotton sportswear. In the process they have influenced cotton growers to use environmentally friendly methods and influenced other competitors to join hands in creating a viable business ecology around organic cotton. Andersons Inter floor is another shining example of an Ecological organisation. The Tatas are a business group that are governed by a strong commitment to values. They are serious about their 'Corporate Social Responsibility' initiatives and support a large number of philanthropic activities. But, can these organisations that are essentially focused on the viability of their businesses, go beyond a 'mature interdependence' of their own value chain? Is it realistic to envisage Tata Motors, collaborating with Suzuki or Hyundai, to ensure a 'zero' waste process in the entire automotive sector? Would such collaboration end up becoming an exploitative oligopoly?

Many organisations today interact and inter depend with others very deeply. Co-makership is the best practice in innovation. Experts from, say, the parent automotive company and from a carburettor manufacturer, and probably researchers from universities, form a team that designs the fuel injection system of the new car. In order to bring this into production, a software solution provider from India is designing the car's new controls; a seat manufacturer in China is designing the new upholstery. Who do these teams belong to? Obviously, a Clockwork idea of an organisation where there are clear boundaries does not apply. Even a Network paradigm has to be extended to comprehend this phenomenon. James.F.Moore in his book 'Death of competition'[1], uses metaphors drawn from nature to explain business realities, and uses the term 'ecologies'. These 'ecologies' are set up for a purpose, after which they are disbanded. For this process to be effective, the individuals must act from a clear Network paradigm – mutuality of purpose, and the purpose being 'wealth creation'. Obviously, such a group will function with the least amount of human waste and friction, if all its members have truly transcended Clan, Arena and Clockwork paradigms in themselves. Definitely, in the example we have taken,

[1] *The Death of Competition: Leadership and Strategy in the Age of Business Ecosystems* Harper Business, 1996, ISBN 0-88730-850-3

people from many races, religions and nationalities are involved. Is there a real transcending at the individual level? Is there any investment made to discover the most optimal way to work together? In all probability, many of the individuals act from a personal Arena (what's in it for me?), manage and subordinate their Clockwork (religious/nationalistic belongings and ideology) and participate in the market competition that this so called ecology is part of. But these purpose driven Networks are not acting from the Values of the Ecological paradigm of thinking.

The survival drives based on fear, search for security, and impulsive desires, have been modified and placed in different containers. Feelings like greed, envy and pleasure are clearly evoked by the organisations in the process of attracting buyers, investors, and employees. The Network paradigm is then only a mutually convenient way, an efficient way of maximising personal gain. Can such a paradigm lead the way to an intelligent solution to today's crisis?

> To usher in an Ecological way, the world will require many people at a truly spiritual level, Bodhisattvas to lead, anchor and help the transition.

A true realisation of an Ecological way of living and thinking would knock the bottom out of the idea of a 'viable individual', of a 'viable fragment', that is not intimately concerned about the well-being and viability of the whole interdependent earth–Gaia. The paradigms Arena, Clockwork and Network, have emphasised the idea of the individual and channelled the fears and desires of the individual to social, political, and organisational processes. Is it conceivable that an Ecological transformation will happen in the near future? What will motivate action in the Ecological paradigm? Given the fact that the powerful motivators of greed, envy, personal acquisition and the like, are the root of the negative impacts of the way we live today, will this be replaced by compassion and true 'reciprocal altruism' at the scale and intensity required to redesign economics, redirect technology and redefine politics? Is there a leader, or a collection of people or a process that can truly confront the myths and collective collusions of Clan, Arena, Clockwork and Network? Can they manage the reaction, rage, dependence and a loss of anchor that this confrontation and questioning will cause and transform these energies into the processes that usher in an equitable and sustainable future?

To usher in an Ecological way, the world will require many people at a truly spiritual level, Bodhisattvas to lead, anchor and help the transition. One Gandhiji and one Mandela will not do. Many people playing significant roles in organisations and in society have to display a spirit of true service and not be motivated by the power and privilege that the role provides.

Are Aurobindo and Krishnamurti the new leaders? They are people who seem to have transcended the ego, its fears, desires, prejudices and limitations. Are Mahatma Gandhi and Nelson Mandela the new leaders? They have confronted oppressive colonising regimes, with an approach that asserted the new without falling into the trap of reactivity and hatred. The Bill Gates and the Mittals are great entrepreneurs and are certainly great exponents of the 'Network', but do they have a vision beyond a predatory organisational worldview that sees maximisation of profits and top line growth as paramount? What is the model of sustainable development that will be articulated by the new Arjuna for the world?

Perhaps in looking for individuals as leaders and role models, we are barking up the wrong tree. Arjuna is deploying leadership qualities only when he is questioning the foundations of the existing mind-set that led to the Mahaabhaarata war. The dialogue between Krishna and Arjuna is the 'Leading edge', the moment when dharma of the *Yuga (the millennium)* is being redefined. This dialogue is profoundly meditative and therefore, capable of transforming Arjuna, and through him, the process of 'creative destruction' unfolds. Is 'Leading' then a verb, an action that comes alive from time to time? Is 'Governing', a more time dictated action where Yudhishtra, Bhima, Nakula, and Sahadeva with their abilities to sustain society for long periods of time, become the more relevant models? Or is it perhaps a dynamic balance between all of them?

It is clear that, expecting one person to be a 'leader' who can constantly be both 'horizontally' deeply aware of the 4 quadrants of collective living (Refer Chapter 2), as well as profoundly insightful 'vertically', is untenable. We will have to wait eternally for the next 'Krishna' to take birth! Perhaps it is more useful to look at how balanced each of us can be in inducting the '4 quadrants' in our minds and in our action. This is the direction Ken Wilber suggests. It will also be necessary to design and enliven forums and processes where the 'leading edge consciousness' can come alive and transform the participants who are in an intense enquiry. Dr David Bohm suggests this direction in his various writings and dialogues.

Personal practice and preparation that helps us develop these potentials is an essential prerequisite.

If one is to bring the Mahaabhaarata alive today in one's consciousness and action, it cannot just be a dramatic representation that happens once in a while. We must view the Mahaabhaarata and the five archetypal 'heroes', as potential personas in our minds. Personal practice and preparation that helps us develop these potentials is an essential prerequisite. Simultaneously, designing organisations that have not only structures and systems, but also spaces and forums where these five orientations can take a collective form and expression, becomes another building block.

It is imperative that a relevant way of looking at wealth, technology, markets and human relationships emerges today. It is also important that we attempt to design organisations that can foster the emergence of new leadership and 'leading edge' consciousness. May a thousand Arjunas bloom!

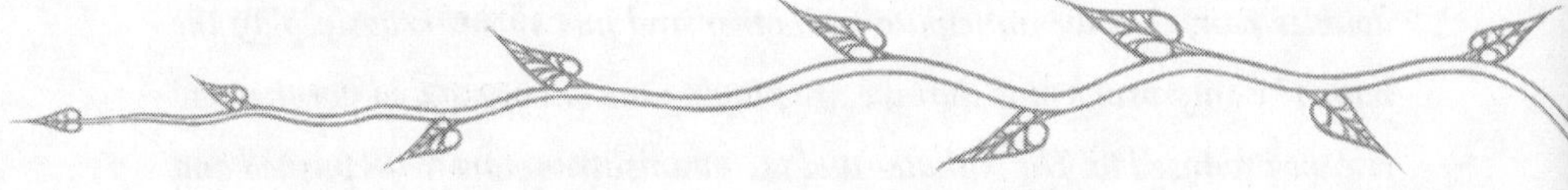

After a few months of intense work and excitement, Ranjan came home on a weekend looking troubled. Sanam waited for Ranjan to go through his routine of getting locked up in his study, furiously writing notes, and working things out for himself, before asking him what was wrong. "I was meaning to share this with you Sanam," Ranjan began, "this inner transformation stuff is not very easy. As you know we are sitting down every couple of weeks in a dialogue and reflection forum, as we call it these days. What we discover is that it is not only individual propensities that we need to look at, but also the dynamics between us. Arun Natarajan, our Angel investor says that all five hero archetypes exist inside us, but, we get more proficient in one or two of them and find it difficult to express the others. So whenever there is time and clarity in our actions we are practising the new behaviours, but when there is pressure we are falling back."

"Isn't that great?" Sanam responded. "I mean you are recognising it. I did not have peers around me when I tried on my new 'Self', and it took me a long time to see how I was falling back." Ranjan perked up. "Ok, you asked for it," he said, with a lot more energy, "Let me share with you my latest reflections." "Saptaparni has given us two very interesting questions to use in our sessions. The first is to ask ourselves the question 'In doing what I am doing, what am I really doing?' Our pattern for the dialogue and reflection sessions is to explain to the group a critical live event that we wish to examine. Whoever wishes to start, describes it like a drama. He is a character in the drama however he names people, including himself, as though they are characters. We then ask the key question of all the players in the drama. This usually throws up huge insights. Let me give you an example: there was a discussion I had triggered with the R&D group, asking for their reflections on what they saw as ways to go forward. The session started well, but slowly wound down. As we examined the various transactions, it became clear to all of us, that Jagan and I are a tandem team. When we are together, I slip into emphasising the Bhima in me, and Jagan the Sahadeva! We are so comfortable playing like a seasoned doubles pair, that we anticipate each other and just spontaneously play the ball. The only problem is that we are playing the old game and not the new one we promised to! The Nakulas and the Yudhishtras start to get pushed and

slowly start to adjust and accommodate. All of us are getting pulled into our habitual roles. The going seems smooth, except that it is ineffective for the goal of creating many more 'team players and challengers'. When we shared this in the forum, it became clear that among the six of us we had set up a pattern. Shanti and Afsal became 'supportive'; Raj tried to raise issues and then settled down to 'small improvements', as he called them. Rashmi was comfortable and rattled off all kinds of alternatives. We had been doing this for a long time, and this was the prototype of the cultural patterns across the organisation. What we then had to do as a group was spend some quiet time and come back with alternative behaviours. We ask ourselves, "How was I part of the problem, and how can I be part of the solution?" This is the second 'money-back-guarantee-asthra (weapon)' as AS called it that will transform us. Here we allow anyone to play any part and this is really refreshing, funny and insightful. Unexpected possibilities surface and those parts of myself that I am blind to, or have difficulty with, are the easy alternatives that others see. We then set out what we call the 'Smiles per hour' contest among ourselves. We give ourselves a smiley each time we enact an appropriate new behaviour. The winner gets an extra beer in the next forum. This is great fun, but I can tell you that being a Nakula and listening before I speak, letting all the ideas come forth, see how I can evoke more ideas before I speak, is really tough for me! But the great discovery is that often others state many ideas I have, and the acceptance becomes easy. I just have to say yes. This is not my idea of heroism, but it is certainly great for teamwork.

"There have been some painful and interesting discoveries. Shanti always thought she was very people-oriented. It came through that she is a Yudhishtra, and very role-bound and idealistic. So she sits and listens to people and does all the right things, but ends up acting from her head and from the rules. She is really reeling from this discovery. She wants to attend one of Saptaparni's Theatre Labs and do some serious work with herself. 'God that's the part of my mother I so dislike', she burst out when she saw this side of herself. 'I have read all about how deep the family socialisation is and how we often take up the behaviours of people we feel oppressed by and hide them from ourselves'. Afsal has had to face up to being too much of a Nakula, doing all kinds of contortions

to keep the financials looking good. He needs to be a Yudhishtra and push all of us into a discipline. Rashmi and I have realised how we get carried away, become emotionally charged and treat all rules like red rags!!"

"AS told you when you started that the 'shadow play' will not be pretty. What you celebrate as team work might actually be collusion, he had said, and you were very annoyed," Sanam reminded him. Ranjan smiled like a child caught with his hands in the cookie jar. Both Sanam and Ranjan laughed a lot at this point and hugged each other. "It has been a tough six months but we will make it Sanam!" Ranjan said, his voice thick with emotion, "I will lead the company to fulfil its destiny." As he sat down, there were tears in his eyes. Sanam held his hands and said, "We will create the land of our dreams Ranjan, and we will create a Camelot".

Ranjan was simultaneously excited and sombre. "We have taken a clear step out of the old path and set out on the new, Sanam. I am feeling elated, but feeling anxious too. We were hanging on to the old patterns not knowing what to chop and what to retain. We have decided that we will become a global product company and we will lead the eco-system by licensing the small operators. We have decided to keep a few clients going on an 'end-to-end' throughput. We will design new products and applications with a degree of client involvement, make the products and service them. This entire throughput will be our R&D, 'innovate the product and the delivery'. Then we will outsource all the routine parts and the core product, as a black box to our associates. We have decided not to get more specific than a clear statement of who we will be, and how we will work. We started that way and kept moving ahead since we were very responsive. We are still the most innovative company in the field. Like Afsal said, 'we are moving out of our auto rickshaw and designing an SUV. We know the space and we can drive it best'. For the next one year our targets are clear. Our investor Arun is thrilled too. Most importantly, we have said that creating response capability at the 'Dream, decide, design and deliver' operational base will be nurtured by the culture of the 'Panchayat'.*"*

"Let me guess," Sanam interjected, "You are going to ensure that the operational systems are energised by a culture that emulates the Paandava army".

"That's the idea, but this will take a very modern form," Ranjan responded. "The process will go something like this. Any of us from the top management can call for a 'strategic breakthrough Panchayat'. The idea can come from anywhere, but if it comes through chats with our own people, that's great. This 'breakthrough initiator' will come to the meeting with sufficient 'homework' done on the numbers, trends and probabilities. We then dialogue on it till we say 'go or no go!' with a powerful convergence. If in three meetings, over two weeks, we can't arrive at a consensus I will take a call either to study further, run a pilot or drop it. Let's say we are all committed to 'go!' Then we frame a goal with a time line. Say, Product X or Service Y from 'concept to first positive cash flow in six months'. Now we will set up the five chairs, one for each of the Paandavas. Bhima's chair is the place from which the person asks, 'How will we ignite and sustain a passion for this goal?' We write our ideas on post-its and put them on a flip chart. Then the Yudhishtra question, 'How will the process become error free, repeatable and scalable'. Ideas should be written down on post-its. Then the next question from Nakula's chair, 'How will the process flow, end to end, create value at each part of the system, what infrastructures do we build?' We then move on to the Sahadeva question, 'How do we establish a learning rigour and create knowledge through the process?' Then we come to the Arjuna question, 'How will this project lead to organisation building and evolution?' The post-its are gathered and categorised, actions distilled and arranged as a throughput system across a time line. Now we take coherent sets of actions, and each of us volunteers to take charge. One of us becomes the orchestrator.

"Now comes the part you will enjoy, Sanam. Each of us not only systematises our tasks and sets out work plans to discuss at the next meeting, we also ask ourselves the three 'role preparation' questions from theatre, that Saptaparni has taught us – 'Who am I?', 'Where am I?' and 'Why am I here?' This is the phase where the invisible but vital part of the design gets addressed – the way in which each of us will play our roles, and make the dream come alive. 'Who am I?' will broadly look at what role I feel evoked to play and how I will relate to the other role holders. For example, one can play an 'expert' role in project 'A', a 'consultant' role in project

'B', while being the 'orchestrator' of project 'C'. 'Where am I?' relates both to the areas of the throughput that one is taking accountability for, as well as sensing the situation, the phase of the project, its relationship to the assumptions we made at the inception. 'Why am I here?' is simply one's ability to see how the project is proceeding towards its goals and making choices to steer the ship towards its intended destination".

"You have gone through the 'Dream, decide and design' stages of the project, so I guess deliver is just the execution," Sanam said. "No, we have decided to do an introspective session along with each milestone review. We will probably ask Saptaparni to facilitate the first few. What we will do there is similar to our retreats. We will look at key events, like the key episodes of a serial and literally describe the scenes. Then we will ask each player in the scene to introspect – 'in doing what I was doing what was I really doing?' 'Was I moving the project to its goal, was I true to the answers we gave to the Paandavas?' 'How was I part of the dysfunctionalities that came up?' 'How can I be part of initiating and nurturing the healthy processes?' While the process looks simple, the practice of a meditative and non-judgmental listening is essential. Only then do we help each other absolve ourselves of any guilt or shame in making mistakes, or letting the team down and move into healing each other and the team."

Who am I?', 'Where am I?' and 'Why am I here?

"That's the turning of the Dharma Wheel," Sanam recollected. "Saptaparni has also talked about creating forums for togetherness, celebration, mourning, recalibration, team-learning and organisational healing, in the retreats. We want to take about six months or more for practising our 'Panchayat', before we go organisation-wide", Ranjan continued.

"The most important parts of these 'panchayats', *is going to be what Saptaparni called the* 'naadi pariksha *(reading the pulse)'. What we will do every six months is to have a total review of the organisation health, by asking the following five questions: 1. How are we taking to the new? We will look at the five voices Shareholder, Customer, Technology, Employees and Society and share the emergent reality. If we have no surprises, we are probably not listening, according to Saptaparni. 2. How are we digesting the new? Are we able to understand the emergent reality, discuss it, and derive its implications*

for Mobile Unlimited? 3. How are we eliminating the old the dysfunctional and the toxic? Are we clear about what will add value to us, and what is creating waste?' This is true, first and foremost, in the hearts of every member of Mobile Unlimited, then in all the operational dimensions, then in our cash flow. 4. How are we disseminating and creating a flow across the organisation? Information, knowledge and resources have to flow appropriately and without eddies and currents. We can't make the waters muddy, before we announce policies. Knowledge cannot be hoarded. This is going to be tough since, except for resource flow, the other two are intangible. 5. How are pride and élan being created and fostered across the organisation? We realised that the moment we rediscovered our dream and the pride we shared in our accomplishments as the top management, our dissatisfactions transformed into a restless energy in search of getting better. Our confrontations took on a vector of 'let's find the right way', and did not create conflicts. We want to make sure all this happens across the whole organisation."

"Do you realise why Saptaparni called it the 'naadi pariksha'?" Sanam asked, "The five questions you have narrated to me are the five Vaayu's that maintain our health according to Ayurveda. You have always wondered why Vaidyar Balan always starts with asking about the toilet habits, perspiration, water intake and length and the smell of the breath. He is checking if the Apaana Vaayu, and the 'toxin eliminating processes' are working well. That's the key to any healing. Yoga starts with teaching exhale along with Aasana postures that help elimination. The intake of the new breath is Praana Vaayu, digestion is Samaana Vaayu and circulation is Vyaana Vaayu. All these four are checked through the various pulse readings the Vaidyar takes." "And the fifth?" "Aha! That's the most difficult and the most important, Udaana Vaayu. This is the subtle breath that not only helps man walk erect it carries the residues of one's Karma. It out-lasts the body and moves across to our next birth." "All that is fine, but how does it relate to Mobile Unlimited?" Ranjan was always a little suspicious of this 'esoteric stuff' as he called it. "Udaana Vaayu is reflected in our ability to hold ourselves in positive regard, and not lose a sense of deep joyousness in living, even when there is adversity. Modern medicine is now recognising this too.

Our antibodies and other healing chemicals are most active when we are joyous. Santosha *(contentment), the word Yoga uses, is not an outwardly expressed thing but a sense of faith in oneself and affirmation in one's own worth, that keeps a zest for life alive whatever the circumstance". "Now I see the connection. Saptaparni asked us in the early part of the retreat if we can take bad news without losing our confidence. He then made us recount our accomplishments, not just external milestones, but intangible things like wisdom. He made us affirm each other by sharing how we valued each other, how we found each other trustworthy and then asked us to say what gave us pride in our collective efforts to make Mobile Unlimited evolve. This helped us a great deal, as we started to introspect. He would close each retreat by asking us to put down how we had valued each person's contribution, even the small ones. I thought it was his way of making the process soft! Now I see that he helped us rediscover our pride, as we went into the process of uncovering our mistakes, and more importantly, our shadows."*

"What about us?" Sanam said as Ranjan was preparing to get up. "Aha! I forgot to mention that we have promised each other that twenty days a month will be the norm, and we will also work out some flexi timings. I promise a really meaningful couple of weeks with you every six months, apart from shorter working days". "How soon will you live up to the promise?" Ranjan smiled sheepishly "I promise I will. I must if I have to really be healthy in body, mind, and spirit, to be part of the leadership team".

Ranjan seemed quiet and thoughtful as he sat for the morning cup of tea with Sanam the next day. The morning sun was soft and beautiful as it lit up the garden. The birds were chirping, some excitedly and some in a lilting melody. "What a beautiful morning!" Ranjan began. "Have I lived up to what your teacher said about good kings and great heroes?" Ranjan suddenly asked Sanam and pulled her out of her reverie. Sanam took a while to get the context of the question. She smiled, drew her shawl close to her body, a few drops of tears wet her eyes. "I guess our Dharma has been shaped in the crucible of the Dharma Sankata we traversed. 'A Dharma Sankata navigated with mindfulness creates

"Have I lived up to what your teacher said about good kings and great heroes?"

the ground for many to live in a way that enlivens the whole context' my teacher always said with conviction. I think we have done this."

"I was thinking about the idea of good kings and heroes, and ..." Ranjan began Sanam seemed to be far away. She turned her attention to Ranjan, "Just one last comment," he began hesitantly, "The idea of leadership that Saptaparni and you have helped me to look at has some very different characteristics from the usual idea. Most books on leadership and teamwork make it very important to name an enemy. This has always bothered me. I think I know why. When I go to my team and name the enemy, I do two things. Firstly, I make them anxious and secondly, I am subtly saying that the wolf is at your door, I am the hero and I am your saviour. I make them dependent on me and fearful and angry with the enemy. I am evoking the Clan and the Arena in their minds. All the other tools and techniques I use are then used from this mind-set, a mind that is creating the global crisis today, the crisis of climate change and of economic models that will exacerbate the problem. The underlying ground of thought that this comes from is the model of the victim, the oppressor and the saviour. My team members are potential victims and I am the saviour. If they don't listen to me, I have the right to oppress them 'for their own good' else surely the wolf at the door will gobble them up. The Arjuna idea is Dharmic because the potential Hero/Leader has to get out of this strangulation-triangulation! The hero takes in the shadow and negative aspects of 'his people' and meditates. He has an insight and with this insight, arises compassion. From this ground of insight and compassion, he works and struggles with his people to find a new ground. There is no hate, no anger, no vengeance and no violence in this process."

"That is sounding like a saint," Sanam pulled Ranjan's leg. Ranjan replied seriously to this. "Maybe, I am talking about a level of thinking that is at least ecological if it is not holarchic. If we have to deal with the global issues we face today as mankind, we need a lot of people at all levels that can go beyond the egotistical idea of country, religion and race. Plato said that kings need to be good philosophers and is this not the central message of the Bhagavad Gita?"

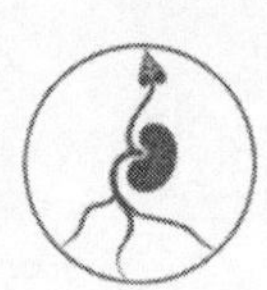

As you approach the end of this conversation, may I help you to set up a conversation with yourself? I would like you to become a *Saakshi*, a dear friend and witness unto yourself. Your mind is contemplative and you are aware of the sweep of your life, its flows, its twists and turns. Your physical body is on its deathbed. You decide to relate the story of the dying person as if he/she is a friend, to the people who have gathered. Will you begin with a song? If so which one? Did your friend write poetry or words of wisdom that he/she kept secret? What were the dreams and aspirations of your dear friend? How did they evolve and change? Who were the people who influenced him/her most profoundly? What did your friend live for, what was he/she willing to die for? Did he/she live or die this way? What were the gifts that your friend was born with? How did he/she deploy those gifts? Did your friend mindlessly feel arrogant or depressed because of what was endowed? Did he/she accept it with humility, and help it grow to its full potential? Did he/she trade with it? Convert it into worldly achievements and acquisitions or did he/she use it wisely for the simultaneous good of the self and of others? Who befriended him/her and why? Who were the enemies, or was your friend unwilling to state convictions and act on them? Who mourns his/her death and why? Did your friend add value and meaning to him/herself through the process of living? What quintessence will the Udaana Vaayu carry forward on its journey?

Notes to myself

1. My commitment to the world around me asks of me to share my insights and enable others to do their tapas and walk their path.

2. Maybe in time, when I have been just 'a good king', this ground that we have tilled and regenerated will also come up against its limits and another Arjuna will have to be born to take up the Tapas and find new ways.

3. A whole year since I began this journey. It feels like many lifetimes, maybe it is. And most satisfying is the way Sanam has been a companion all the way. "Love is to be with your partner as she changes" my literature Professor would say. I think I understand this now. I always thought of an end like a film, a romantic idea I guess. I see now how the horizon keeps expanding. It is not just I, Jagan and my team or our organisation or our stakeholders. It is the way all of us are intertwined and creating a world with every action of ours.

4. I understand the idea of the 'Gaandiva' (Arjuna's divine bow) and why it takes an Arjuna to lift it and string the bow. The two ends of the bow are the eternal ends of the Dharma Sankata inherent in leadership. Namely, the beauty of one's tradition and the potentials of a new way. When Arjuna strings the bow,

he is acknowledging the tension inherent in the present. As he places an arrow and pulls the bow back, he is delving deeply into the tradition, looking at what must be retained and what must be changed. He is simultaneously looking at the new, what is wholesome and what is not. As Arjuna bends the bow, he takes the question deep within, discovers the purity of his intent, accepts the responsibility of making a choice. He aims the arrow towards the future that he will create with the assistance of Krishna who points to the 'way'. He waits for the exquisitely perfect moment when the time is right to release the arrow.

5. What is the arrow? I pondered. This is what it seems like to me today:

I am the arrow,
I am made of earth,
Firm enough to take a stand upon,
But willing to absorb moisture;
I am made of water,
The moisture that will bring the seed alive;
I am made of fire,
The will within the seed that makes it grow;
I am made of air,
The breath that gives praana to the nascent life;
I am made of space,
Where the flower will unfold,
Offering its beauty and fragrance to the world.

6. My commitment to the world around me asks of me to share my insights and enable others to do their tapas and walk their path.

7. "Dukhesheshvanudvighnamanaha...." He whose heart is not distressed in calamities, from whom all longing for pleasure has fallen away, who is free from attachment, fear and wrath, he is a seer whose mind is rooted in truth. (Bhagavad Gita. Ch2.56)

Glossary

LEADERSHIP DHARMA

Arjuna the timeless metaphor

Aasana Postures used in Yoga practice

Abhimanyu Arjuna's young son

Adharma Actions that cause decay and death

Adhikaar Legitimacy and affirmation

Ambalam A sacred space/temple

Amrapalli A courtesan who became a disciple of Buddha

Angulimala A violent person converied by the Buddha into a compassionate one

Apsara Divine dancer

Arangetram The first public dance performance

Arjuna The Paandava hero who was blessed with Lord Krishna's friendship

Ashoka The famous Emperor of the Gupta dynasty who become a Buddhist after the *Kalinga* war. Also a great patron of the Buddhist *sangha*

Asthra A weapon of war

Asura People of extraordinary capabilities that are self-centered and extractive

Avatara Purusha Divine manifestation in human form

Ayurveda The system of medicine indigenous to India

Bala Krishna The form of Sri *Krishna* as a child

Bhaava Expressions in dance that reflect the inner state of the dancer

Bhaavana Mental formations/ visualisation

Bhagavad Gita The divine teaching of Lord Krishna to Arjuna on the battlefield

Bhikku The mendicants and monks of the Buddhist order

Bhima The *Paandava* hero gifted with enormous strength and emotional intensity

Bhishma The great patriarch of the *Kuru* dynasty

Bhooman Foundation; substratum

Bimbisara A powerful king who lived in Buddha's times

Bodhi The tree under which the Buddha sat as he meditated

Bodhisattva Enlightened beings on the path to Buddhahood

Brahmin The priestly class of Hindus

Burning ghats Cremation grounds along the river Ganges

Chakra Energy centers in the body that impact thought, feeling and action the seven chakras are:

Moolaadhaara Situated at the base of the spine; anchors instinct

Swaadishtaana Situated just below the navel; anchors aggression

Manipooraka Situated above the navel; anchors containment

Anaahata Situated at the heart; anchors affection

Vishuddhi Situated at the base of the throat; anchors creativity

Aagnya Situated at the mid-brow; anchors surrender

Sahsraara Situated at the crown of the head; anchors transcendence

Chakravyuha The concentric defensive formation used in the Mahaabhaarata war by the *Kaurava* army

Chandogya Upanishad One of the principal philosophical texts explicating the nature of Reality

Chettiar The trading and banking community of Tamil Nadu

Chittal Spotted deer

Dandia Raas A community celebration through dance that signifies the love of the *Gopis* for Sri *Krishna*

Daya Compassion

Deva The quintessence of the energies and powers that comprise manifest reality; divine beings

Devavrata Devavrata anointed Bhishma because he took an oath to be celibate and gave up his right to the throne so that his father Shantanu would marry Satyavati

Dharma Kshetra The ground on which a value based stand of moral and spiritual significance is taken

Dharma Sankata The dilemma of choosing between alternatives that have an equal but opposite impact on the situation

Dhritarashtra The blind king, the father of Duryodhana and his 99 brothers; Pandu's brother

Draupadi The wife of the *Paandavas*

Drona The great guru of the martial arts who taught both the Paandavas and the Kauravas the art of war

Dukha Sorrow, sadness, suffering

Duryodhana The eldest *Kaurava*, committed to enmity with the *Paandavas*

Dussasana One of the *Kauravas*, renowned for his ability with the mace

Dwaaraka The holy city where Sri Krishna lived

Gaandiva *Arjuna*'s divine bow

Gauthama The birth name of the Buddha

Gopi Krishna The form of Sri *Krishna* as the beloved of the *Gopis*

Hanuman The great devotee of Sri Raama with extraordinary capabilities, who takes the form of a Monkey

Hiranyagarbha The golden womb, the name given to a state of mind replete with illumination

Indra The king of the Gods

Jaraasandha An *asura* with a 'split personality' and a body that manifests the split; He was also a friend of the Kauravas

Jyotisha Astrologer

Kaama The God of desire and passion

Kabir A poet saint who bridged the Hindu and Muslim faith

Kaivalya A state of total oneness with all manifest and un-manifest reality

Kamsa The uncle of Sri Krishna who was greedy and violent and bent upon destroying Sri Krishna

Kapilavasthu The city where Buddha was born

Karma Action, work deed, moral duty, accountability across births for one's actions

Karna The illegitimate son born to *Kunti* before her marriage to Pandu

Kartha The Patriarch of traditional Indian families

Kaashyapa A prominent Brahmin who became an important disciple of the Buddha who canonised the teachings of Buddha

Kathakali The dance-drama form from Kerala

Kauravas The hundred sons of *Dhritarashtra*, sworn enemies of the *Paandavas*

Kavacha & Kundala The armour and earrings made of gold with special protective powers gifted to *Karna* at birth

Koodam A space of shared belonging and dialogue

Koothu Traditional dance-drama of Tamil Nadu

Kshatriya The warrior caste

Kumar Gandharva A renowned Hindustani musician

Kunti The mother of the *Paandava* Heroes

Kurukshetra The geographical location of the *Mahaabhaarata* war, close to modern day New Delhi

Lakshmana Sri *Raama's* Brother. An iconic figure epitomising brotherly love

Mahaabhaarata The epic based on the saga of the descendants of *Shantanu* namely the *Paandavas* and the *Kauravas*

Mandala A space in which opposites and polarities coexist in harmony; often represented as an enveloping circle

Mara The mythical form of negative forces that attacks the *Buddha* as he nears enlightenment

Mohini The beautiful seductress who entices *Arjuna* away from his penance; considered to be a form of Lord *Vishnu*

Moksha The ending of the cycle of birth and death; unconditional freedom

Naadar A community of people in Tamil Nadu renowned for their emancipation as well as their business acumen and community solidarity

Naadi pariksha The study of a person's pulse; a special skill of *ayurvedic* physicians

Nakula One of the *Paandavas* gifted with great healing powers

Naaraayana One of the forms of Lord *Vishnu*

Nataraja The dancing form of Lord *Shiva*

Naatya Shastra Book of aphorisms on the classical dance and dramatic forms of India

Paasupataasthra A divine weapon of extraordinary power attributed to Lord *Shiva*

Pada yatra Walking Pilgrimage

Panchayats Village councils that had a representation from all the communities living in the village

Partha system The traditional accounting system of the *Marwari* community incorporating budgeting and costing

Perundi The grotesque seductress who tries to block *Arjuna* as he prepares for his penance

Pippala The fig tree

Praana Life force/Pneuma

Pragnya Profound knowing

Prakruti The feminine principle of creation

Puja Prayer

Raaga -The system of a specific scale of notes in Indian classical music

Raja Nithi The legitimate conduct of a king

Raja Dharma The conduct of a king founded on a profound insight into the true and the good

Ramana Ashrama The meditation center built in the place where the saint *Ramana* lived and died

Raamaayana The epic based on the saga of *Raama* and *Sita*

Rasa/Navarasa The 9 basic emotions experienced by people namely, *Sringaara* (affection), *Veerya* (courage), *Roudra* (anger), *Bhayaanaka* or *Bhaya* (fear), *Bibhatsa* (revulsion), *Haasya* (humor), *Adbhuta* (wonderment), *Karuna or Kaarunya* (compassion) and *Shaanta* (equanimity)

Rasika Sensitive audience, a person capable of resonating with the performer

Raavana The King of Lanka who was defeated by Raama

Saadhana Deep and continuous practice for self-transformation

Saakshi Mindful Witness

Saathvikam or Satva Gunam A subtle state of mind capable of deep, resonant and insightful perception

Sahadeva One of the *Paandavas* gifted with deep insight

Sakha/Sakhi Friend and confidante

Samsaara The cycle of birth and death

Samskaara Deeply internalised habits and conditioning; socialisation and acculturation

Sangamitra Emperor *Ashoka's* daughter who went to Sri Lanka carrying the message of the Buddha

Sangha A group of people who share a spiritual practice

Sankhya The original philosophy that underpins all later Indian philosophies

Santhosha Deep and abiding joy

Shakuni The advisor of the *Kauravas* and *Duryodhana's* uncle

Shalya Karna's charioteer

Shaanti Parva The 12th chapter of the Mahaabhaarata dealing with the conduct of kings

Sharanya The glow in the sky that precedes sunrise

Shiva One of the trinity of Godheads of the Hindu Pantheon who epitomises creative destruction

Siddharta The name of the Buddha at birth

Sita *Raama*'s wife

Sonadanda An important disciple of the *Buddha*

Sujatha The young girl who befriended the *Buddha* during his meditation

Surya The Sun

Sutaputra A derogatory term used to humiliate a 'low born'

Sutradhar Narrator; An important role in traditional Indian theatre; the person who points to the contextual relevance of the play

Swaraj Self rule, a word made famous by Mahatma Gandhi during the independence struggle

Taala Tempo, beat

Tantra The process of inner transformation especially that of human passions

Tapas/Tapasya Penance

The Four Noble Truths and the Eightfold Path The essential teachings of the Buddha concerning suffering and the way to end suffering

Thulasi A sacred herb often called Indian Basil

Tiruvannamalai A temple town famous for being the place where Saint *Ramana* lived

Vaachikam A harmonious expression where thought, word and action are convergent

Vaanaprastha The third stage of life where the householder retires from active engagement

Vaasana Concentrated seed form of propensities and conditioning

Vaastu The science of design and architecture

Vaidyar An *ayurvedic* physician

Vaayu Air/gaseous forms of the three humours in the body that take up the following forms

Praana Vaayu The force that takes in fresh energy

Apaana Vaayu The force that expels toxins

Samaana Vaayu The digestive force

Vyaana Vaayu The force that distributes digested energy

Udaana Vaayu The force that uplifts

Venuvana The famous Bamboo grove where the Buddha taught his disciples

Vidura The wise brother and advisor of *Pandu* and *Dhritarashtra*

Vishwarupa The all-encompassing form of Sri Krishna that is simultaneously awe inspiring and terrorising

Yoga Sutras The aphorisms of Yoga written by *Pathanjali*

Yudhishtra The eldest of the Paandava heroes

Yuga Millennium

Afterword

As I started writing this book I was drawn into an inner exploration of my own, as expected. But, the life that it has taken once it has left my desk has been even more exciting. Draupadi knocked on the doors when I shared the book with women; Gopal infused a convergence to the narrative and interactive work made its way in when I shared it with Prasad Kaipa and a few colleagues. Finally, Karthikeyan brought in the idea of 'gaming' the various elements of the self discovery process. Now this book is part of a larger offering *"Arjuna's Tool Kit"* that includes games and apps, behavioural profiling for self reflection and a work book that helps one prepare to take on leadership positions!

Dear Reader,

Now that you have read the book, we invite you to take the next step. We have a team of Coaches who can help you progress on your own Leadership Journey based on the insights of the Mahabharata. Please go to our site: www.taotools.com and register yourself with one of the empaneled coaches. If you are already a coach/ facilitator and you would like to be empaneled, write to the author: raghu@totallyalignedorganization.com

We would be delighted to help you fulfill your aspirations.

Raghu Ananthanarayanan

Mobile : 919840296363